Below and overleaf: The battle of Kirkee was fought in 1817, when the small British force guarding the Resident at the court of the Mahratta Prince, known as the Peshwa, was attacked by the Peshwa's entire army of 26,000 men with fourteen guns. Some of the four guns of the Bombay Artillery can be seen firing from their flanking positions; and the Mahratta cavalry are shown charging the left flank, where they became entangled in a marsh and were shot to pieces by the combined fire of guns and muskets. This setback, combined with the determination of the British force to get to grips with a horde that outnumbered it by nine to one, caused the whole Mahratta army to lose heart and quit the field. (By permission of the India Office Library and Records.)

2

Firepower

Weapons effectiveness on the Battlefield, 1630–1850

by

Major-General BP Hughes CB CBE

SARPEDON
New York

Published in the United States by
SARPEDON

Copyright © 1974, 1997 by Major-General BP Hughes

First published in the UK in 1974 by
Arms and Armour Press
Now published in the UK in 1997 by
Spellmount Ltd
The Old Rectory, Staplehurst, Kent TN12 0AZ

Library of Congress Cataloging-in-Publication Data available.

ISBN 1-885119-39-9

Manufactured in Great Britain.

10 9 8 7 6 5 4 3 2 1

Contents

Acknowledgments

The writing of books such as this would be barely possible without the help of the librarians and staffs of military libraries, and I must therefore first acknowledge with gratitude all that I have so often received from Mr D. W. King until recently of the Library of the Ministry of Defence, from the staff of the Prince Consort's Library, from the Service Historique de l'Armée in France, and from the Director and staff of the National Army Museum. Nearer home, I am particularly grateful to Major R. St G. G. Bartelot, Miss Wood and Mrs Jones of the Library of the Royal Artillery Institution, who have helped so much in the extraction of information from the records in their care.

It has been of the greatest help to me to receive the kind criticism and advice of General Sir James Marshall-Cornwall and Brigadier O. F. G. Hogg, both of whom were good enough to read my manuscript and provide most valuable suggestions for its improvement. The former made available his profound knowledge of the period of the Napoleonic wars; and the latter is, of course, one of the greatest authorities on old ordnance.

I am also most grateful to Major F. Myatt, the Director of the Weapons Museum at the School of Infantry, who was kind enough to read the manuscript and give me the benefit of his very extensive knowledge not only of the Peninsular campaign but also of the tactics and armament of that period.

Lastly, I must thank all those whose works have been consulted and of whom mention is made in the bibliography. In this connection, perhaps I might be allowed to express particular thanks to my friend Mr Jac Weller, whose admirable descriptions of Wellington's battles and of the armament and tactics of his time have thrown so much light on the ways in which armies fought in those days.

Introduction

Of the many aspects of the warfare that was waged with smooth-bore firearms, there is one that has received remarkably little attention from military historians. The weapons of that period have been described with meticulous care in many excellent works – every detail of their appearance, mechanisms and methods of use are fully recorded and illustrated; their scales of issue and their rates of fire are known; and there is no doubt about the ways in which they were used. What is missing, however, is an assessment of the effect or, more brutally, the lethality of the various weapons and combinations of weapons as they were used on the battlefield.

How effective was a volley of the muskets of a battalion? How many men were killed or wounded when five hundred muskets were fired at fifty yards range? How many casualties could be accounted to a battery of guns operating in support of that battalion? And in what ratios did guns and muskets inflict casualties on the enemy?

Those questions have never been satisfactorily answered – though some of the information required to provide the answers has always been available, even if not always complete. There are, of course, excuses for a lack of attention to this matter. Contemporary writers were too close to the events they were describing. The rate of development of the weapons was slow, and their effectiveness had remained unchanged for long periods and was well understood by writers and readers alike. It was unnecessary for historians and critics to remind their readers of the number of bullets or shot that could be delivered in a given time by a particular force, or to describe their effectiveness and the areas over which they produced their effect. The unknown and incalculable factors were what they were required to describe and analyse, and they could rely on their readers to visualise the effect of the weapon-power against which their story was told.

Those writing in the twentieth century face a different problem. Many of their readers are unfamiliar with the performance of the weapons of the past but are probably well acquainted with the very different performance of the armament of the present day. It is therefore disappointing for them to find so little attention devoted to the actual performance of the weapons of earlier times in the modern works

dealing with those periods, for without a knowledge of that performance they cannot easily obtain an accurate picture of what happened in a particular battle. (A notable exception is David Howarth's *A Near Run Thing,* which describes the physical and moral effects of the weapons in use at Waterloo.)

It is not suggested, of course, that the results of battles can be calculated mathematically from any such assessment, no matter how accurate. The qualities of courage, determination and fortitude, the inspirations of leadership, patriotism and, in some cases, hatred of the enemy or of his cause have had effects that cannot be determined by any mathematical formula. But in any battle, and at every stage of any battle, there was always a calculable amount of firepower available to both sides; and though disparities in that respect may have been partly eliminated by the greater skill, dash, endurance or sheer courage of some of the combatants, the result was affected by the weapon-power deployed.

In the event that these remarks should be thought to constitute an impertinent criticism of the great historians, it must be freely acknowledged that Fortescue, in particular, frequently refers to the relative weapon-power and related tactics of the British Army and its enemies. But even he makes little or no direct reference to the effectiveness of their weapons – either overall or, still less, in such a way as to show their relative effects on the target. Much information can, of course, be extracted from his great work by careful study; and his excellent maps make it possible to determine the locations of the small arms with considerable accuracy since the positions of the infantry are always clearly shown. On the other hand, the locations of the artillery are rarely shown in any detail on the maps, nor are its movements on the battlefield always described. This is a great handicap to those seeking to determine an effect that varied so greatly with the range at which, and the direction from which, the guns were shooting. It also makes it impossible to assess the effect of artillery and infantry acting in combination, on which the results of so many battles turned.

Period
This book covers the whole of the period from the middle of the seventeenth century to the middle of

the nineteenth century, and there are three good reasons for such a choice.

The first is that the middle of the seventeenth century is a convenient starting point because it saw the first formation of regular land forces and the appearance of permanent professional armies.

Secondly, the period chosen was one of stability during which the primary weapons of all armies – the flint-lock musket and the smooth-bore muzzle loading ordnance – remained in service in much the same form. There were changes, it is true, in their rates of fire, their mobility and, to a lesser extent, their accuracy; but the period can be regarded as that in which the smooth-bore armament reached the peak of its performance.

Thirdly, it was in the middle of the seventeenth century that – thanks largely to the genius of Gustavus Adolphus – the artillery began to play a significant part in battles. Furthermore, it was at that time that firearms became the primary weapon of the infantry instead of being mere adjuncts to the pikes of previous years. And shortly afterwards, those great captains the Duke of Marlborough and Frederick the Great showed how the handling of smooth-bore armament could be improved and how tactics could be adjusted to take advantage of its powers. Their ideas and the tactics they evolved carried over to the first half of the nineteenth century, when the ultimate development of smooth-bore weapons was achieved.

Unfortunately, the records of nearly all the battles in the early part of this period do not give enough detail to make it possible to assess the ratios in which the various weapons contributed to the result. Without accurate information on the numbers and precise locations of all the weapons concerned, their expenditure of ammunition – or at least the duration of their engagement – and the casualties caused by each of them such an assessment cannot be made. The number of weapons employed is usually known and the locations of the small-arms are normally known; but the locations of artillery are often very vaguely recorded. Surprisingly, the exact duration of their engagement is rarely mentioned: and the division of casualties into those caused by guns and those inflicted by small arms is practically never known. Indeed, it is only for the last hundred years of this whole period that some complete records of all the

data required are available.

Nevertheless, although convincing evidence of performance in the seventeenth and eighteenth century may be hard to find, a number of incidents in, or phases of, certain battles give some indication of the effectiveness of the firearms of that time; and it is possible to compare the somewhat tentative conclusions drawn from that period with the more reliable assessments provided by the better records of the nineteenth century.

Sequence

The book commences with a brief description of the armoury of the period which, because there are so many admirable works dealing with the weapons of the seventeenth, eighteenth and nineteenth century, is intended to serve as no more than a reminder of the weapons that were in use.

This is followed by an appraisal of the theoretical performance of those weapons at their target, both individually and collectively.

An examination is then made of those circumstances which inevitably degraded the theoretical performance of all weapons in battle, leading to a realistic estimate of the performance which could be expected in practice.

Finally, the events of a number of battles are examined in order to apply a practical test to the statements of performance that have been deduced.

Authorities

1. Ordnance: Most early authorities of the seventeenth and eighteenth century quote maximum ranges of ordnance as single figures, and there seems to have been no attempt to define the accuracy that was achieved at the target. Those ranges were merely a guide for the fire, which was applied empirically – accuracy probably not being definable for the weapons of those times.

A single interesting record appears in Colonel Alfred Burne's *More Battlefields of England,* in which he states that the shot marks made on a church tower before the battle of Roundway Down in 1643 can still be seen. These, fired at a range of six hundred yards, show a pattern of fourteen rounds in a space two feet square. The tower, of course, presented a vertical target, and the spread on the horizontal plane would have been less impressive; but this one record, compared with those of later times, seems to indicate that the accuracy of the piece was not markedly less in the seventeenth century than that of its counterpart in the nineteenth century.

Dating from the end of the eighteenth century, there is a great deal of evidence on the performance of smooth-bore ordnance. Of this, three main sources of technical data have been used. The first – hereafter referred to as the 'British Records' – consists of the detailed records of firing trials carried out in Great Britain under the direction of the Master General of the Ordnance between 1770 and 1813, now in the library of the Royal Artillery Institution at Woolwich. The mean figures of performance resulting from the trials were published as official range tables in the various editions of the *Bombardier and Pocket Gunner*.

The second source of information is William Müller's *The Elements of the Science of War,* published in 1811. Not to be confused with John Muller, who wrote the more famous *Treatise of Artillery* in 1768, William Müller was an officer of the Engineers of the King's German Legion. And his was a most useful and comprehensive treatise, in two volumes, covering all aspects of the warfare of his times. It includes information on the ordnance of all European nations and gives some of the most detailed analyses of performance, based on trials, that can be found anywhere. These records are referred to as 'Müller'.

The third technical record is a series of reports on trials carried out by the Madras Artillery of the Honourable East India Company between 1810 and 1817. The results of these trials were recorded by Lieutenant Colonel Henry Trim, Director of the Madras Artillery Depot, whose manuscript is held in the library of the Royal Artillery Institution. The trials involved the firing of many thousands of rounds at many ranges and at many types of target by all natures of ordnance. There are annoying gaps in the record, particularly at short ranges, but this is understandable since a great deal of the trials work was experimental and sought to discover the points at which the equipment ceased to be effective. Nevertheless, much useful information can be extracted from this record; and it is valuable in that it compares the slightly different equipments of the British, Bengal, Bombay, and Madras artillery. These records are referred to as the 'Madras Records'.

A great deal of useful information on the performance of the weapons of the French Army, including comparisons with those of other nations, can be found in *Artillerie de campagne française pendant la guerre de la révolution,* by Matti Lauerma (1956). This is a most comprehensive and valuable work. References to it bear the author's name.

2. Small arms: Both Müller and Lauerma give information on the performance of muskets, and advantage has also been taken of the works of W. W. Greener and Colonel H. C. B. Rogers on that subject. A useful but perhaps slightly prejudiced authority on rifle performance is Ezekiel Baker, who designed the rifle issued to the British Army.

3. General: Many other authorities have been consulted, and their works are listed in the bibliography; but one deserves special mention here: *The Influence of firearms on tactics* by 'an officer of superior rank'. The author was, in fact, the great von Moltke, and his work is a most valuable and penetrating study of the development of tactics as a result of the introduction and subsequent development of firearms.

The great British historians of the period of the Napoleonic wars – Oman, Napier and Fortescue – are frequently quoted, the author's surname only being used in each case.

1. The weapons

Infantry

1. Muskets: By the middle of the seventeenth century the musket was well on its way to becoming the primary weapon of the infantry. Throughout the whole of the time that the musket was in service, the efforts of the designers had been directed towards progressive improvements in the reliability and speed of actuation of a series of different firing mechanisms. The original version, operated by a hand-held slow match, was improved by fastening the slow match permanently to the lock in the matchlock. The wheel-lock followed, in which the priming powder was fired by a spark caused by a mechanism similar to that of a modern cigarette-lighter. Finally, in the last half of the seventeenth century, the flintlock appeared and was to remain in service for another two centuries. As the method of firing was improved, so also was the weapon lightened and shortened: thus by the time the flintlock appeared it had become possible to dispense with the rest from which its heavier predecessors had been fired and to discharge it from the shoulder, like a modern rifle.

The flintlock musket, a smooth-bore weapon loaded from the muzzle, fired a spherical bullet of lead that was propelled by a charge of gunpowder. Firing was effected by a trigger that released a spring-loaded flint to strike a steel surface and cause a spark to ignite the priming gunpowder in a pan over the touch hole.

As previously mentioned, the main aim of designers in the sixteenth and seventeenth century had been to increase the reliability and rate of fire of the musket. Improvement in accuracy and range was of secondary importance at that time. The cumbersome processes entailed in loading, priming and firing the early muskets – to say nothing of the necessity of clearing the bore of fouling at frequent intervals – meant that the musketeers were helpless and useless during the long intervals that elapsed between firings. It was therefore the custom in those early days to deploy them in formations many ranks deep so that the front rank, after firing, could move to the rear for loading and those who had loaded could move forward to the front rank for firing.

The great Gustavus Adolphus was much concerned with the problem of improving the rate of fire of the musket – which, in his time, was the wheel-lock. He lightened its construction and abolished the rest from which it had previously been fired; but more significantly, he caused the gunpowder to be enclosed in a cartridge case made of paper. This greatly improved the accuracy of measurement of the gunpowder charge and, as a result, not only gave more uniform ballistic performance but also increased the rate of fire. In its turn, this enabled the depth of formations of musketeers to be reduced to six ranks.

Once the cartridge had been introduced, the process of loading the musket – which was to remain unchanged throughout the period – was as follows. The soldier took a cartridge from his pouch (which, in the British Army, held sixty), bit off its end and poured a small quantity of the powder from it into the pan over the touch hole. He then rammed the cartridge – which contained the bullet as well as the gunpowder – down the bore of the musket with his ramrod, cocked the lock, and was ready to fire. An alternative method, used in some armies, was to ram the entire cartridge down the bore so that some of the gunpowder was forced into the touch hole to prime the piece.

Frequent clearing of the fouling that accumulated in the barrel naturally reduced the rate of fire. By the end of the eighteenth century and during the Napoleonic wars the flintlock musket could be fired five times in a minute by a single man working independently. When fired in controlled and collective volleys, as was normal in battle, a rate of fire of between two and three volleys per minute could be attained.

As long as the weapon was smooth-bored and fired gunpowder, which inevitably fouled the bore, the designer was always faced with the choice of improving range and accuracy or increasing the rate of fire. The former could be achieved only by making the bullet a tighter fit in the bore, but the latter demanded a loosely fitting bullet that could be easily rammed. In the conditions of the time, improvement of the rate of fire invariably took precedence. Thus the British Brown Bess musket, which armed the British infantry from the middle of the eighteenth century to the middle of the nineteenth century, had a barrel of No 11 bore measuring 0.76 inches in calibre and a bullet of No 14 bore that was 0.71 inches in diameter. The windage, or gap between the bullet and the bore, was therefore one-twentieth of an inch – and it was deliberately made so large in order to simplify loading and thus reduce the time it took. Although resulting in considerable inaccuracy and lack of range, those disadvantages were accepted in order to provide the highest possible rate of fire at short range.

The French musket of corresponding date was slightly smaller in calibre (0.70 inches) and fired a lighter bullet (twenty-two to the pound compared to the British fourteen). It is possible that it had a marginally longer effective range than Brown Bess, but Oman considered that the greater weight of metal in a British volley was significant in battle. In any case, all the muskets of the time were designed primarily in the interests of a high rate of fire at the expense of range and accuracy – to the extent that no sights were provided on the Brown Bess, which was aimed merely by looking along the barrel.

The effectiveness of the musket is discussed on page 00. Suffice it here to state that its maximum effective range was between 100 and 200 yards. It must not be forgotten, however, that the 'stopping power' of its enormous bullet was formidable indeed. As one contemporary writer put it, 'it would stop a bison in its tracks'; and a man hit by it would almost invariably have been incapacitated if not killed.

2. Rifles: Rifled small-arms, in which the bullet (which was at first spherical and not elongated) was stabilised by being spun in flight, had been invented by the middle of the sixteenth century. Their accuracy was superior to that of the musket but, perhaps a little surprisingly, the range of the early rifles was not markedly longer than that of the smooth-bore musket. Rifles, however, suffered from one serious disadvantage: the bullet had to be rammed in from the muzzle, the soft metal of which it was made being forced into the grooves of the rifling. This required considerable effort even when the bore was clean; but when the bore became fouled after firing, the necessary force increased to a point where it became impossible to load without first clearing the fouling. Consequently, the rate of fire and the reliability of the rifle were appreciably lower than those of the musket.

As opposed to their use for sporting purposes, rifles were not used seriously in war before the middle of the eighteenth century. It is said that it was the effective use of sporting rifles by the American forces in the War of Independence that first encouraged their use by skirmishers and snipers, who could take advantage of their greater accuracy for their special tasks. But whatever the origin of the idea, a proportion of the infantry of most countries was being armed with rifles towards the end of the eighteenth century – albeit a small and somewhat irregular proportion. Of the British infantry in the Peninsula, the only battalions armed with rifles were those of the 95th Foot and some of the 60th, though some of the light battalions of the King's German Legion also had them. The French Army had none at all in the Peninsula. Therefore, although some rifles may have been deployed in the British skirmishing line, the number was small and they were unlikely to have had a great effect on the total firepower.

The weapon used in the British Army was Baker's rifle, which had a calibre of 0.653 inches and fired a bullet weighing 350 grains.

3. Pikes and bayonets: In the middle of the seventeenth century the infantry was still armed with the pike as a complementary weapon to the musket. Indeed, until about that time the pike had been the more important of the two. Massed formations of infantry armed with their very long pikes had presented solid barriers that were impervious to attack by either mounted or dismounted troops while firearms were in their infancy. But improvements in the newer weapon gradually led the musket to predominance. By the end of the sixteenth century, pikes and muskets had begun to be used in approximately equal numbers; and Gustavus Adolphus took things a step further by forming whole battalions of musketeers only, employing twice as many muskets as pikes.

The ascendancy of the firearm continued until, at the beginning of the eighteenth century, the combination of a sufficiently reliable musket with a fixed or fixable bayonet – bayonets having been introduced into the British service in 1672 – finally eliminated the pike as a separate weapon.

Though the bayonet is not a firearm, it is necessary to take its use into account when seeking to analyse battle casualties. It could be the final arbiter in an action – as it was in the capture and recapture of the Flèches and the Great Redoubt at Borodino; but it was generally impossible to assault unshaken

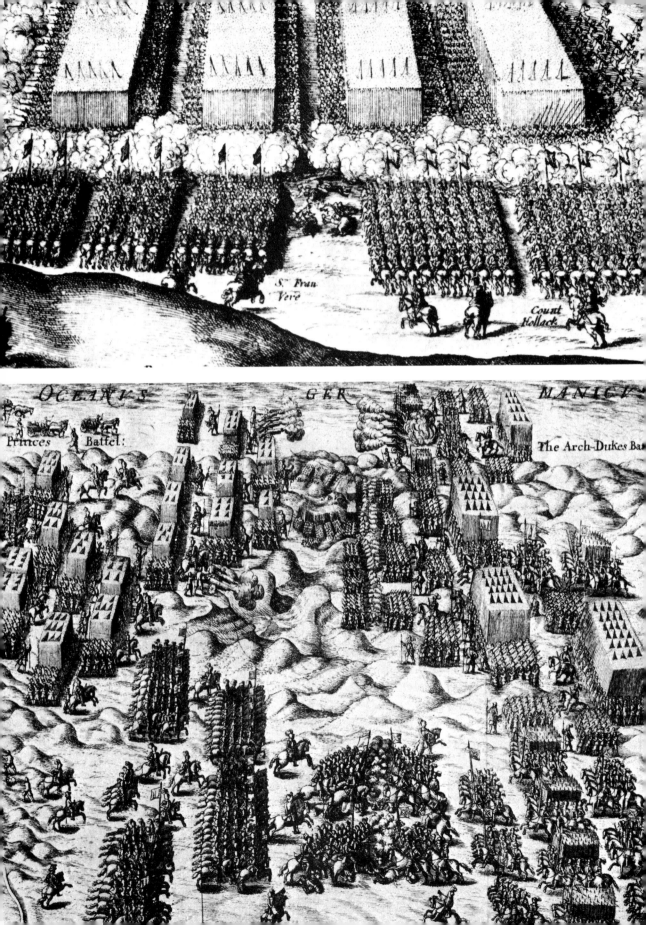

infantry with the bayonet alone. Firearms had to reduce the cohesion of the defending ranks first and shake the resolution of the men forming them. Even then, it was often the threat posed by the bayonet rather than its actual use that swayed the final issue. A bold attack with the bayonet without any preliminary musket fire was often carried out in the wars in India, however, though rarely without artillery support; but in Europe there was a tendency to discourage premature hand-to-hand fighting, in which control could be lost. There are several instances in which, as at Talavera, troops subjected to very heavy musket fire at point-blank range could not be restrained from surging forward to attack their enemy with the bayonet. But this could lead to confusion if the enemy was unbroken and if, as happened in the French column formation, considerable reserves of unshaken troops were waiting behind the firing line. The bayonet was therefore mainly used to confirm a result that had already been very largely completed by firepower.

Cavalry

The advent of firearms caused considerable changes in the armament of the cavalry. By the beginning of the seventeenth century the cavalry had given up its traditional lance and had, for the most part, adopted a short firearm – the pistol (some cavalry being equipped, however, with a long firearm – the arquebus). But by the middle of the century, Gustavus Adolphus had realised that cavalry armed with a pistol, with an effective range of only fifteen yards, was no match for unbroken infantry armed with muskets. He therefore withdrew the pistols and replaced them with swords. And the sword remained the primary weapon of the cavalry throughout the rest of the period, though a pistol or a carbine was also carried in a secondary capacity. Several nations armed some of their cavalry with lances instead of, and in some cases in addition to, swords.

Throughout the period there was a distinction, not always clearly drawn, between light and heavy cavalry. The light was generally employed for reconnaissance and skirmishing duties, and the heavy was used for shock action on the battlefield. This distinction was encouraged by the difference between horses of a stamp suitable for fast work over long distances

and heavier horses whose weight was of value in shock action.

Artillery

The weapons with which the artillery was armed, properly described collectively as 'ordnance', were of three separate kinds: guns, howitzers, and mortars – to which could be added rockets as an alternative armament used to a limited extent by some artilleries. These separate types of ordnance were made necessary by the fact that it was impossible to design a single all-purpose weapon to perform all the tasks demanded of the artillery.

A gun was designed to impart the highest practicable muzzle velocity to its projectiles, not only to give them the greatest possible range but also to increase their hitting power. This demanded a long piece, so that the gases produced by the exploding propellant charge could act upon the projectile for as long a period as possible. At the same time, with the ratio of charge weight to projectile weight as high as it could be, the calibre – or size of the bore – was limited by the ability of the metal of which the piece was made to withstand the stresses placed upon it. The gun therefore had to be long and thin, its length being between fourteen and twenty-four times its calibre.

Howitzers were required to throw as heavy a projectile as possible on a curved trajectory and were therefore of larger calibre than guns; but since a high muzzle velocity was not essential, they could be shorter in the barrel. Generally, they were between four and six times their calibres in length. As a large propellant charge was not required, though the calibre was large, the small charge could operate more efficiently if it was confined – as it usually was in howitzers – in a small chamber at the rear end of the bore.

Mortars exaggerated the characteristics of howitzers, being designed purely for high-angle fire. But they were rarely used in the field and need not be considered here. Rockets were also used to only a very limited extent from 1806 onwards; solely in the British and Indian services. No information of any value is available on the physical effect of their very erratic performance.

From the time in the fifteenth century when it first became possible to cast the pieces, or tubes, of ordnance in solid metal, there was very little change in their design for four hundred years. The length of the piece was shortened as gunpowder was made to burn more quickly and more efficiently, and a more truly cylindrical bore was achieved when it became possible to drill the solid metal. Apart from these improvements, however, the design remained constant from the middle of the seventeenth century to the middle of the nineteenth century.

By the beginning of that period, the sizes of pieces had become standardised throughout Europe; but there were two different sequences of calibres. The British, Austrian, Danish, Prussian and Russian artilleries used 3-, 6- 12- and 24-pounder (pr) guns, the figure indicating the weight of the projectile: and the French and Spanish used the sequence 4-, 8-, 12- 16- and 24-pr. The French introduced a 6pr gun at the end of the eighteenth century, but it was in service to a limited extent only during the Napoleonic wars. There was also a 9pr gun in the British service until about 1750, when it fell out of use. It was reintroduced in 1808 when the French 8pr was found to outmatch the British 6pr gun. The French 8pr gun was, in fact, very nearly the equivalent of the British 9pr as the French livre weighed 1.1 English pounds.

Howitzers in the British and French artilleries were classified by their calibres, the British having 4⅖-inch, 5½-inch, 8-inch, and 10-inch and the French having 6-inch and 8-inch. The other European powers used an extraordinary and confusing system under which their howitzers were defined by the weight of a stone shot that would have fitted their bores. Stone shot was not used after the middle of the seventeenth century, but this method of classification was retained after it had become obsolete. There were 7pr, 10pr, and 25pr howitzers in the Austrian, Danish and Prussian artilleries.

In general, the bigger the calibre of a piece and the heavier its projectile the longer its maximum effective range and the more destructive its fire. At the same time, the heavier pieces required heavier carriages with reduced mobility. Ordnance larger than the British 18pr gun and 8-inch howitzers were regarded as siege artillery. They are therefore beyond the scope of this book and will not be considered further here.

The majority of projectiles fired from smooth-bore ordance were spherical in shape and were propelled by a charge of gunpowder enclosed in a flannel bag, usually loaded separately from the projectile. The charge was ignited by a 'tube' containing an inflammable composition, which was placed in a hole in the breech called the 'vent' and to which a smouldering 'portfire' was applied when the order to fire was given. The tube was made either of tin or from a goose quill.

Although the appearance and design of the pieces of all guns and howitzers underwent few changes between 1650 and 1850, there was a considerable amount of development of the carriages on which they were mounted. The stages of this development can be described as follows.

Until the end of the sixteenth century it had been accepted that artillery possessed limited mobility and that, though it was useful in siege operations and static warfare, it could not be expected to accompany armies in the field. No mobile substitute for the ponderous carriages of early days had then been designed. But from the beginning of the seventeenth century attempts were made to bring light guns to the battlefield, and some light carriages – at first not very robust – were made for small guns (see page 47). The result of this innovation was that for the next two hundred years the mobile artillery of an army was split into two echelons. The first, containing the lightest guns and howitzers, was permanently attached in small numbers to battalions of infantry and sometimes to regiments of cavalry; and the remainder, including the heavier natures, formed the 'park of artillery', kept under central control though not neccessarily deployed as an entity.

The carriages used in the seventeenth century were all of 'double bracket' pattern, consisting of a heavy wooden axle-tree and a 'trail' made of two substantial baulks of timber set on edge and parallel to one another. These were called 'brackets', and they were connected to each other by three or four crosspieces called 'transoms'. The brackets and transoms formed a right-angled parallelogram that was bolted to the axle-tree at its front end – its rear end resting on the ground in action. The piece was supported between the brackets, its trunions resting in two semicircular grooves known as 'trunnion holes'. Strips of metal, called 'capsquares', prevented the piece from jumping out of the trunnion holes.

Until about the middle of the eighteenth century the piece was elevated or depressed by handspikes, used as levers, under the breech and held in the required position by wedges, known as 'quoins', between the breech and the centre transom. This clumsy arrangement was replaced by a screw-threaded rod working in a capstan-headed nut secured to the transom. The upper end of the rod was generally bolted to an eye cast under the cascable of the piece, but in some cases it ended in a flat plate on which the breech rested. The first reference to the use of such gear in the British service appears to be a record of 6pr and 12pr guns so fitted – described as 'Ordnance light brass, mounted on travelling carriages complete with limbers, ammunition boxes and elevating screws'[1] – being sent to North America in the force under the command of Major General Braddock in 1754. It could have been in service some years before that, but probably not before 1750.

The double-bracket carriage remained in service in all artilleries until the end of the eighteenth century. Its chief disadvantage was the weight on the rear end of the massive trail – so considerable that traversing the gun had to be carried out by at least two men using long handspikes, thus slowing the rate of fire and degrading the accuracy of laying.

Several major improvements, mostly to the carriage, were made to ordnance during this period. The first was the product of Gustavus Adolphus' inventive mind. Seeking a degree of mobility as yet unknown, he designed a light gun and carriage that weighed only 650lbs in all and could be drawn by two men or one horse. The piece of the gun consisted of a tube of copper wound with hempen cord, the whole enveloped in leather. Two such guns were attached to each battalion.

This light gun was later replaced by a brass piece of conventional design at the expense of more weight; but this Swedish light 4pr gun remained in service as a very serviceable little equipment for one hundred and fifty years and was, in fact, used by other countries including France.

Some important reforms were carried out in the French artillery during the eighteenth century. In 1732 General Vallière standardised the design of all

French pieces, although he did not extend that process to the carriages. (At that time, the French artillery used howitzers to a very limited extent.) And in 1767 a much more extensive series of reforms was carried out by General Gribeauval. He produced the famous 'Gribeauval System', which embraced not only the simplification and standardisation of the equipments – including their carriages – but also their attendant wagons and, indeed, the organisation of the artillery arm as a whole. It was Gribeauval-pattern guns and howitzers that armed the French artillery during the Napoleonic wars – and very serviceable equipments they were. Their double-bracket trails were shorter and lighter than those of earlier days to the extent that it was possible for the commander of a gun detachment to traverse the gun himself, using two short handspikes.

The last big change in the design of carriages during this period took place in the British artillery when, in 1792, General Congreve designed an entirely new form of carriage in which a single pole-like structure replaced the double-bracket trail. This placed the centre of gravity of the whole equipment further forward and lightened the weight on the trail so that one man could traverse it unaided. Both the rate of fire and the accuracy of laying were thus greatly improved; and additionally, it reduced the turning circle of the carriage when in draught.

This last point introduces the method of transportation of gun carriages. The problem of their movement to and from their gun positions had been solved since the sixteenth century by the use of a limber – a two-wheeled vehicle to which the trail of the gun could be secured and to which the animals which drew it could be harnessed. In its simplest form it consisted merely of an axle-tree and a pair of wheels; and the combination of the gun carriage and limber formed an articulated four-wheeled vehicle with considerable cross-country mobility.

The animal best suited to the draught of artillery equipments in civilised countries has always been the horse; but the weight of even the lightest carriages and the need to be able to move over broken ground demanded the use of more than one horse for each carriage. In the middle of the eighteenth century carriages were still so heavy that a team of fifteen horses was thought necessary for a 12pr gun, and even

1. Dickson Papers.

a 6pr required seven horses. As the carriages were made lighter the number of horses was correspondingly reduced until, by the time of the Napoleonic wars, teams of six or eight horses were normally used for all field guns and howitzers.

In the seventeenth and early eighteenth century, gun teams were hired for a campaign and were accompanied and driven by their own civilian drivers. By the end of the eighteenth century, however, this arrangement had been found to be unsatisfactory and enlisted soldiers – amenable to discipline – were provided to drive the teams, which now consisted of troop horses belonging to the army. At first, the drivers and horses in both the French and the British artillery were provided from a corps of drivers or artillery train and were merely attached to, not forming part of, the batteries they served.

But efforts to improve the mobility of the artillery were continuous, and a particular example of this was the creation by Frederick the Great of specialised 'horse artillery' in 1759. Such units were organised and equipped for rapid movement, one of their features being that the drivers were permanent members of the unit instead of being attached from a separate corps. They were particularly suited to the support of cavalry, though Frederick also used them as a mobile reserve of artillery which could be quickly moved to any part of the battlefield. This example had been followed by most other powers by the end of the century.

It can be generally stated that until the end of the eighteenth century the artillery, in conveying its heavy carriages to the battlefield, had some difficulty in keeping pace with the other arms. By the end of the century, however, the field artillery had attained a mobility comparable to that of the arm it was required to support. This seems to indicate that enough horses of suitable quality were constantly available; but that was not always the case. The British artillery, for example, was much hampered in the early stages of the Peninsular campaign by a serious shortage of horses – as a result of which some guns could not take the field at all. In general, however, it can be assumed that horse and field batteries were able to keep up with infantry and cavalry without trouble.

The combination of a light gun or howitzer, its limber, and a team of six or eight horses gave excellent cross-country performance. Some obstacles – particularly those with a vertical face – were impossible to negotiate; but experienced gunners could be relied upon to find a way round them or even, by the enthusiastic use of pick and shovel, to make a passage through an offending barrier. Fords to a depth of four feet could be negotiated; and rivers of greater depth could be crossed by swimming the horses and ferrying the carriages and men on rafts, which could be made with surprising speed by experienced men. There are few instances of it having been impossible to bring guns into action in the best positions because of difficulties with the ground.

It was, in fact, often on the infamous cart tracks that passed for roads that the artillery – in common with the other arms – had the greatest difficulty in movement. But a gun detachment had considerable spare manpower to help its gun teams, and tools to improve the roadway or remove obstacles were readily available on the carriages. The length of a day's march was usually dependent upon such matters as the location of water or shelter at its proposed end, but ten to fifteen miles a day was practicable. And there are many records of forced marches in which distances of forty or fifty miles were covered in twenty-four hours.

It remains to describe the actions necessary to the service of the gun in order to appreciate how the effectiveness of fire could be affected by the degree of efficiency shown. Five men were required to serve a light smooth-bore gun with full efficiency, excluding those required to bring up its ammunition. The essential tasks of each of them were as follows:

1. Command, supervision and laying: A non-commissioned officer was required to command the detachment, supervise its work and direct the fire, both tactically and technically. He had to lay the gun himself and observe the effect of the shot, making such adjustment to subsequent rounds as might be required.

2. Sponging and ramming: The piece had to be swabbed out after each round had been fired. This was done with a long 'spongestaff', after which the propellant charge and then the projectile had to be rammed down the bore from the muzzle. The ramming was done with the same spongestaff reversed. All of these tasks were carried out by the 'spongeman', who stood in front and to the right of the muzzle of the gun.

3. Serving the vent and priming: The passage of the sponge down the bore forced a current of air out of the vent, and if any smouldering residue from the last charge was left in the bore there was a danger of it exploding and injuring the spongeman. Such explosions were by no means rare when the drill was faulty, and they usually resulted in the spongeman losing an arm. To guard against this, the vent was stopped by the 'ventsman', who placed his thumb – enclosed in a leather thumbstall – over the aperture of the vent. The ventsman also had the tasks of inserting the 'pricker' down the vent to puncture the bag in which the charge was enclosed, in order to make ignition more certain, and then inserting the tube. In the British service he stood to the right of the breech of the gun; in the French artillery he stood to the left.

4. Loading: The fourth member of the detachment, standing in front of and to the left of the muzzle, placed first the charge and then the projectile into the bore for the spongeman to ram home. He was called the 'loader'.

5. Firing: The fifth essential gunner, called the 'firer', fired the gun with a smouldering portfire that he applied to the tube in the vent. The portfire, which burned for about half an hour, was ignited from the linstock – a slow match that was kept burning on the gun position throughout the action. The firer stood to the left rear of the breech in the British artillery, and to the right in the French artillery.

Though the gun could be served in an emergency by a smaller number of men than five, it is clear that the service would then have been correspondingly less efficient and the rate of fire lower than that normally attained. There was, of course, a variable number of other men in the detachment whose duties were to bring up ammunition, set fuzes and hand the rounds to the loader, and they could be called upon to replace casualties on the gun. But the detachment, as a whole, could not suffer more than one or two casualties without loss of efficiency.

All pieces of ordnance were laid – that is, directed at their targets – visually, and this involved three processes. The gun had first to be aligned on its target

in azimuth – a process called 'traversing' in the British artillery; it had then to be aligned in the vertical plane so as to compensate for the target being above or below the gun; and finally, a further elevation of the piece, known as 'tangent elevation', had to be applied to compensate for the vertical distance that the projectile would drop in flight due to the pull of gravity.

On going into action for the first time, the gun was traversed on its platform to align it on the target, to which end the double-bracket trail had usually to be moved by two men under the commander's direction – the block trail being adjusted by the commander himself. Thereafter, after firing, before laying could begin again, the first task was to run the gun up to its firing platform, from which it would have recoiled some four to six feet when the previous round had been fired. The field gun weighed the best part of a ton, so this called for some muscle-power on the part of the detachment.

No tangent elevation was required at short ranges of up to about 350 yards, but even so the gun had to be aligned in elevation. Before elevating screws were brought in during the second half of the eighteenth century, this required the breech to be raised or lowered with handspikes and held in position by the quoins – with obvious failings in speed and accuracy. The elevating screw effected a great improvement.

Before 1700 the laying of the piece in elevation, including the application of tangent elevation when necessary, was effected by the layer looking over the 'line of metal' – the centre line of the top surface of the piece – and judging the amount of elevation by eye. The accuracy of laying was later improved by the provision of lines scribed on the side of the breech, which indicated quarters of a degree of elevation when aligned with a foresight on the side of the muzzle. But the final improvement for both line and elevation was the introduction of the 'tangent sight' at the end of the eighteenth century. This device, placed in a hole in the base ring of the piece, had a moveable cross-piece with a notch in it. The cross-piece could be set on a scale to apply the tangent elevation required for any range, and the notch was used as a hind-sight in conjunction with a fore-sight on the swell of the muzzle.

This combination of accurately adjustable sights

and reasonably fine elevating gear was used during the Napoleonic wars with considerable efficiency. Moreover, some trials carried out in 1971 on three old 6pr guns in the Rotunda Museum at Woolwich gave some interesting and relevant results. In the first place, it was clear that with the elevating gear clean and properly lubricated and the bolt securing the elevating shaft to the cascable well fitting, the gear worked remarkably smoothly and virtually no backlash was perceptible. Tests were then made with a modern field clinometer, and it was found that one complete revolution of the elevating screw altered the elevation of the piece by thirty, forty and sixty minutes in the cases of the three guns tested – the amount depending on the pitch of the screw. Taking the mean reading of forty minutes, it was found that laying for elevation could be carried out to within one-twentieth of a turn of the screw – that is, to within two minutes. This accuracy was certainly better than that which could be obtained when laying with the naked eye over open sights; and it seems likely that accuracy in laying the smooth-bore equipment was not degraded by any inefficiency in the elevating gear once this was introduced.

However smooth and accurate the gears may have been, the accuracy of fire ultimately depended on the skill of the layer. Both fore-sight and hind-sight were crude instruments and, however accurately the tangent elevation may have been applied to them, the alignment of the gun on the target with the naked eye must always have taxed the skill of the layer very highly. Nevertheless, layers were very experienced men and there is ample evidence that fire could be applied accurately at surprisingly long ranges. The observation of the fall of each shot would be taken into account by the layer, and he would have a considerable knowledge of the ways of his gun and the errors to be expected in its trajectory. Indeed, it is probably fair to assert that the errors of the gun were always greater than the technical errors of experienced layers.

The most significant improvements in the design of ordnance during the last two hundred years of the smooth-bore era were the introduction of the elevating screw and the tangent sight. Use of the former must have increased both the rate of fire and the accuracy of laying to a very considerable extent; the latter must have improved the accuracy of laying at the longer ranges, which had previously been largely a matter of guesswork. Both of these inventions can be assumed to have been perfected by 1780 and may have been in use slightly earlier.

Right: Although the first of these photographs shows action towards the end of the nineteenth century and on a coast-defence gun, it provides an admirable illustration of the way in which all smooth-bore pieces were laid before the introduction of the elevating screw. The two gunners on either side of the breech are levering it up and down by means of their long wooden handspikes while the Number One is looking over the sights and directing their efforts until the gun is accurately laid on the target. The gunner kneeling behind the breech will then push the quoin between the breech and the transom, or cross-member, of the carriage to hold the piece in the required position. This cumbersome and complicated process, requiring the combined efforts of four men, restricted the rate of fire and the accuracy of laying. The second photograph shows the vertical elevating screw that was introduced in the middle of the eighteenth century and effected a great improvement in both the speed and the accuracy of laying by providing continuous fine adjustment in the hands of one man.

Pictorial section:
The development of small-arms

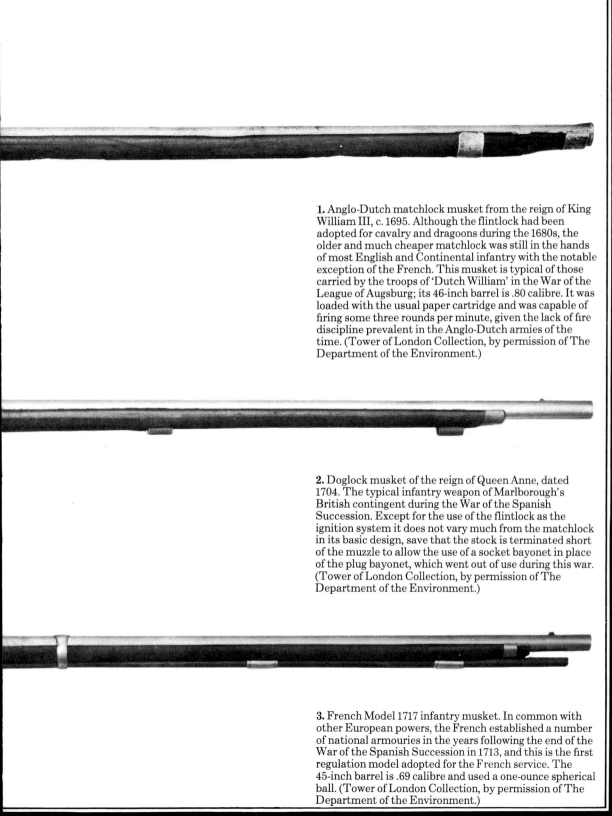

1. Anglo-Dutch matchlock musket from the reign of King William III, c. 1695. Although the flintlock had been adopted for cavalry and dragoons during the 1680s, the older and much cheaper matchlock was still in the hands of most English and Continental infantry with the notable exception of the French. This musket is typical of those carried by the troops of 'Dutch William' in the War of the League of Augsburg; its 46-inch barrel is .80 calibre. It was loaded with the usual paper cartridge and was capable of firing some three rounds per minute, given the lack of fire discipline prevalent in the Anglo-Dutch armies of the time. (Tower of London Collection, by permission of The Department of the Environment.)

2. Doglock musket of the reign of Queen Anne, dated 1704. The typical infantry weapon of Marlborough's British contingent during the War of the Spanish Succession. Except for the use of the flintlock as the ignition system it does not vary much from the matchlock in its basic design, save that the stock is terminated short of the muzzle to allow the use of a socket bayonet in place of the plug bayonet, which went out of use during this war. (Tower of London Collection, by permission of The Department of the Environment.)

3. French Model 1717 infantry musket. In common with other European powers, the French established a number of national armouries in the years following the end of the War of the Spanish Succession in 1713, and this is the first regulation model adopted for the French service. The 45-inch barrel is .69 calibre and used a one-ounce spherical ball. (Tower of London Collection, by permission of The Department of the Environment.)

4, 5. British Long Land Pattern musket, dated 1747. The characteristic British musket used during the War of the Austrian Succession, the Seven Years' War, and the War for American Independence (with a 42-inch barrel, and known as the Short Land Pattern). By the time of the Seven Years' War (1756–63) many of these muskets had been altered to have a steel ramrod in place of the brass-tipped wooden rod used until that time. The 46-inch barrel is .78 calibre, and the ornate furniture is of cast brass. The Duke of Cumberland's introduction of Prussian drill and discipline greatly improved the fire discipline of the British Army, and it was this musket with which the new drill was carried out. (Tower of London Collection, by permission of The Department of The Environment.)

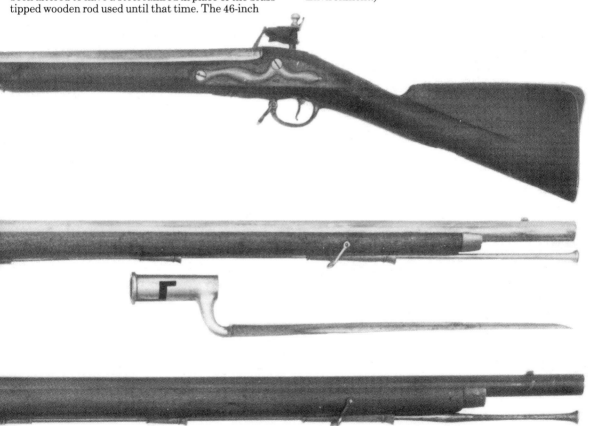

Austrian flintlock muskets. **6.** Model 1722, the first regulation design adopted for the Austrian infantry – the type used at the Battle of Mollwitz. The Model of 1745 was the first to use band-fastened barrel and iron ramrod. **7.** Model 1754 is an improved version of the Model 1745. Note the much stronger construction and the heavy iron ramrod. This was the infantry musket of the Austrian armies of the Seven Years' War. The barrel of the Model 1722 is $45\frac{1}{2}$ inches, and that of the Model 1754 is one inch shorter; the calibre of both is .74. (Tower of London Collection, by permission of The Department of the Environment.)

These photographs show the problems facing a gunner when laying with the naked eye at targets at various ranges. To avoid obscuring the target, the tangent sight has not been fitted; and the elevation of the piece has been exaggerated to show the line of metal. The men are shown at ranges of 250, 500 and 600 yards from the gun, and it will be seen that even at the moderate fighting range of 600 yards accurate laying was a task that called for some skill. It must also be remembered that the gun had to be completely relaid after it had recoiled on firing and had been run up again to its original gun-platform.

Furthermore, absent here is the smoke that would frequently have obscured the target and through the gaps in which the gun had to be laid with great rapidity.

1: 250 yards, single rank.
2: 250 yards, double rank.
3: 500 yards.
4: 600 yards.

3

4

2. Theoretical performance of the weapons

Before any attempt is made to assess the effectiveness of smooth-bore weapons, two general points have to be appreciated.

It must first be remembered that all fire was 'direct fire' – that is to say, it was necessary for the firer or the layer to see the target from his position standing, kneeling, or lying at his weapon. Furthermore, there were no optical aids such as telescopic sights: all aiming was done with the naked eye.

The limitations of the naked eye on the battlefield were well defined in the *Artillerist's Manual* of 1839–59 as follows:

Good eyesight recognises masses of troops at 1,700 yards: beyond this distance the glitter of arms may be observed. At 1,300 yards infantry may be distinguished from cavalry, and the movement of troops may be seen; the horses of cavalry are not, however, quite distinct but that the men are on horseback is clear. A single individual detached from the rest of the corps may be seen at 1,000 yards but his head does not appear as a round ball until he has approached up to 700 yards at which distance white crossbelts and white trousers may be seen. At 500 yards the face may be observed as a light coloured spot; the head, body, arms and their movements, as well as the uniform and the firelock (when bright barrels) can be made out. At between 200 and 250 yards all parts of the body are clearly visible, the details of the uniform are tolerably clear, and the officers may be distinguished from the men.

The plates opposite show the view over the sights of muskets and guns aimed at men at various distances, giving some idea of the problems presented to the soldier in aiming and laying. It is obvious that the infantry soldier was not called upon to fire at ranges at which his target could not normally be clearly seen but that the gunner may well have had some difficulty in laying on troops at the longer ranges to which his equipment could shoot.

The second general point is that no single smooth-bore weapon could produce fire comparable to that of modern automatic or quick-firing arms. It was impossible to sweep an area so as to deny it to an enemy without concentrating an inordinately large number of smooth-bore weapons for the task. And even then, the area covered could never be large and could never be regarded as absolutely impassable by determined men operating in depth. Each musket or gun must be regarded as an individual 'single shot' weapon capable of a maximum rate of fire of not more than two or three shots a minute – a very different picture

from that of the rapid firing weapons of today.

A good example of this limitation of the power of smooth-bore armament is provided by the story of the British attack on Bladensberg, before Washington, in 1814. The attacking infantry had to cross a river by a single narrow bridge that was within both gun and musket range of the American forces. Though casualties were certainly suffered, the fire of six guns and several hundred muskets was not able to prevent the British infantry from crossing the bridge in a way that unsubdued modern weapons would have made quite impossible.

The musket

The musket of the eighteenth and nineteenth century, with its heavy spherical bullet, its large windage and its low muzzle velocity (that of the French fusil was 320 metres per second), had a poor ballistic performance. Its bullet followed a trajectory that became excessively curved and erratic at all but very short ranges. Greener [1] states that the bullet dropped five feet vertically over a distance of 120 yards from the muzzle. As a result, it was just possible for a good marksman to hit a man at 100 yards: a volley could be fired with some chance of obtaining hits on a mass of troops at 200 yards: but at 300 yards fire was completely ineffective and the bullet was no longer lethal [2]

Colonel H. C. B. Rogers [3] quotes *To all sportsmen,* by Colonel Hanger, written in 1814, in which it is stated even more pessimistically that '(Brown Bess) . . . will strike a figure of a man at 80 yards - it may even be at 100, but a soldier must be very unfortunate indeed who shall be wounded by a common musket at 150 yards provided his antagonist aims at him: and as to firing at a man at 200 yards with a common musket you may as well fire at the moon and have the same hope of hitting your object. I do maintain and will prove whenever called upon that no man was ever killed at 200 yards by a common musket by the person who aimed at him.'

It seems likely that the ballistic performance of the musket was even lower in the eighteenth century than in the nineteenth . Lauerma, quoting Rouquerol.[4]

1. W. W. Greener, *The gun and its development,* p.624.
2. Lauerma, p.32.
3. *Weapons of the British soldier.*
4. *L'artillerie au debut des guerres de la revolution.*

estimates that between 0.2 and 0.5 per cent of the bullets fired hit their targets, and he repeats a statement of the times to the effect that to kill one man it was necessary to fire at him seven times his own weight in lead. These were practical as opposed to theoretical figures, however, and it will be seen later that there was a considerable difference between the two.

There must have been some improvement in the performance of the musket between 1650 and 1850, but it is clear that throughout the whole period it was a very short-ranged weapon and that the zone in front of a line of infantrymen in which an enemy was vulnerable to their fire was no more than 200 yards in depth. The improvement in performance was almost entirely in the rate of fire.

In spite of the low performance of the musket, it was rarely possible to make a direct assault on unshaken infantry with the bayonet. A fire-fight at close range – and often at very close range – had almost always to be carried out in an attempt to break the enemy's cohesion; and it was usually only after prolonged musketry had reduced both the enemy's firepower and his will to resist that the attacker could move forward to occupy his objective.

The fire of the muskets was delivered in controlled volleys by whole battalions, by sub-units of the battalion or, in the early days, by ranks. Rank firing was used when the rate of fire was slow in order to produce fire as continuous as possible over a wide frontage. The selection of the frontage over which volleys were to be fired depended on the tactical situation at the time, but it was also often dictated by the visibility. Thus the opening volley in a fire-fight would probably be fired by battalions, but the smoke cloud that then enveloped the battlefield would cause subsequent fire to be delivered by sub-units.

The maximum volume of fire was produced by deploying the infantry in line so that all the muskets could be fired at once. In the eighteenth century the line was three ranks deep, but by 1800 – though the French retained three ranks – the British Army was using a formation two ranks deep. Oman, in *Wellington's Army*, assumed that only the front two ranks of the French formation fired; and in theory, certainly, the third rank passed its loaded muskets forward and reloaded the empty ones that were passed back. But there seems to

be little doubt that in the stress of battle all of the front three ranks in the French Army fired simultaneously.

The establishment of battalions varied in the armies of different nations and at different times; and the actual strengths available in battle were usually considerably lower than the establishments. Thus at Waterloo the average strength of the Allied battalions was no more than 570 men, and of these some would have been in the light company. It would therefore not be misleading to assume a strength of 500 muskets for an infantry battalion. A British battalion, formed in line in two ranks at 22 inches per file, had a frontage of about 150 yards, and its theoretical firepower is shown in diagram 1.

Each bullet being effective on only one line of flight, a better picture of the firepower can perhaps be given by expressing it as a theoretical total of 1,000 to 1,500 bullets per minute over a frontage of 150 yards, or 6 to 10 bullets per yard per minute.

Finally, it remains to determine the theoretical effectiveness of this fire. Apart from the derogatory remarks already quoted, a number of records exist of trials with muskets that were carried out in c.1800. Picard, in *La Campagne de 1800 en Allemagne*, gives the mean error of the French fusil of that time, fired from a fixed rest at 150 metres, as 75cm in height and 60cm laterally. He goes on to give the following results of fire delivered under battle conditions by trained soldiers against a target measuring 1.75 metres by 3.00 metres:

Range	Percentage of shots hitting
75 metres (82 yards)	60%
150 metres (164 yards)	40%
225 metres (246 yards)	25%
300 metres (328 yards)	20%

Müller gives a set of figures for fire against a target representing a line of cavalry, with an interesting distinction between 'well trained men' and 'ordinary soldiers'. These, which require degrading to show the results against a line of infantry, are as follows:

Range	Percentage of hits obtained	
	By well trained men	By ordinary soldiers
100 yards	53%	40%
200 yards	30%	18%
300 yards	23%	15%

Diagram 1. The firepower of an infantry battalion in two ranks.

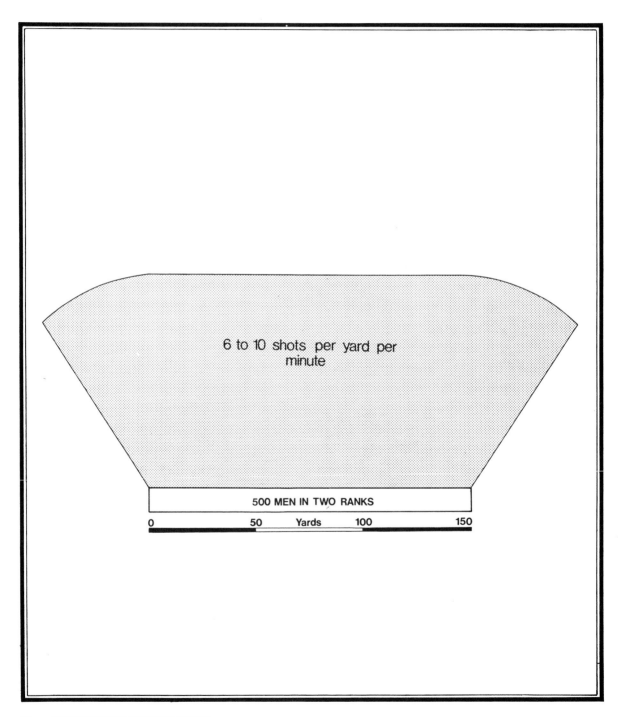

6 to 10 shots per yard per minute

500 MEN IN TWO RANKS

0   50   Yards   100   150

Greener, in *The Gun*, gives figures for the percussion musket – which was only marginally better than the flintlock as regards range and accuracy – as follows:

Range	Percentage of hits against a target 6 feet by 20 feet
100 yards	75%
260 yards	42%
300 yards	16%
400 yards	4·5%

The first two of these records seem slightly suspect at long range in that the reduction in effectiveness falls off less steeply as the range increases; but after allowance has been made for the different targets assumed, their mean gives a picture of theoretical performance as shown in diagram 2.

These figures indicate that, in theory, a battalion 500 strong firing two volleys during an attack by infantry over 100 yards of ground might expect to obtain some 500 to 600 hits from the 1,000 musket shots that could have been fired during the attack. It is emphasised, however, that this must be regarded as an entirely theoretical estimate since casualties on such a scale can never have been inflicted; but it serves as an indication of what might have been attainable under absolutely perfect conditions.

The rifle

The rifle, which appeared only in the period of the Napoleonic wars and was not in service during the campaigns of the earlier part of the eighteenth century, was a considerably more accurate weapon than the musket. But its range, though longer than that of the musket, was not as long as might be expected. The British Baker's rifle was 'deadly in the hands of troops up to 200 yards, dangerous between 200 and 300 yards in the hands of a marksman'.[1] Baker himself claimed the certainty of a hit at 200 yards, a good chance of one at 300 yards when the wind was neglible, and an occasional hit at 400 to 500 yards.[2] The plates here show the results of trials carried out with Baker's rifle at ranges of 100, 200 and 300 yards. These, again, were carried out under perfect conditions – most of the rounds having been fired from an immovable rest. They did show, however, that the rifle was very

1. *English guns and rifles*, George.
2. *Remarks on rifled guns and fowling pieces*, Baker, 1823.

appreciably more accurate than the musket and had about twice its effective range.

Artillery

Before the effectiveness of artillery can be studied, it is necessary to examine the different projectiles it fired and what they achieved at their targets. In spite of the complication they caused, different projectiles were required because, just as it had proved impossible to design a single all-purpose type of ordnance, no one pattern of projectile could be found to operate efficiently at all ranges and at all targets.

1. Round shot: The primary projectile of the gun, as opposed to the howitzer, was round shot. Throughout the whole period during which smooth-bore ordnance was in service, seventy to eighty per cent of the ammunition held in the field for all guns was of that type; and it is clear that a greater reliance was placed on it than on any other projectile.

Round shot were solid cast iron spheres, or 'cannon balls', the weight of which defined the size and classification of the guns from which they were fired. But when considering the effect of a shot at the target, it is interesting to visualise its size as well as its weight. The diameter of the smallest commonly used was just under three inches, and that of the largest used in the field was about four and a quarter inches.

Round shot had two purposes: to breach the walls of fortresses in siege operations, and quite simply to destroy men, horses and equipment in the field. In the latter role, even when of small size, it was devastating to those who stood in its path and within its range. It could shatter a gun carriage or wagon and slice men or horses in half, doing either in a noisy and frightening manner. There are records of as many as forty men having been killed by a single shot at a range of 600 to 800 yards, all having been in the line of fire at the time. The close formations adopted by all troops in order to concentrate their own firepower made them vulnerable to round shot and made the evasion of a shot seen to be approaching them virtually impossible. Müller states that, within effective range, one shot fired at right angles to a line of infantry could be expected to kill three men, 'but four or five are sometimes wounded'.

It is important to appreciate the effect of the weight of the shot. There was little difference between the

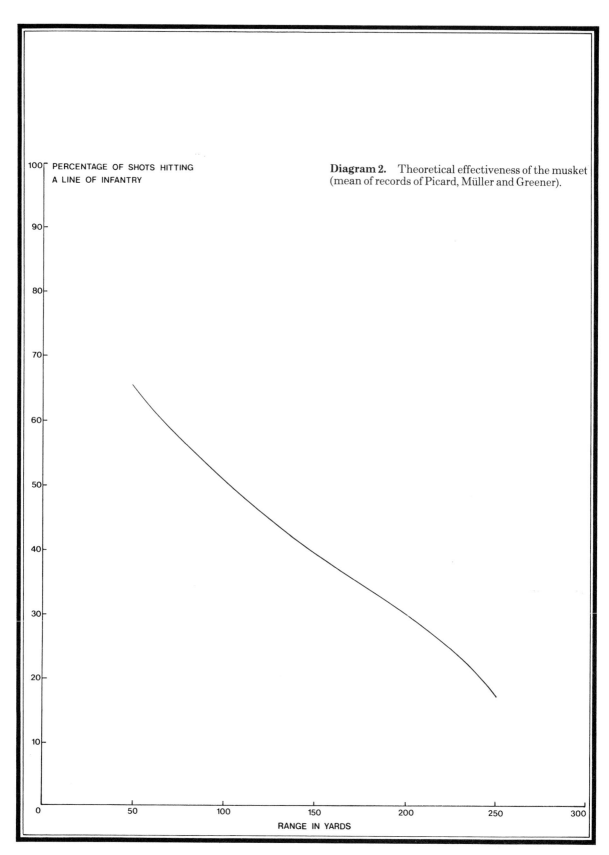

100 PERCENTAGE OF SHOTS HITTING
A LINE OF INFANTRY

Diagram 2. Theoretical effectiveness of the musket (mean of records of Picard, Müller and Greener).

RANGE IN YARDS

Below: Records of trials carried out with Baker's rifle in 1800, 1803 and 1805. From *Remarks on Rifle Guns* by Ezekiel Baker, 1823.

Bottom of page: The Baker rifle.

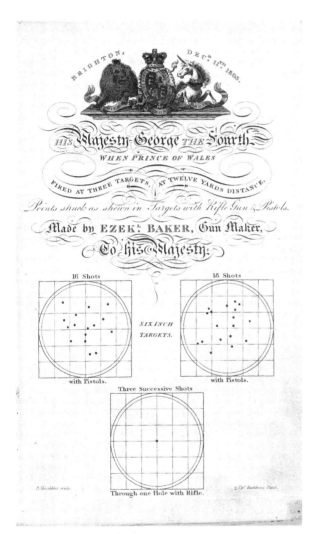

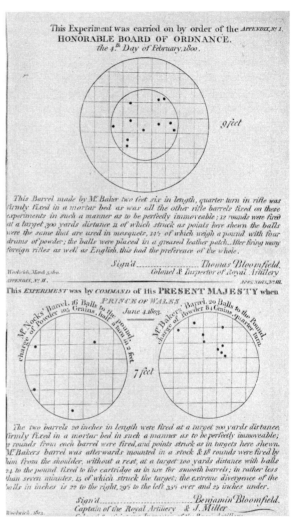

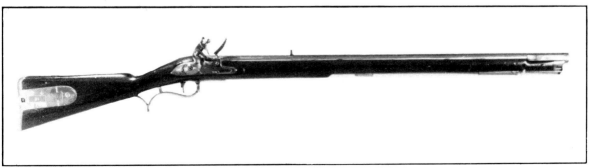

muzzle velocities of all the guns used in the field, but the heavier the shot the greater was its remaining velocity – that is, its velocity at the target [1] The destructive power of the shot depended on its kinetic energy, which varies directly with the weight but according to the square of the velocity. The heavy shot was therefore possessed of appreciably more hitting power than the light shot. Again according to Müller, in relation to a 3pr shot a 6pr shot was fifty per cent more effective and a 12pr was twice as effective. It is a point worth bearing in mind when studying the battles.

There are, indeed, many examples of the effect of heavy shot in battle throughout the whole of the smooth-bore period. One of the earliest was at the battle of Minden in 1759, when the 12pr guns of Captain Macbean's company had a decisive effect. But the most striking instance was the engagement of Russian field guns by the two 18pr guns of the British siege train at the battle of Inkerman. The heavy shot of the British guns overpowered and destroyed in succession the guns of a large battery of Russian field artillery, whose return fire was largely ineffective.

Before the Peninsular campaign, a preoccupation with colonial wars in difficult country led to the arming of the British field artillery mainly with light 6pr guns. In the Peninsula, however, the British Army found itself facing the 8pr and 12pr guns of the French artillery – which meant, with the French livre equivalent to 1.1 British pounds, that the French 8pr was almost as heavy as the British 9pr. This outgunning of the British artillery led to the reintroduction of the 9pr as the standard armament of the field artillery. Furthermore, the Duke of Wellington rearmed half his Horse Artillery troops with 9prs for the Waterloo campaign – accepting a certain reduction in mobility to obtain a greater effect at the target. Jac Weller considers that this substitution of the 9pr involved a considerable reduction in the rate of fire. The running up of the heavier 9pr carriage, which recoiled further than the 6pr, would have been more laborious, but it seems unlikely that when the gun detachments were fresh the rate of fire would have been more than marginally slower than that of the lighter equipment.

1. At 1,000 yards range: 18pr – 840 fps; 9pr – 690 fps; 6pr – 450 fps (Madras Records).

During the preliminary bombardment at the battle of Gujerat, the 9prs fired 52 rounds per gun to the 6prs' 77, but the 24pr howitzers fired 60 rounds per gun to the 12prs' 42 [Madras Records]. Moreover, at Waterloo, Sandham's Company and Mercer's Troop, armed with 9pr guns, fired 183 and 116 rounds per gun respectively; and Webber Smith's Troop, in action in much the same locality and armed with 6pr guns, fired 110.

One other important effect of heavy shot must be noted. When time permitted – as in the preparation of a defensive position – field works would sometimes be constructed particularly to protect gun positions, and they provided almost complete protection against any shot smaller than a 9pr. It was therefore frequently necessary to employ even heavier calibres if the guns behind them were to be neutralised effectively.

In assessing the effect of round shot, it is helpful to visualise the trajectories or paths that they followed after leaving the gun muzzle. Diagram 3 shows the path followed by a shot fired from a horizontal gun, the vertical scale being exaggerated thirty times.

It can be seen that the shot fell steadily from the height of the muzzle till it hit the ground at the point known as 'first graze'. It then bounced, or ricocheted, and continued to the point of 'second graze', after which some eighty per cent of the shot ricocheted again. During the whole of this flight the shot was below 'man height', and any man or horse in its path would have been hit. The application of a small amount of elevation, up to say a quarter of a degree, would have moved the point of first graze 100 to 200 yards further from the gun, but the trajectory would still have been entirely below man height.

Diagram 4 shows the effect of applying greater amounts of elevation.

Provided that no friendly troops were in the line of fire, it was possible to use the ricochet effect of point-blank fire at ranges of up to 800 yards, as shown in diagram 3; but this tended to be inaccurate and it reduced the hitting power of the shot at the target. It was normally better to bring the first graze on to the target as shown in diagram 4; for although, in that case, the first part of the trajectory would be above man-height, it can be seen that at ranges of less than 900 yards there was still a zone of appreciable depth before and after the point of first graze within which a man could be struck. It was undoubtedly this long zone of effectiveness that caused reliance to be placed on round shot as the primary projectile of the gun – compensating, as it did, for errors in trajectories and eliminating the effects of inaccuracies in laying.

A study of these diagrams also shows that, unless the guns were sited on markedly higher ground than that occupied by the troops they were supporting, it was normally impossible to fire over the heads of friendly troops except at very long range. The trajectory was too flat to permit this; and it must also be remembered that the guns could not be laid visually unless there was a clear line of sight from the gun to the target.

The linear effect of round shot made it far more destructive if it could be fired at its target in enfilade – that is, in a sweeping line from end to end – and the gunners were constantly seeking gun positions from which enfilade fire could be developed, particularly at the longer ranges. This, and their inability to fire over the heads of the infantry, led to the occupation of gun positions that were usually on the flanks of the troops supported.

2. Common shell: Round shot were not fired from howitzers, the lower muzzle velocities and higher trajectories of which would have made them ineffective. Instead common shell were fired; and these were the primary projectiles of howitzers in all artilleries other than the British[1] Common shell were hollow spheres of iron containing a charge of gunpowder that was exploded, after a predetermined time of flight, by a fuze. The fuze contained a train of powder – the length of which was adjusted when the fuze was set – ignited by the flash of the howitzer's propellant charge.

Fuzes could not be set sufficiently accurately to burst a shell in the air above a target deliberately, but a form of air-burst was sometimes effected by causing the shell to ricochet and burst after first graze. It required a reduced charge, but that presented no particular difficulty.

It must not be thought that a shell filled with gunpowder produced a destructive effect comparable with that of a modern shell filled with high explosive.

1. British trials in 1779 established that common shell could also be fired from guns but they were not normally fired from field guns, which carried no shell in their ammunition echelons.

Diagram 3. Trajectories of a 9pr gun at 0° elevation (mean of 50 shots, Madras Records 1813); 6pr ranged about 100 yards less.

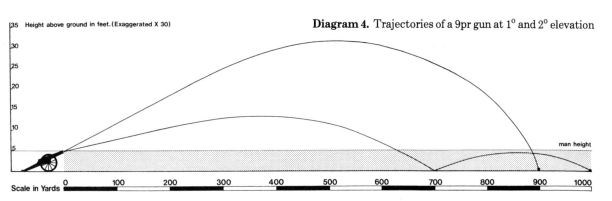

Diagram 4. Trajectories of a 9pr gun at 1° and 2° elevation

Nevertheless, even the small powder-filled shells of field howitzers produced unpleasant bursts with appreciable lateral effect. The high trajectories of howitzers enabled them to be fired over the heads of friendly troops, as happened when Bull's Troop of the Royal Horse Artillery cleared the wood at Hougoumont during the battle of Waterloo – the wood at that time being occupied by both sides. Howitzer fire could also be developed against troops behind cover.

Field howitzers were normally found either singly or in pairs in each fire unit, and it is therefore clear that during the relevant period much more reliance was placed on light guns than on light howitzers – which means, in effect, that the round shot was considered a more effective projectile than the common shell.

3. Spherical case or shrapnel shell: There was one type of projectile that was used only by the British artillery during the Napoleonic wars – the spherical case shot, which had been invented several years earlier by Lieutenant Henry Shrapnel, R.A., and was ultimately given his name at the request of his descendants [1] It consisted of a hollow iron sphere filled with bullets and also containing a bursting charge of gunpowder. The charge – ignited by a fuze similar to that used in common shell – blew open the shell at a predetermined point on the trajectory, ejecting the bullets from the case so that they continued to travel along the shell's path towards the target. Diagram 5 shows the effect of shrapnel shell and the importance of it bursting at the correct point on the trajectory.

Shrapnel, which was fired from guns as well as from howitzers, was most useful at long range, where the spread of the bullets could compensate for errors of the gun.[1] A drawback, it is true, was that well-trained men were needed to set its fuzes accurately; but there is evidence that the French, who had no comparable projectile, found it effective and disliked it. Between thirteen and nineteen per cent of the ammunition of field guns was shrapnel, and field howitzers carried as much as fifty per cent.

4. Case or canister shot: The last type of projectile fired by guns and howitzers was case shot, which consisted of a tin case containing a number of loose bullets and of a size to fit the bore. The case merely held the bullets together during their passage up the bore. When it emerged at the muzzle, the bullets were released to continue their deadly passage over the immediate frontage of the gun position. The

1. Invented in 1784. Accepted after trials in 1792 and 1803 (Ordnance Select Committee, 3 June 1803). First used at Surinam April 1804.

1. 6pr shrapnel (27–85 bullets per shell) had a spread of from 250 yards at point blank range to 150 yards at 1,000 yards.

Diagram 5. The problems of firing shrapnel shells.

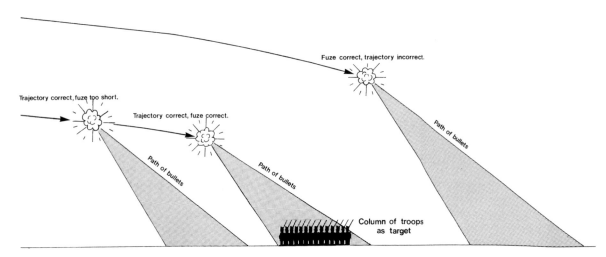

Fuze correct, trajectory incorrect.

Trajectory correct, fuze too short.

Trajectory correct, fuze correct.

Path of bullets

Path of bullets

Path of bullets

Column of troops as target

lethal range of the bullets was limited, however, to a maximum of 500 yards. Case shot was therefore purely a close-range projectile and was intended primarily for use in repelling the last stages of an assault. It was sometimes used offensively too, but the small quantity of case shot held (28 rounds per gun for the British 6pr and 16 rounds per gun for the 9pr) naturally limited its employment for that purpose.

Most artilleries used a heavy and a light version of case shot – the light case of the British 6pr gun holding 85 $1\frac{1}{2}$-ounce bullets and the heavy case holding 41 of $3\frac{1}{4}$ ounces, other calibres being in proportion. The large bullets of heavy case ranged further than the light ones, and there are instances in war – and records of trials in peace – of fire being delivered with heavy case at ranges of up to 600 yards. The extreme range of light case bullets was normally taken to be 250 yards, and it was the British practice to limit the range of all case shot to about 350 yards. But the French artillery seems to have used it at rather longer ranges, particularly in attack.

The bullets of case shot spread out somewhat rapidly at the muzzle, Müller having recorded a spread to a circle whose diameter was 32 feet per 100 yards of range. As many of these bullets
of range. As many of these bullets drove harmlessly into the ground or passed above man-height, case shot could not be regarded as a very efficient form of projectile. But though there was a waste of effort that increased with range, there is little doubt that it was a damaging projectile at short range. It was particularly effective against the large target presented by cavalry; and at very short range it was possible to fire two rounds of case, or one of case and one of round shot simultaneously.

5. Grape shot: Many contemporary writers refer to the use of grape shot in the field. It consisted of nine very large bullets wired together, and could be regarded as an extreme form of heavy case. Although it was certainly used by light iron guns against ships' boats, for the holing of which it was very effective, its heavy bullets would not have been as destructive as lighter ones at normal fighting ranges in the field. No record of grape shot appears in the published scales of ammunition carried by field artillery in the British service, but there are several references to the undesirability of firing it from brass guns owing to the damage that it would cause to their bores. It is possible that it was used by the artilleries of other powers, but it seems likely that the word 'grape' was used loosely and incorrectly when referring to case shot and may also have been used to indicate heavy case as opposed to light case.

Rates of fire

In 1646 Master Gunner William Eldred stated, in *The Gunner's Glasse*, that a maximum of ten rounds an hour could be fired from a gun, and that after forty shots had been fired an interval of an hour must be allowed to cool the piece. The rate of fire at that time was restricted not only by the weight of the carriages and by the clumsy gear used for elevating and depressing the pieces but also – and, in the master gunner's mind, more significantly – by what may be called a lack of endurance in the early cast pieces themselves. They could not, with safety, withstand the shock of firing when they became overheated after prolonged or too rapid firing.

This danger receded as the technique of casting gun barrels improved, and it is probably accurate to state that in the first half of the eighteenth century the rate of fire was limited mainly by the delays arising from running up the gun and relaying it with handspikes and quoins. Gun barrels were known to burst, on occasion; but such accidents usually occurred in siege operations after prolonged firing. There are few recorded instances of guns bursting in the field.

After the introduction of the elevating screw and the tangent sight, in the 1760s, the rate of fire was greatly improved. And on the fully developed smoothbore ordnance of the nineteenth century it was possible for a well-trained gun detachment to fire as many as eight rounds a minute from a light gun. A considerably slower rate of fire was insisted upon in practice, however, so that the interlocking movements of the gun drill could be performed without danger of mistakes that could lead to premature bursts of the highly explosive cartridges. A rate of fire of two rounds a minute was therefore laid down for all projectiles other than case, with which three rounds a minute was permissible.

Scales of ammunition

The standard rates of fire may also have been laid

down with an eye to the amount of ammunition held in the field, which was clearly not unlimited. In the British and French services the scales were as follows:

Table showing the scales of ammunition held by British and French guns about 1800

BRITISH

	Round shot	Shrapnel	Heavy case	Light case
Light 6pr gun				
Gun axle box	8	–	–	–
Gun limber	32	–	5	5
Wagon limber	32	–	4	4
Wagon body	60	20	5	5
Total	132	20	14	14
			Total rounds per gun 180	
9pr gun				
Gun limber	26	–	3	3
Wagon limber	26	–	3	3
Wagon body	36	12	2	2
Total	88	12	8	8
			Total rounds per gun 116	

FRENCH

	Round shot		Heavy case	Light case
4pr gun	118		24	26
			Total rounds per gun 178	
8pr gun	137		40	20
			Total rounds per gun 197	
12pr gun	153		24	26
			Total rounds per gun 203	

Authorities: British: *The Bombardier and Pocket Gunner;* French: Lauerma.

These were the amounts of ammunition immediately available on the gun position, held in what was called the 'firing battery'. A small amount of additional ammunition was held in the 'first line' ammunition wagons, which were normally not in such close touch with the gun line.

It will be seen from these figures that there was enough ammunition in the firing battery to enable about one hour's continuous firing to be carried out at the laid down maximum rate. Continuous firing for such a long time, however, would very rarely have been either possible or required in support of infantry or cavalry. But the records show that when the artillery was required to undertake counter-battery fire an hour's bombardment of hostile gun positions was often too short to neutralise them effectively. It is therefore clear that when counter-battery work was required, the supply of ammunition had to be carefully watched to ensure that shortages would not occur if the guns were later called upon to engage more menacing enemy infantry or cavalry.

Records of trials

The trials examined at this stage are those that were carried out in peacetime in order to determine the theoretical performance of the equipments. Such trials were carried out with meticulous attention to the conditions, and they included records based on accurate observation and measurement of all aspects of the performance achieved. As was explained in the Introduction, three sets of records are drawn upon here and are referred to as the British Records, Müller, and the Madras Records.

1. The zone of the gun: The area into which all the shots from a gun will fall, when the gun is laid in exactly the same way for each shot, is known as the 100% zone, and that into which half the shots can be expected to fall is the 50% zone. The first point to be studied is the size of the zone over which the errors of a gun and its projectile caused a number of rounds to be spread at the target.

Müller gives 'differences of ranges' – an obscure term that might mean either half the 100% zone or its full length – as 28% of the range for a 6pr gun. At the same time, he attributes to the 3pr gun the remarkably small error of 3% of the range. This seems much too small to be acceptable and may well be a misprint.[1] If it is assumed that Müller intended his 'difference' to mean the whole 100% zone, this would give a zone of 140 yards at 500 yards range. The British Records and the Madras Records are not so pessimistic, putting the 100% zone as about 10% to 15% of the range. That figure seems to be well supported and applicable to all equipments.[2]

It would be unwise to be too dogmatic about the exact size of the zone of round shot at short ranges with flat trajectories since it was the long zone within which the shot was below man-height that made the projectile so effective. Errors in the point of first

1. Nevertheless, the 3pr gun was well known as an accurate performer (see British Records).
2. Lauerma confirms this figure for French guns.

graze did not diminish its lethality. At the longer ranges, a 100% zone of 100 to 150 yards can be assumed at 1,000 yards range.

Some records suggest that errors in line were generally greater than those in the vertical plane. Müller stating that they were three times as great.[1] This was not significant against linear targets but affected such shooting as that against individual guns.

2. The effectiveness of round shot: Müller gives the number of hits that could be expected when round shot were fired at a single line of infantry at right angles to the line of fire. The figures, obtained by firing at a screen six feet high and counting the holes made in it by the shot, are:

[1]. This is not confirmed by the British Records, which put the average line error as 2 feet at 400 yards.

Gun	Range	Percentage of rounds fired that took effect
3pr	450 yards	100%
	750 yards	34%
	1,100 yards	20%
6pr	520 yards	100%
	950 yards	31%
	1,200 yards	17%
12pr	600 yards	100%
	950 yards	26%
	1,300 yards	15%

These results relate to a target representing a single line of men. The penetrative power of the shot must be remembered, however, when translating the number of hits against a screen into the number of casualties to be expected in a formation more than one rank deep – particularly a column.

The Madras Records, which are very extensive and

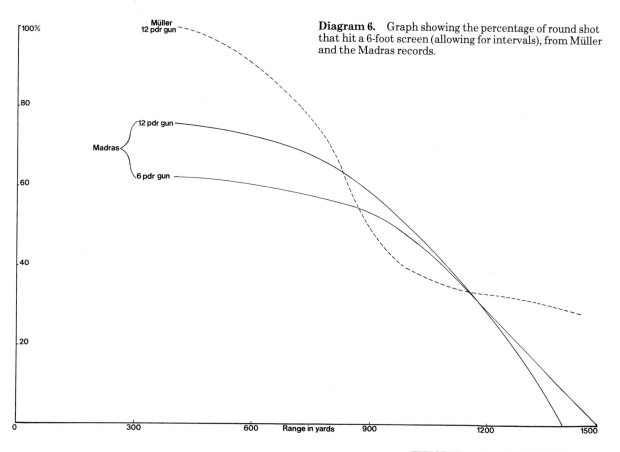

Diagram 6. Graph showing the percentage of round shot that hit a 6-foot screen (allowing for intervals), from Müller and the Madras records.

Right: Facsimile of a page of the British Records of trials fired with case shot from a $4\frac{2}{5}$-inch howitzer. The records show the number of bullets that hit screens at various ranges. These are some of the early records, dated 1770-71, but they show the accuracy in the compilation throughout. It will be seen that, in these cases, the shot proved to be almost totally ineffective at 400 yards but that an average of 33% of the bullets of the $4\frac{2}{5}$-inch howitzer's case shot hit the screens at 200 yards.

based on the expenditure of many hundreds of rounds, confirm these figures but do not claim 100% effectiveness at short range. Müller's results and those of the Madras Records are shown graphically in diagram 6.

Lauerma considers that the light British guns, although more mobile than the French, were less accurate than the French equipments. This may well have been so: the French guns had a smaller windage than the British and that would have given them greater accuracy and more range, which is borne out by the fact that the French artillery tended to engage at rather longer ranges than the British.

There can be little doubt of the ability of the smooth-bore gun to put the percentages of its shots shown in diagram 6 through a target screen at the various ranges shown. But it is clear that there was a range beyond which it ceased to be profitable to fire round shot because the results would not have justified the expenditure of ammunition. That range varied with the type of target and the tactical situation. It was often profitable to fire round shot at columns or masses of men and horses at long range to take advantage of its penetrative power: but the diminished chance of a hit at long range limited the effectiveness of fire against linear targets such as gun positions unless they could be taken in enfilade. In this connection Müller records trials of fire against embrasures that presented targets similar in size to those of single guns. These trials, using a 6pr gun, established that 50% of the shots hit the target at 520 yards range and 25% hit it at 850 yards. The heavier guns produced the same results at ranges that increased with the calibre.

Clearly, it would be impossible to define a single fixed range beyond which the light guns were ineffective. In general terms, however, their maximum effective range can be taken to have been between 800 and 1,000 yards.

3. The effectiveness of shrapnel shell: Shrapnel shell is the one projectile of which the records of effectiveness are scanty and somewhat contradictory. Müller does not mention it at all, and there is little information in the Madras Records. The British Records, however, include particulars of a number of practices carried out at Sutton Heath in 1812, covering the firing of a little over one hundred rounds from light equipments at longish ranges and

indicating a very low performance. Between 2% and 17% of the bullets fired are recorded as having hit the target screens at ranges of between 700 and 1,500 yards. The Madras Records, though not extensive, suggest that on average about 10% of the bullets were effective – adding the interesting information that the spread of the bullets in range was between 160 yards at short range and 100 yards at 1,000 yards.

The number of bullets in each shell, depending on the weight of the bullet used (which varied considerably), was:

6pr gun	from	85 to 27
9pr gun	from	127 to 41
12pr gun	from	170 to 63.

The ballistic performance of the shell itself was similar to that of the round shot, but the effectiveness of the bullets depended on the accuracy of both the setting and burning of the fuze. Errors could also occur through an inaccurate estimation of the length of fuze required and from the difficulty of determining by visual observation from the gun position whether the selected fuze length would give a correct burst.

In spite of the apparently rather low figure of effectiveness there is no doubt that shrapnel was used extensively in the British Army at long range, where the spread of the bullets produced a better effect than a plunging round shot. Whinyate's Troop, for example, fired 236 shrapnel shells as opposed to 309 round shot at Waterloo. Shrapnel would have been most effective when fired in the larger shells of the field howitzers, which contained more bullets than those of the guns. The $5\frac{1}{2}$-inch howitzer's shrapnel shell, for example, held 153 bullets and was probably more tolerant of fuze errors because its remaining velocity was lower than that of the gun. There is a record of Major Norman Ramsay, in action at Waterloo on the left of Bull's Troop, sending a message to his old Troop Commander Major Bull to say that the shrapnel of his six heavy $5\frac{1}{2}$-inch howitzers was very effective in the wood beyond Hougoumont (perhaps the first recorded instance of flank observation).

It may be concluded, theoretically, that shrapnel shell was a profitable alternative to round shot or common shell at the longer ranges, and that some

Experiment with Case Shott carried on in the presence of the Right Honourable General Conway in the Years 1770. 1771.

4⅖ Inch Howitzer — Weight 2.1.4 — Length 1 fod. 10 Inch

Nature of Ordnance (Pdrs)	Weight of Powd. (lb.oz.dr)	Shott Nat	N°	Tot. Wt. (lb.oz.dr)	Elevation (Deg.)	1st Target dist 200 Yards Thro'	1st Target Hitt	2d. Target dist 400 Yard Thro'	2d. Target Hitt	3d. Target dist 600 Yd. Thro'	3d. Target Hitt	Total N°	Remarks
0.8.0	1¼		61	6.0.4		.. ..	12 2	..	1	..	.. ..	15	Woolwich
	1½		74	8.1.10		.. ..	7 2	..	..		..	9	
	2		61	8.0.14		1 1	14 4	..	..		..	20	
	1¼		61	6.1.2		3 ..	6 2	.. ..	2		..	13	
	1½		74	8.0.12		1 .	10 8	..	1		..	20	
	2		59	8.0.6		2 1	13 6	.. ..	2 1	.. ..	.. ..	25	
	1¼		61	6.0.8		. 1	11 8	.. ..	2 1	.. ..	..	23	
	1½			..		.. ..	.. ..	..	..	..	..	..	
	2		60	8.0.2		1 ..	10 3	..	..		..	14	
	1¼		61	6.0.4		2 ..	20 5	..	7 2	.. ..	.. ..	36	
	1½		73	8.0.0		1 .	9 2	..	..		..	12	
	2		59	8.0.8		1 .	17 3	..	..		..	21	

ten per cent of the bullets contained in the shell could be expected to take effect. This would mean that the effect of round shot and shrapnel was comparable since both an accurately laid round shot and a correctly fuzed shrapnel shell could be expected to cause several casualties in a massed target.

4. The effectiveness of case shot: The effectiveness of case shot was tested by firing it at a screen 100 feet wide (representing the frontage over which the fire of a battery would normally be developed) and 8 feet high to represent cavalry or 6 feet high to represent infantry. Müller quotes trials establishing that 41% of the bullets of British 6pr case shot were effective at 400 yards and 23% were effective at 600 yards. The French 8pr gun is said by him to have recorded rather over 70% at 500 yards and 80% at 875 yards, but these figures seem confused and suspect.

The Madras Records are voluminous, well over a thousand firings being recorded including comparative trials of British, Bengal, Bombay and Madras shot. They, and the British Records, produce a picture of effectiveness that is shown in diagram 7.

It seems reasonable to conclude that, taking the British 6pr gun as an example, the following numbers of bullets could be expected to have taken effect on a line of infantry at the ranges shown:

Range	Per round fired
200 yards	55 bullets of light case
400 yards	36 bullets of light case
600 yards	6 bullets of heavy case

This means that a battery of British 6pr guns, discharging rather more than 500 bullets in a single salvo at 200 yards range, could have expected to obtain some 300 hits. In the number of bullets fired, this would have been the equivalent of a single volley of musket shots fired by a battalion of infantry 500

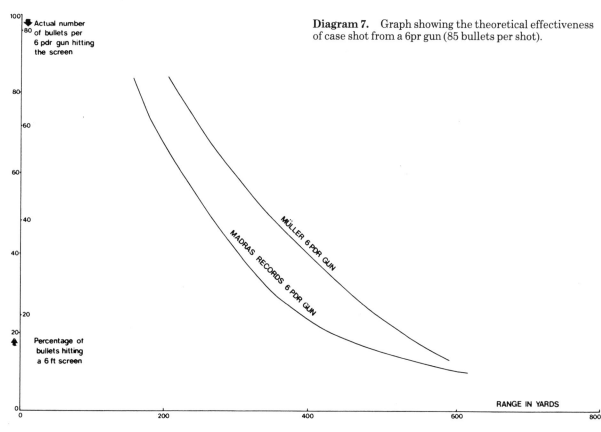

Diagram 7.   Graph showing the theoretical effectiveness of case shot from a 6pr gun (85 bullets per shot).

Diagram 8. The use of different projectiles at various ranges.

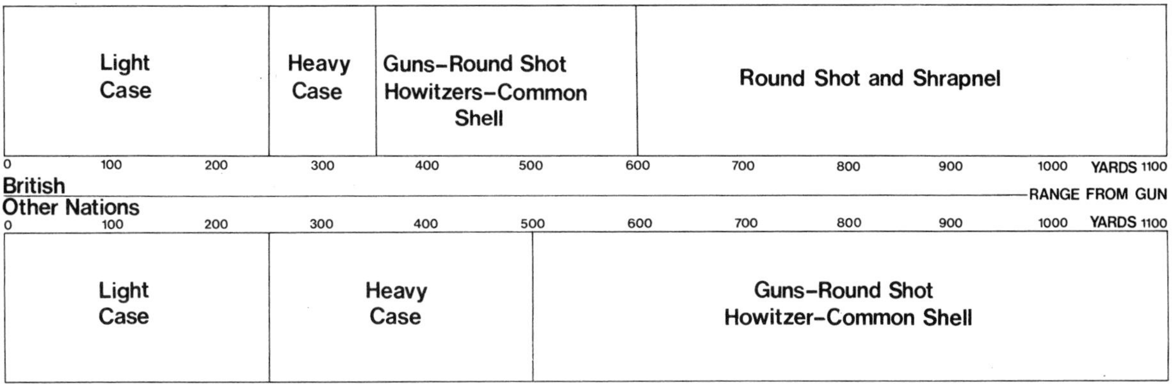

Light Case	Heavy Case	Guns–Round Shot Howitzers–Common Shell	Round Shot and Shrapnel

```
0      100      200      300      400      500      600      700      800      900      1000    YARDS 1100
British
Other Nations                                                                                 RANGE FROM GUN
0      100      200      300      400      500      600      700      800      900      1000    YARDS 1100
```

Light Case	Heavy Case	Guns–Round Shot Howitzer–Common Shell

strong. Muskets were effective at a range of 100 yards or less, and case shot could be fired with effect up to 350 yards. The correct combination was, therefore, to use guns at the longer ranges and muskets when the range had closed sufficiently to enable them to fire effectively.

The use of the different weapons

The foregoing analyses show that there was a series of 'range bands' within each of which one type of projectile was the most effective. This can be seen in diagram 8.

Estimates of overall effectiveness (guns only)

Müller finally works out in a detailed calculation the number of casualties that one gun could be expected to inflict under ideal conditions during attacks on the area of a gun position by a formation of infantry and a formation of cavalry, taking into account the different speeds of their movements and excluding the use of shrapnel shell. Fire is assumed to have been opened at an exaggeratedly long range of 1,700 yards and to have been maintained up to the last 60 yards, though a realistically small credit is given for the effect of fire at a range of over 1,200 yards. The results are shown in diagrams 9 and 10.

Müller assumes a rate of fire appreciably higher than that laid down in the British manuals. Whereas he expects the guns to fire 22 rounds each against the cavalry attack, the British calculation allows only 11 rounds; and Müller's 55 rounds per gun against the

infantry corresponds to a British estimate of 36 rounds.

The British calculations suggest that Müller's casualty figures are optimistic. Nevertheless, there is no doubt that – given a clear field of fire and good visibility – well trained and unsubdued artillery could inflict casualties of the order of those shown above at ranges of 800 to 1,000 yards; and their fire could be most destructive when their targets were within short range.

In general, the artillery of the smooth-bore period was more effective in defence than in attack largely because attacking infantry and cavalry were bound to adopt formations that made them vulnerable to artillery fire during the last stages of an attack, and also because its fire became more effective as the range to the target decreased.

In the opening stages of an attack, when supporting artillery was required to provide fire at long range, the effectiveness of that fire depended very much on the extent to which it could be developed in enfilade against the linear targets presented by the defenders. As the attack moved forward, the supporting artillery moved forward on its flanks and hoped to be able to continue to fire at decreasing ranges. During the final stages of an attack, however, it was almost always impossible to avoid the masking of the artillery's fire by the assaulting troops – although the guns could still harass the enemy's flanks.

The number of rounds British artillery was expected to fire in the face of attacks by cavalry and

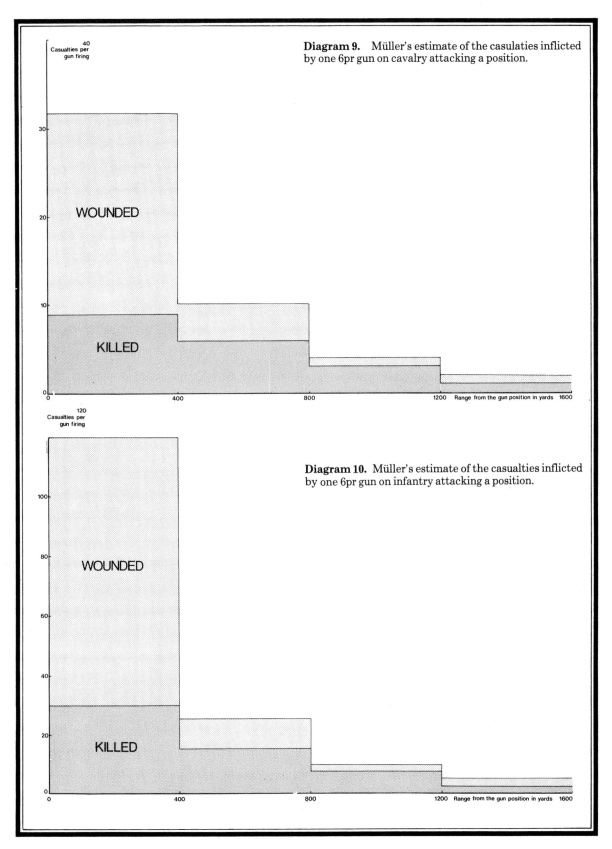

40
Casualties per
gun firing

30

20
WOUNDED

10
KILLED

0
0   400   800   1200   Range from the gun position in yards   1600

Diagram 9. Müller's estimate of the casualties inflicted by one 6pr gun on cavalry attacking a position.

120
Casualties per
gun firing

100

80
WOUNDED

60

40

20
KILLED

0
0   400   800   1200   Range from the gun position in yards   1600

Diagram 10. Müller's estimate of the casualties inflicted by one 6pr gun on infantry attacking a position.

infantry on the vicinity of gun positions were as follows. (The calculation is taken from *The Artillery Officer's Assistant,* a training manual of the Madras Artillery dated 1848; but this was copied from similar Royal Artillery training instructions.)

Attack by cavalry
First half mile at the trot, second quarter at a canter, last quarter at a gallop.

Range from guns	Rounds fired per gun
1500–650 yards	7 spherical case
650–350 yards	2 round shot
350– 0 yards	2 case shot
	Total 11 rounds

Attack by infantry

Range from guns	Rounds fired per gun
1500–650 yards	19 spherical case
650–350 yards	7 round shot
350–100 yards	8 case shot
100– 0 yards	2 case shot
	Total 36 rounds

It should be noted, however, that the Indian artilleries used a higher proportion of spherical case, or shrapnel, than the Royal Artillery since the formations they engaged were usually more dispersed than were European armies. The 'Royal' 6pr and 9pr guns held only 20 and 12 rounds of shrapnel per gun respectively and would have fired round shot instead.

The battle of Ramilles, showing the way in which Marlborough caused his army to move into battle.
(By permission of the National Army Museum).

Pictorial section: The development of artillery

Below: A corresponding gun and howitzer in the British series of smooth-bore ordnance. The gun is the 3pr firing a three-pound shot with a calibre of 2.913 inches. The howitzer, with a calibre of $4\frac{2}{5}$ inches, fired a shell of $8\frac{1}{2}$ pounds weight. The characteristic long slim shape of the gun can be compared with the shorter and thicker howitzer. This gun's maximum range is given as 1,200 yards at 4° elevation, the howitzer's being 900 yards at 11°.

Right: Some of the implements used in the service of smooth-bore ordnance. These photographs of original specimens held in the Rotunda Museum at Woolwich show:
1,2. The portfire holder and portfire with which the gun was fired.
3. The pricker, pushed down the vent to puncture the bag of the cartridge to make ignition more certain.

4. The thumbpiece worn by the ventsman to protect his thumb when serving a hot vent.
5. The portfire cutter, usually fixed to the trail. It was used to cut off the end of the burning portfire when firing had ceased.
6. The handspike inserted in the loop above the trail eye, with the aid of which the carriage was traversed in action.
7. The spongestaff with which the piece was swabbed and the shot, or shell, and the charge were rammed down the bore.
8. A powder scoop, used to handle loose powder before the advent of cartridges.
9. The linstock holding a slow match, which was kept burning on the gun position and from which the portfires were ignited.

Below right: Photographs of original round shot, common shell, and spherical case shot in the Rotunda Museum.

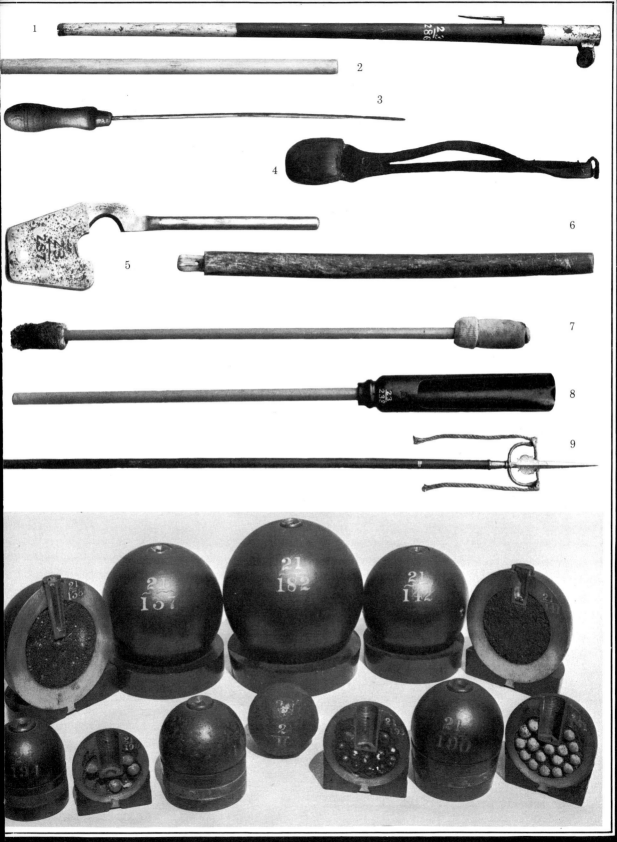

THE DEVELOPMENT OF ARTILLERY

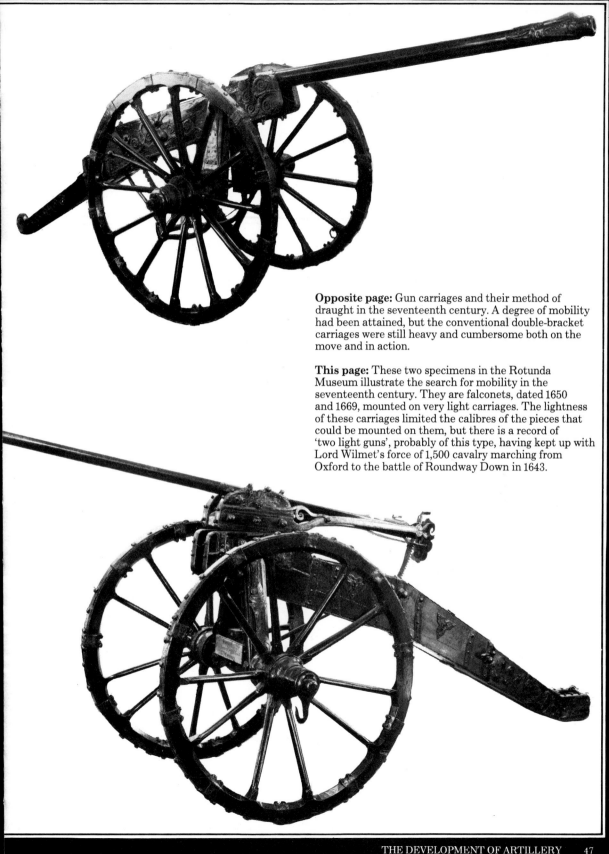

Opposite page: Gun carriages and their method of draught in the seventeenth century. A degree of mobility had been attained, but the conventional double-bracket carriages were still heavy and cumbersome both on the move and in action.

This page: These two specimens in the Rotunda Museum illustrate the search for mobility in the seventeenth century. They are falconets, dated 1650 and 1669, mounted on very light carriages. The lightness of these carriages limited the calibres of the pieces that could be mounted on them, but there is a record of 'two light guns', probably of this type, having kept up with Lord Wilmet's force of 1,500 cavalry marching from Oxford to the battle of Roundway Down in 1643.

Below: A contemporary drawing of the carriage of a 12pr field gun of c. 1735, the date of which was confirmed by an expert's view that the paper it is drawn on was made in Amsterdam in 1730; and one of Colonel Albert Borgard's sketches of a field gun and carriage of c. 1720. Little change had taken place since the previous century: the carriages were still heavy and cumbersome, with characteristically long trails.

Right: German and French carriages of the eighteenth century.

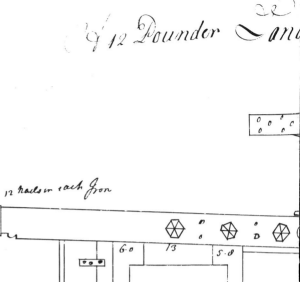

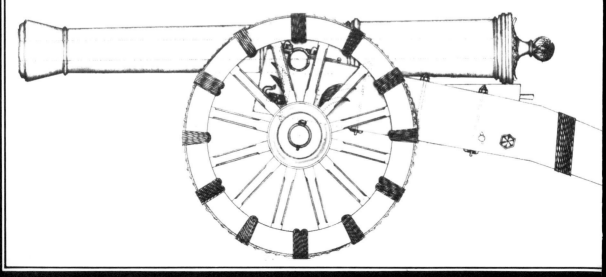

AN PROFFELL OF AN HOLLANDS SIX POUNDER

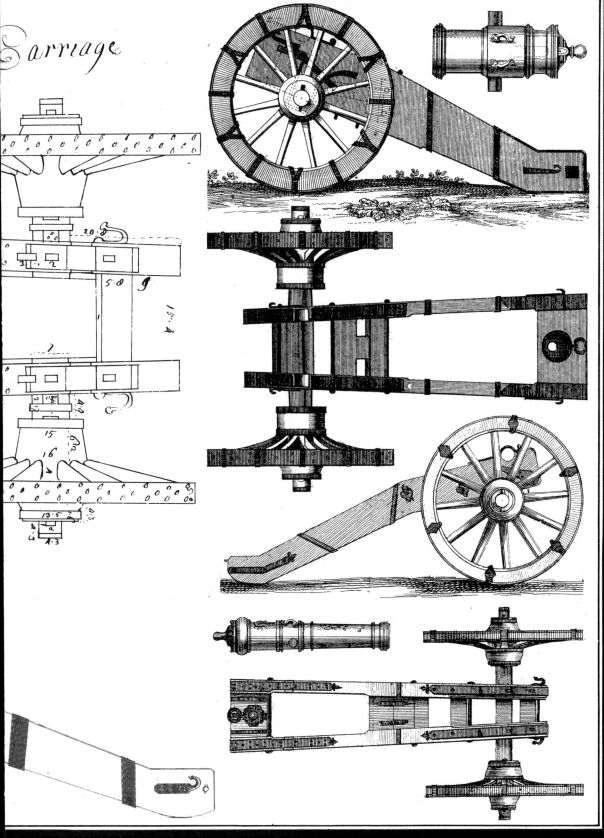

Carriage

Below: A French 6pr carriage of the late eighteenth century, from Gribeauval's *L'Artillerie de France,* 1792.

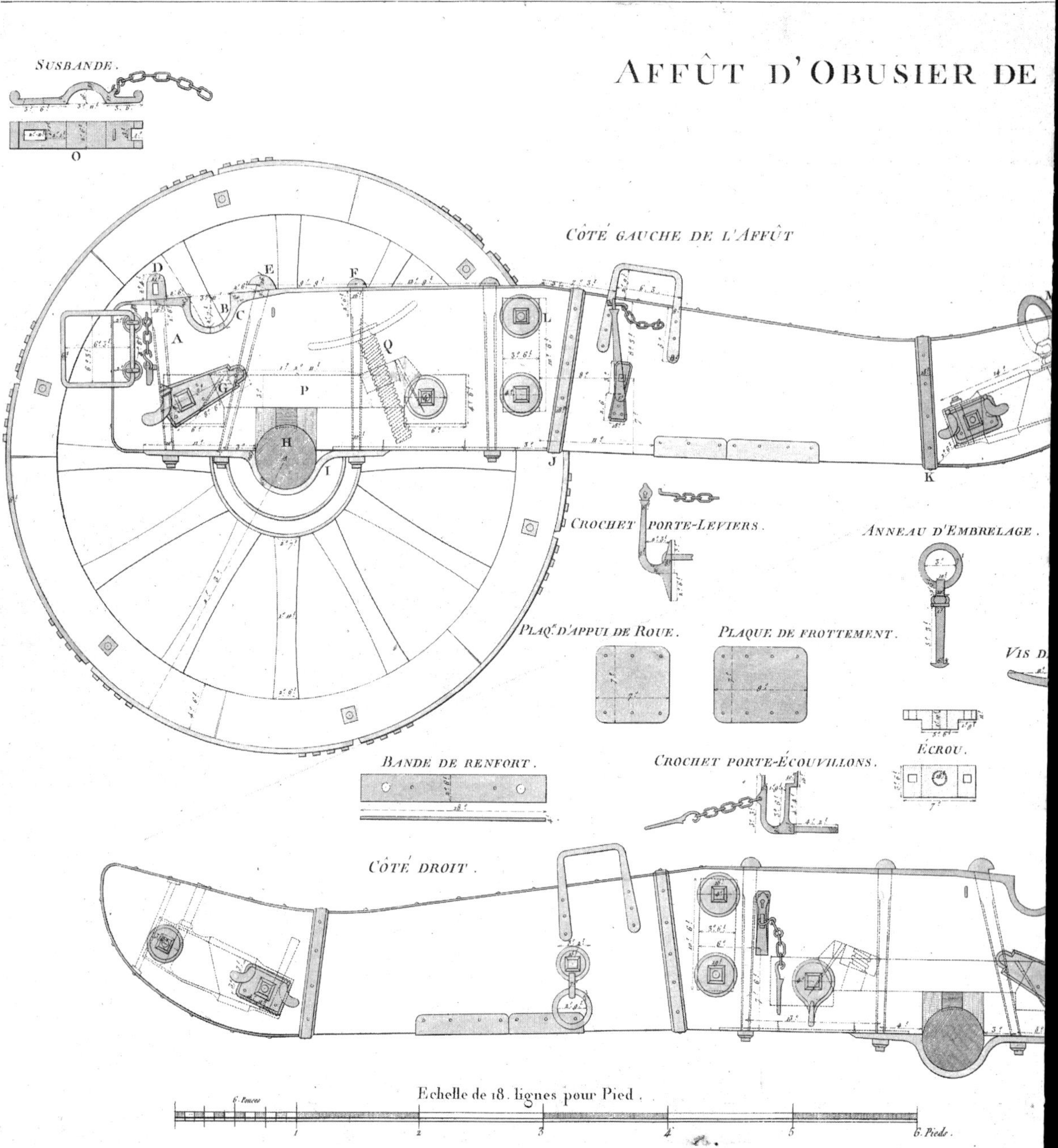

AFFÙT D'OBUSIER DE

SUSBANDE.

O

CÔTÉ GAUCHE DE L'AFFÙT

CROCHET PORTE-LEVIERS.

ANNEAU D'EMBRELAGE.

PLAQ.^E D'APPUI DE ROUE.

PLAQUE DE FROTTEMENT.

VIS D.

ÉCROU.

BANDE DE RENFORT.

CROCHET PORTE-ÉCOUVILLONS.

CÔTÉ DROIT.

Echelle de 18 lignes pour Pied.

6 Pouces.   G. Pieds.

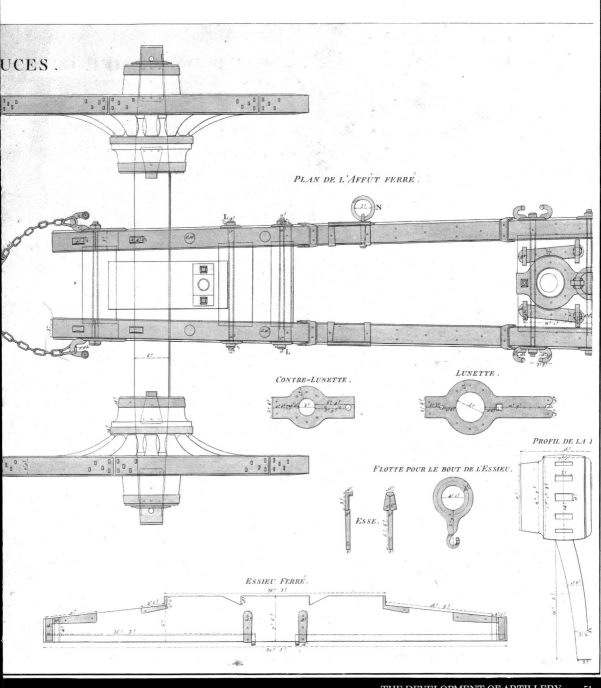

UCES .

PLAN DE L'AFFUT FERRÉ.

CONTRE-LUNETTE .

LUNETTE .

PROFIL DE LA

FLOTTE POUR LE BOUT DE L'ESSIEU.

ESSE .

ESSIEU FERRÉ.

Plan and elevations of a British 9pr brass gun, carriage and limber of the early nineteenth century, from Straith's *Treatise*

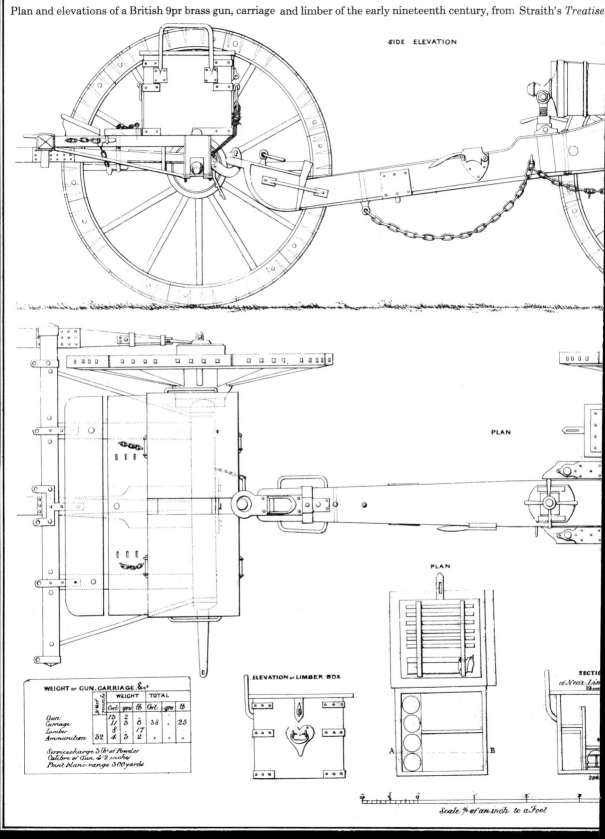

SIDE ELEVATION

PLAN

PLAN

ELEVATION or LIMBER BOX

SECTION
of Near Lim

WEIGHT of GUN, CARRIAGE &c?		WEIGHT			TOTAL		
	Number	Cwt	qrs	lb	Cwt	qrs	lb
Gun		13	2				
Carriage		11	3	8	38		25
Limber		8		17			
Ammunition	32	4	3	2			

Service charge 3 lbs of Powder
Calibre of Gun 4·2 inches
Point blanc range 300 yards

Scale ⅜ of an inch to a Foot

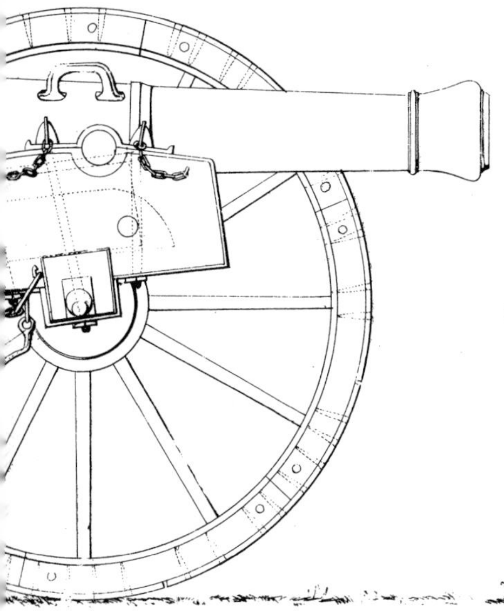

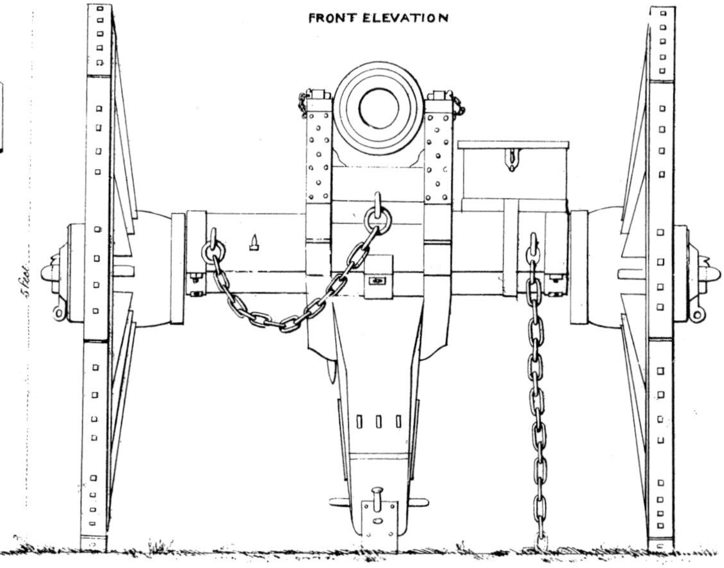
FRONT ELEVATION
5 Feet

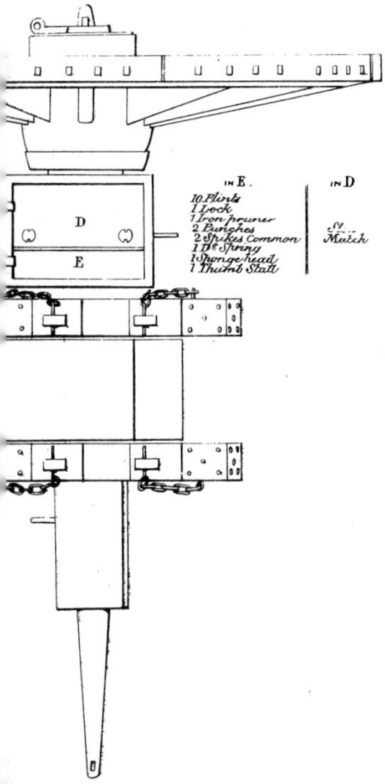
D
E
in E.
10 Flints
1 Lock
1 Iron pruner
2 Punches
2 Spikes Common
1 D^o Spring
1 Sponge head
1 Thumb Stall
in D
Match

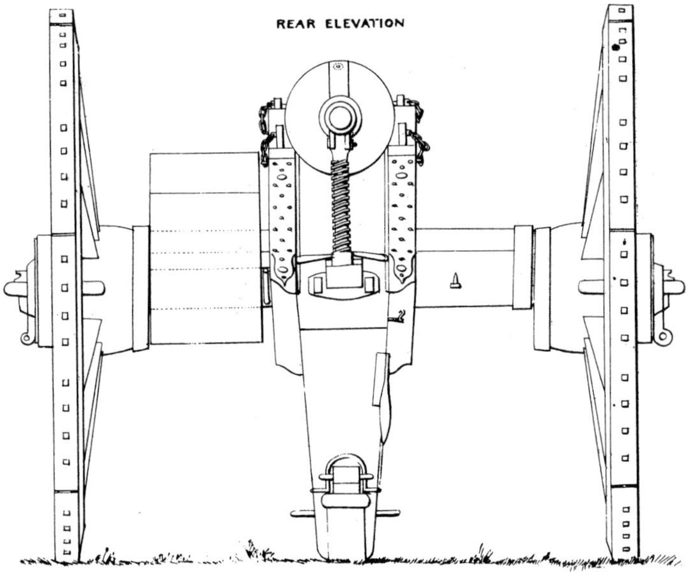
REAR ELEVATION

NEAR LIMBER BOX		MIDDLE BOX	OFF LIMBER BOX	
4 C Case 1 Auger 1 C Screw 2 Files 1 Funnel 2 Fuze Boxes 1 Knife 1 Mallet 2 Needles 1 Pincers 1 Sawset 1 Scissors 1 Setter 1 Worsted	6 Solid Shot 8. 3lb Cartridges 6 Portfires } 1 Saw } on lid 6 Spherical Case 8. 3lb Cartridges 6. 3½ oz Bursters Quick Match 2 Fuze Bags 6 in each	1 Washer 1 Linch Pin 2 Couples 1 Rammer head	6 Solid Shot 8. 3lb Cartridges 6 Portfires } S. Ion match } on lid 6 Solid Shot 8. 3lb Cartridges	4 Com: case 1 Tube pocket 100 Tubes 1 Tin Primer 1 Hammer

PRINCIPAL DIMENSIONS OF GUN AND CARRIAGE

			Feet	Inches
Length of Gun			6	0
Diameter of	Base Ring		1	0½
	First Reinforce		..	11
	Second Reinforce		..	10
	Neck		..	7½
	Swell of the Muzzle		..	10½
	Face of Piece			7¼
Length of	Bracket		4	6
	Trail	from rear of Bracket	5	10½
		between cheeks	3	8
	Nave		1	7¾
	Axletree Arm		1	3¾
	Axletree bed outside cheeks		1	0½
Diameter of Wheel			5	6
Diam^r.	Nave	Butt end	"	11½
		Pack stroke	1	1
		Small end	..	10¼
	Axletree arm	at Shoulder	..	2¾
		small end	"	1 6/10
Breadth of Felly or tire			"	2¾
Depth of Felly			..	4¾
Breadth between cheeks of Carriage			..	10½
Thickness of cheeks ... d^o			..	3½
Depth at breast ... d^o			..	11
Depth at rear of bracket ... d^o				8
Length of Splinter Bar of Limber			6	2

Plan and elevation of a British light 6pr gun, from the
Shuttleworth collection of plates (c. 1811).

Below: The standard light gun and howitzer of the British Army in the period of the Napoleonic wars – the light 6pr gun and the light 5½-inch howitzer. Both specimens are in the Rotunda Museum: the piece of the former is dated 1796, and the laminated trail is of the same date. The wheels, in their original form, were replaced in 1862. The carriage of the howitzer is an exact copy of the original.

Right: One of the French 9pr 12pr 8pr guns captured at Waterloo.

A general view of the battle of Oudenarde showing the
armies fully deployed for combat. (By permission of the
National Army Museum.)

3. Inefficiencies of the battlefield

The theoretical performance of the various weapons of the smooth-bore period was inevitably degraded by the conditions obtaining on the battlefield; and that such a degradation occurred is evident from the figures of theoretical effectiveness given in Chapter 2 which, if achieved, would have resulted in few remaining alive after any engagement. The extent of the degradation and the periods during which it applied can only be matters of speculation, but it is necessary to appreciate the factors that could have affected efficiency before the course of particular actions can be analysed.

There were two ways in which the degrading factors operated. The first was in the reduction of the theoretical performance of the weapon so that it was less destructive to the target, and the second was in the impeding of fire or preventing it from being applied when the target would otherwise have been vulnerable.

The animate target

The most important reduction of the theoretical effectiveness of any weapon arises from the difference between an inanimate target – in the trials quoted, a continuous target representing a line of troops – and a living target. In the first place, the trials target is usually stationary whereas the real one is often moving. But more significantly, there are many gaps in and around a line of men even when they are in close order. Practice and trials in later times were carried out against rows of dummies shaped like individual men; but the results given in Chapter 2 were obtained against continuous screens, which must have exaggerated the effectiveness of the fire considerably.

There can be few today with actual battle experience who have failed to be surprised on occasion when, by all the force of scientific calculation, the enemy should have been wiped out but was not. The alternative of unexpectedly heavy casualties when fire seems to be ineffective occurs more rarely, and all experience shows that a considerable reduction of theoretical lethality is invariably found when the target consists of living, moving and reacting human beings. But if this is true of the far more efficient projectiles and much more rapidly firing weapons of the twentieth century, it is clear that the slow firing single-shot firearms of the smooth-bore period must have been affected to an even greater extent by the inevitable drop in theoretical performance.

Technical failures

There was a danger of several technical failures that could affect the quality of the fire of all weapons using gunpowder. The method of loading the musket (described on page 10) invited inaccuracies in the amount of powder used, causing variations in the performance of the weapon – particularly with regard to range. The firing mechanism, with its crude method of priming, was also by no means reliable and misfires occurred frequently.

Lauerma states that at the end of the eighteenth century fifteen per cent of musket shots misfired even in dry weather. The incidence of misfires must have been appreciably higher in the wet conditions in which so many battles were fought. It would therefore seem likely that nearly a quarter of the musket shots ordered to be fired never left the muzzle.

The artillery was less affected by misfires. In all but the very early days its charges were contained in bags, and the drill ensured that they were sheltered from rain by the gunner who brought them up to the gun. Moreover, it was possible to insert a fresh tube without danger and without much delay if the priming failed. There must have been misfires, but they should not have reduced the effectiveness of fire to any great extent.

There was, however, one technical difficulty that may sometimes have affected the service of the guns. This arose from overheating after prolonged rapid firing. In the early days of the seventeenth century it had led to a danger of the piece itself bursting, and the rate of fire had therefore been severely restricted to avoid that risk. But even when better-cast pieces were in service and a higher rate of fire was permissible, an overheated piece was difficult to handle. The vent became so hot that it was impossible to load a fresh tube without it exploding prematurely; and it also became impossible to serve the vent, even though the ventsman wore a leather thumbstall to protect his thumb. It was this danger that led to the order prohibiting the use of guns singly –exemplified by a disastrous occasion in the First Afghan War, in 1841, when a single gun of the Bengal Horse Artillery became too hot to fire and the force it was supporting lost heart and was routed.

Human error

The physical inefficiencies of individuals varied with the state of training of a man and his unit; but the slow rate of fire of the 'single shot' weapons of the time placed a premium on the accurate aiming or laying of each round. Insofar as that was concerned, the gun layers of a well trained unit were highly experienced and reliable men who had reached the rank of sergeant after long service. However crude their apparatus may now appear, they were undoubtedly capable of hitting their targets within the capabilities of their gun. All the records of theoretical performance already quoted took into account layers' errors – every round fired on trials having been laid in the same way as a round in battle, though admittedly without the disturbances.

The type of inefficiency most difficult to assess is that which arose from loss of nerve in the stress of battle. Relevant to this is an account left by Lieutenant Godfrey Pearse, of the Madras artillery, of an incident during the siege of Multan in 1849. Pearse was then in command of a battery of large siege pieces engaged in breaching the wall of the fort to enable the storming parties to enter; and his five heavy guns and three huge howitzers were methodically blasting away the revetment when a large and highly menacing body of Sikhs, armed to the teeth, suddenly emerged from the fort and charged towards the battery. Pearse gave the order to load with case shot, and as soon as the enemy was within range he ordered the battery to fire. There was a huge multiple flash and a vast cloud of white smoke – but when the smoke cleared, it was seen that only three men had been hit by the 916 bullets discharged. What had happened was that in the stress and nervous excitement of the moment the layers had been careless in the task of depressing their great pieces from the elevations at which they had been bombarding the fort and had not brought them down to the horizontal. Consequently, practically every bullet in their case shot had passed harmlessly above the heads of the enemy.

It certainly took strong nerves to aim a musket or lay a gun accurately when the enemy was charging at a position and there was time for only one or two rounds before the charge struck home. There must have been instances of failure in this respect; but individual failures were less serious in an infantry unit than in a gun detachment, where five men had to operate at full efficiency all the time. Here, again, training and discipline told – as also did the instinct of self-preservation – and it would be unwise to assume that good regular units could not be relied upon to man their weapons efficiently in the face of danger.

Apart from possible loss of nerve, sheer fatigue must also have played a part. In most cases, the infantry arrived at battlefields after long and tiring marches – frequently in atrocious weather and without food – and must often have reached the stage where the heavy musket tended to droop at the 'present'. Indeed, many shots must have been wasted as a result of tired muscles. Gun detachments, on the other hand – though they may not have had to march to the battle – were physically fully extended in action. Each gun recoiled from four to six feet when it was fired, after which its ton weight had to be run up by the manpower of its detachment. Even the tasks of sponging and ramming required appreciable effort, and there was constant movement backwards and forwards to bring up ammunition. The whole of the gun detachment had a series of strenuous tasks to perform in battle, and the men must have been tired by the end of the day. Mercer relates in *The Waterloo Diary* that by the end of the action his detachments were no longer physically able to run up their guns, which were then in a tangled mass with their trails interlocked. There can therefore be no doubt that efficiency must have suffered towards the end of a long action.

One more difficulty was the decentralisation of control, which was inevitable in battle and which certainly led to an imperfect distribution of fire. In general, the infantry soldier would fire at right angles to his line – but it was impossible to ensure that the fire of a whole unit would be distributed with mathematical accuracy over the whole front. The guns, too, laid individually by their Numbers One, must sometimes have produced an imperfect distribution of battery fire. There must have been gaps in the fire pattern in some places and overhitting, particularly by the bullets of case shot, in others.

Ground

The ground over which a battle was fought must naturally have affected the visibility, and hence the vulnerability, of the troops taking part in it. Covered approaches, dead ground and the screening provided by woods or undergrowth would give protection from fire, which always had to be aimed visually; but such cover affected the attacker and the defender in different ways. Uneven, broken or obstructed ground presented difficulties to attacking forces, who needed to preserve a rigid formation in order to bring their weapons to bear effectively. To them, the value of such cover would be greater during the approach to the assault than during the assault itself. For the last few hundred yards of an assault, the tactics of the time made it necessary for both infantry and cavalry to be fully exposed to view – and, therefore, to fire.

Cover from view, and also the protection from fire that some cover could provide, was of more value to the defenders than to the attackers throughout a battle. There was a tendency to regard the ability to stand upright under fire as a virtue to be encouraged, but it is noteworthy that it was Wellington's practice to withdraw his infantry behind a crest during a preliminary bombardment to avoid unnecessary casualties before the actual assault. At that time it was also customary to make infantry lie down while they were under artillery fire and unable to use their weapons. Thus the target presented by infantry holding a defensive position must often have been very different from that of the six-foot screen against which trials results were recorded.

Gun positions had to be entirely in the open and in full view of the enemy if the guns were to fire effectively. No form of indirect fire, permitting the guns to shoot from behind cover, had yet been developed. High ground was sometimes used by artillery to provide gun positions from which it was possible to shoot over the heads of friendly troops, but such siting was somewhat frowned upon in the manuals – probably because it reduced the effect of shot by shortening the lethal zone and causing the shot to bury itself. Nevertheless, positions on high ground were occupied to advantage by the French artillery at Talavera and the British artillery at Salamanca.

In general, then, it may be said that – except in the case of gun positions – natural cover could often reduce the effect of fire at long range. At close range, however, all arms on both sides had to be in sight of and therefore vulnerable to each other.

One other aspect of cover is the protection that could be obtained from field works specially constructed for the purpose or from things such as banks or walls of which advantage could be taken on the battlefield. The protection from fire that a quite small bank of earth could give was considerable, and the infantry was trained to take advantage of such protection provided that they could shoot over it. The artillery did not deliberately seek that kind of cover, but it was not ignored when it happened to be available. The use of the sunken road along the ridge at Mont St Jean at Waterloo is a good example of the protection that such features could provide. Deliberately made or adapted field works were often used in battle, though the amount of time and labour needed to construct them usually limited their scope in mobile warfare to strong-points and single redoubts. A redoubt would be virtually impervious to a 6pr shot, and an embrasure in it would provide only a very small target – though a shot passing through it could disable the gun behind it.

Ammunition supply

Another factor that must have affected the firepower of armies was the reliability of the supply of ammunition.

The British infantryman carried 60 rounds on his person, and that seems to have been sufficient for the needs of most battles; though there are certainly instances of shortages in prolonged fighting, particularly with regard to isolated posts. Replenishment was from the first line transport of the unit.

Typical holdings of ammunition for field artillery were between 120 and 200 rounds per gun (British 9pr and 6pr) in the firing battery, and between 160 and 220 including the first line wagons. But all ammunition was extremely inflammable, and there were many instances of fires that caused a whole wagon and its contents to explode. At the battle of Ferozeshah in the first Sikh war, for example, 500 rounds of ammunition were lost in that way.

However, though there are several records of anxiety regarding the availability of artillery ammunition on the part of commanders – such as that

The smoke of battle in the days of gunpowder. From the moment that the first firearms were discharged, the whole battlefield was permanently enshrouded in smoke; and it was through the fleeting gaps in that dense white cloud that most of the fire was delivered. The seizing of the right moments to fire and to reload demanded great skill and experience on the part of the officers and non-commissioned officers in command of the fire units. (By permission of the National Army Museum.)

recorded by Mercer at Waterloo – there are few instances of units actually running out of ammunition during a battle. Thus at Waterloo – a prolonged and severely fought example – a total of no more than 10,000 rounds of artillery ammunition was fired by 78 British guns and howitzers, giving an average expenditure of 129 rounds per gun. The highest expenditure recorded was that of Sandham's company, which fired 183 rounds of 9pr and $5\frac{1}{2}$-inch howitzer ammunition. The average is well within the 163 rounds held for the 9pr gun, though it admittedly does not take into account losses due to the destruction of wagons and their contents.

Allowing for the factors already mentioned that would often have retarded the rate of expenditure, it must be concluded that the scales of ammunition were adequate – a view supported by the fact that those scales remained virtually unchanged throughout the whole of the last century of the smooth-bore period. Nevertheless, economy had to be practised. At Waterloo, for example, Wellington forbade the engagement of the French artillery by the artillery under his command in order to ensure that adequate stocks of ammunition would be available to deal with the more dangerous attacks of infantry and cavalry.

Smoke
One of the most significant obstructions to fire on all the battlefields of the smooth-bore period was undoubtedly the dense clouds of white smoke that gunpowder produced when it exploded. An entire line of infantry would be obscured after a volley, and batteries of guns firing continuously would be enveloped in the smoke of their own discharges. The extent to which the smoke persisted depended on the atmospheric conditions, but there must have been instances of intermittent or even continuous obscurity that prevented anything like the maximum theoretical effectiveness of the weapons in action. The musket, operating at short range, would have been less affected than the gun; but even so, there must have been frequent occasions when the carefully timed volleys of the infantry could not be fired because the target was obscured by smoke.

The artillery would have been impeded not only by the smoke around its guns but also by that created

around its targets. The longer the range at which a weapon was required to fire the more it must have been impeded by the swirling clouds of smoke enveloping the battlefield. For this reason it would normally have been impossible for artillery to maintain its maximum potential rate of fire for long periods.

Atmospheric conditions and the direction of the wind are rarely recorded in the accounts of battles, though they must have decided the persistence and movements of the vast smoke-screen that both sides created. Exceptionally, almost all accounts of Talavera mention the fact that smoke from the French batteries drifted continuously over the whole of the battlefield and obscured the view of both sides. But it is possible that the presence of smoke was so universal that it was accepted as an inevitable hazard and was therefore not considered worthy of special mention. Nevertheless, account must certainly be taken of the fact that all targets would frequently have been obscured by it, even if only intermittently.

It is also worth noting that the often unpredictable movements of the smoke haze in which all battles were fought called for a high standard of fire control. To time and order a tremendous first volley was easy enough when the air was clear and the enemy plainly visible; but in the later stages of a clouded battle, a nice judgment was required as to what size of sub-unit could best take advantage of gaps in the smoke and when their volleys could best be fired.

Conclusions
Taking all these circumstances into consideration, it is interesting to see how the figures of theoretical performance given in Chapter 2 could be adjusted to give those that might be expected on the battlefield.

Müller claimed that some fifty per cent of musket bullets were effective at 100 yards range. If a misfire rate of twenty-five per cent is assumed, and if the performance is reduced by a factor of two to allow for other inefficiencies and impediments, it would seem that not more than fifteen per cent of the rounds that could have been fired were likely to have been effective.

In the case of artillery, it should be possible to make a more reliable assessment of the impediments to its potential firepower if the duration of an engagement and the number of rounds actually fired are known. This can be done from the records of the battle of Waterloo, certainly not with complete accuracy but with enough evidence to reach an interesting conclusion.

At Waterloo, three separate series of attacks were made on the Allied position on the ridge of Mont St Jean. A British battery near La Haie Sainte could have engaged all three. The first series, by d'Erlon's and Reynier's corps, began at 1.30pm with an uphill attack through standing crops and over very wet ground from a starting line 1,200 yards from its objective. Whereas the artillery would ideally have been expected to fire 36 rounds per gun at such an attack, it seems wiser to assume 50 rounds per gun as the unimpeded ideal because of the slow speed at which it must have been delivered.

There followed a period of perhaps an hour in which the rear ranks of the French column pressed forward to replace those who had fallen and hand-to-hand fighting took place. During this phase the guns' fire would have been impeded by the mixture of enemy and friendly troops, and in some cases the detachments may have been withdrawn. Another 30 rounds per gun could possibly have been fired during this period.

The second series of attacks consisted of continuous charges by the cavalry, and it is difficult to decide the length of time during which the guns could have been firing in a situation of such confusion. The gun detachments were withdrawn into the protection of the infantry squares at the last moments of each charge, but Mercer recorded the appalling damage that his last salvo of case caused at 30 yards range. According to the drill books, a single cavalry charge was expected to receive 11 rounds per gun. It might therefore be fair to assume that each gun could ideally have fired some 60 rounds during the period of the cavalry charges.

Last came the attack of the Imperial Guard, which could ideally have received 36 rounds per gun during the attack and another 30 rounds per gun in the confusion after it.

Therefore, assuming no impediments, the allied artillery at Waterloo concerned with all three attacks could have fired:

Against d'Erlon's and Reynier's Corps	80 rounds per gun
Against the cavalry	60 rounds per gun
Against the Guard	66 rounds per gun
	206 rounds per gun

Some other firing would have taken place during the battle even though engagement of the enemy's artillery was forbidden, and so it seems reasonable to put the maximum number of rounds that could theoretically have been fired at 250 per gun.

The average number of rounds actually fired was 129 per gun. It therefore seems that the impediments to firing due to smoke and other interruptions must generally have led to the artillery's expenditure of ammunition being not more than half of what could have been fired under perfect conditions. Thus a single, simple, deliberate attack by infantry could be expected to receive about 20 to 30 rounds from each gun that was within range.

As far as round shot is concerned, a distinction must be drawn between the number of shots expected to find the target – as shown in diagram 6 – and the number of casualties inflicted. Each shot hitting a body of men or horses in close order would normally cause two to four casualties, so that the guns could expect to kill or wound, on average, more than one man for every round fired at 600 yards range or less.

As regards case shot, the number of casualties inflicted in practice on a body of troops in close order could not be more than the number of bullets shown as effective in diagram 7; and it was certainly reduced by the probability of more than one bullet hitting one man. When allowance is made for the many eccentricities that must have occurred, it is certainly necessary to assume that not more than half the bullets reaching the target caused casualties. Thus a single salvo of case shot from a battery of six 6pr guns at 200 yards range, discharging a total of 510 bullets, could have been theoretically expected to obtain 300 hits. It seems likely that, in practice, no more than fifty per cent of these hits would have caused casualties. The small bullet is a much more capricious performer than a large shot, however, and there must have been wide variations in the practical effect of case shot in battle.

Pictorial section: Artillery Drill

Load.

This series of drawings is taken from an early nineteenth-century drill book of the Madras Artillery. They show the movements of the members of the gun detachment in the service of the gun, the figures above each man indicating his number in the detachment. The interlocking of the actions of all four members of the detachment made it essential to restrict the rate of fire in order to avoid the very real risks of accidents due to premature ignition of the charges.

Hunsley delt.

No 6 is supposed to cover left wheel
at 5 yards in rear of it

Porter lithr.

This is the new muster limber
now issuing.

Advance *Spunge*

one two three

Spunge

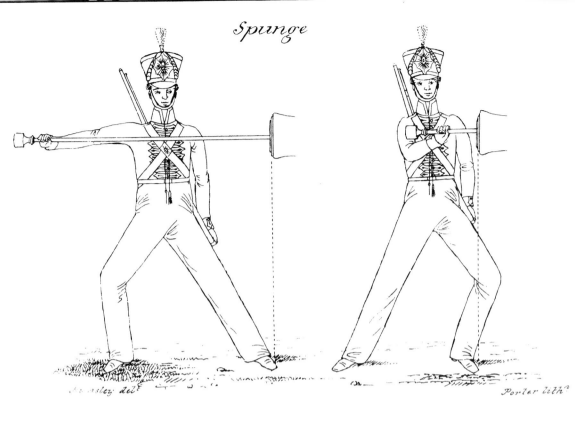

Ram home Cartridge.

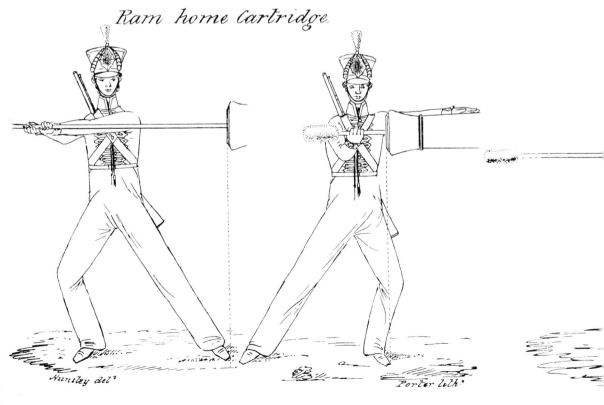

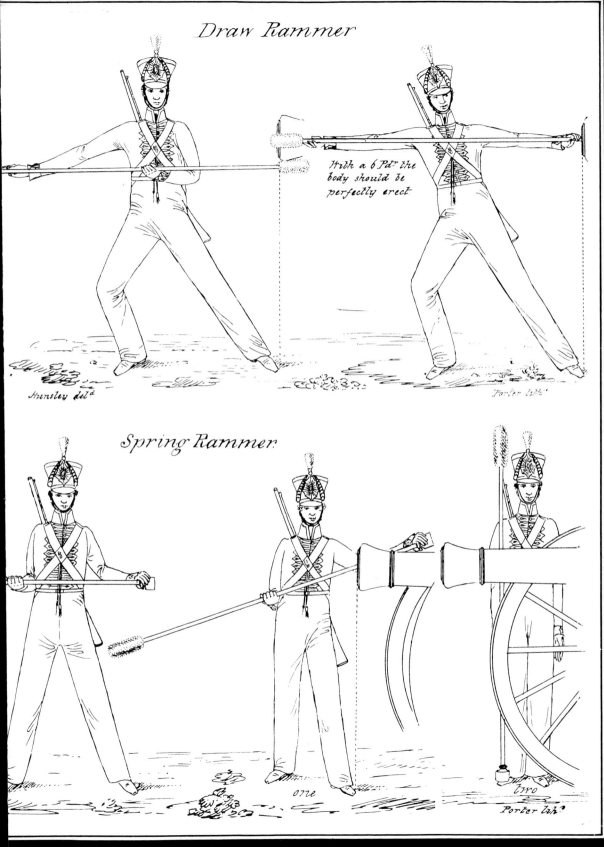

Draw Rammer

With a 6 Pdr the body should be perfectly erect.

Hunsley delᵈ

Porter lithᵒ

Spring Rammer

one

two

Porter lithᵒ

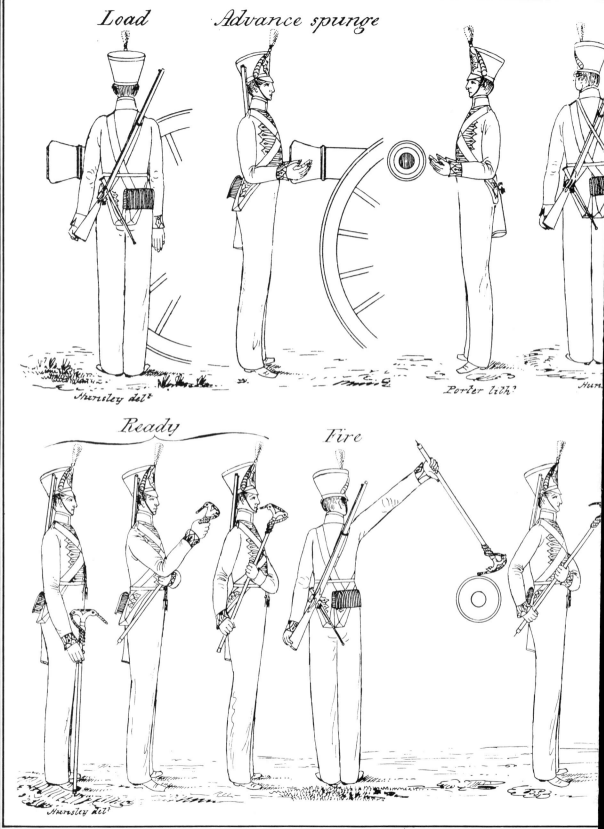

Load   Advance spunge

Hunsley del.ᵗ   Porter lith.ᵗ   Hun

Ready   Fire

Hunsley del.ᵗ

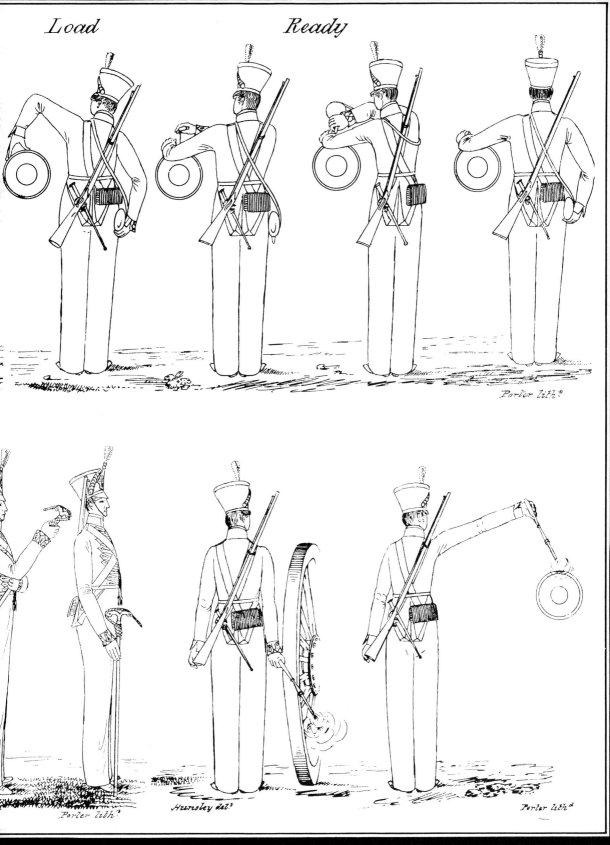

Load   Ready

Porter lith?

Porter lith?   *Hansley del?*   *Porter lith?*

4. The seventeenth and early eighteenth century

The only convincing test of the speculations so far propounded is to apply them to what actually happened on the battlefield – examining a number of battles, and incidents in battles, to determine from them the extent to which the various weapons contributed to the result.

As already pointed out, such assessments demand accurate information on three matters. In the first place, it is essential to know the numbers and exact locations of the short-range weapons of the time. In general, information on this – and, indeed, on other aspects of the battles – becomes more accurate as time moves on. Concerning the initial positions of the infantry and cavalry, there is usually a reasonably accurate record; and such matters as frontages can be checked with the known strengths of units. In particular, the initial positions of the British infantry and their enemies are always most accurately recorded in the maps of Fortescue's great history. The positions shown were carefully checked by the author on the ground, and they will always be found to tally precisely with his records of the units' strengths. He and other historians can rarely show on their maps the movements made during the battles, but these can usually be determined from the text.

It is entirely another matter, however, to discover exactly where the guns were; for it was customary on the part of even the greatest historians to show the guns on their sketch maps in a series of rather conventional symbols, without much attempt at accuracy of location and often without any identification of units. Furthermore, it was difficult to indicate the number of guns without exaggerating the frontage of the gun positions. This lack of precise information is partly due to the custom of the times by which part of the artillery tended to be attached to infantry units or formations and was expected to 'conform to the movements of the infantry'. When there is no other information, it is sometimes necessary to assume that the artillery was doing just that; but this vagueness about exact numbers and precise locations of the guns, coupled with their short range, often makes it difficult to assess the effectiveness of their fire. From the period of the Peninsular war, however, there is, fortunately, better evidence of the location of the gun positions occupied by the Allied artillery in a small number of battles. A Lieutenant

Unger of the artillery of the King's German Legion, who was serving during the Peninsular campaign, made a series of sketch maps showing the exact locations and moves of the artillery in the battles in which he took part. The original of only one of those maps survives, in the library of the Royal Artillery Institution, but there are printed copies of two others and copies of his notes on the battles. These records are of Talavera, Albuera and Bussaco, and they are of the greatest possible value in analysing the performance of the artillery of that time.

Another useful record of the initial positions of the artillery in the battles of the eighteenth and nineteenth century is contained in *Alison's History of Europe*, of which the Atlas by Alex Keith Johnston shows the gun positions with some accuracy – though the movements that took place during the battles are not shown. And there is one other series of actions for which not only the initial positions of all arms are shown but also all their subsequent movements: the historians of the Sikh wars in the 1840s took some pains to record this information in their sketch maps which, though sometimes complicated to read, are a valuable source of information on the firepower that was available.

In general, therefore, it may be said that it is usually possible to discover how many weapons were in action; that this information is usually more precise for small arms than it is for artillery; and that the information on both improves towards the end of the smooth-bore period.

The second piece of information that is required before effectiveness can be determined is the amount of ammunition expended – but, frustratingly, this information is very rarely to be found. Exceptionally, the expenditure of every battery of British guns at Waterloo is known; but even domestic historians such as Duncan and Dickson rarely mention the amount of artillery ammunition expended in battles as opposed to sieges. The rare occasions on which there was a shortage of ammuniton are mentioned – such as at Albuera, in the case of the infantry, and at Ferozeshah in the case of the artillery – but all that can be stated with confidence is that in one battle it would normally have been impossible to fire more ammunition than was carried by each man in the infantry and by the firing battery wagons in the artillery.

An estimate of the amount of ammunition fired can be arrived at by considering the duration of an engagement in relation to the rates of fire known to have been possible. Such timings, again, are rarely recorded precisely (though Oman is helpful in this respect), but informed guesswork can sometimes be carried out from a knowledge of the distances covered and the normal speed of movement.

Lastly, it will be appreciated that no accurate assessment of the effect of fire can be made without information on the number of casualties resulting from it. The casualties suffered by a whole force during and often, significantly, just after a battle are generally recorded, and there is usually a separate record of the casualties inflicted on each unit. But there is a very understandable absence of records of the proportions in which casualties were attributable to artillery or small-arms fire – and it would probably be unreasonable to hope for accurate information on this point since the medical services were not organised to provide it until after the Crimean war. There are, however, certain phases of a comparatively small number of battles in the period for which – by the accident of history – the number of casualties inflicted by guns and muskets were recorded separately. Attention is naturally focused on them here.

The first appearance of firearms

At the beginning of the period, firearms had not yet assumed the dominant position they were to occupy a hundred years later. By the middle of the seventeenth century both guns and muskets were in the field, but their state of development limited the reliance that could be placed on them and they were not the primary armament of the land forces. At the same time, the ways in which they were introduced and the ways in which they were used were very much bound up with the tactics of the time.

The story of the development of those tactics is extremely complicated and diverse, and opinions are often divided not only on the facts but also on the reasons for changes. Nevertheless, with the dangers of over-compression and over-simplification fully realised, it is essential to include here a short summary of the way in which war was conducted tactically – without which it is impossible to understand the tasks the weapons were called upon to perform. In-deed, to obtain a clearer idea of the ways in which firearms were woven into the armoury it is necessary very briefly to look back a few hundred years.

At the beginning of the fourteenth century the mounted knight was supreme on the battlefield, his social superiority and his ability to equip himself expensively consolidating that position. Foot soldiers, armed only with pikes and similar weapons for hand-to-hand combat, supported the mounted warriors and provided a firm base for the army as a whole.

Then came the English archers, armed with the long-bow. Their arrows forced the mounted knights to adopt heavier armour; but even then, horses were still vulnerable to the new weapon. The supremacy of the mounted arm was thus seriously challenged, leading to the use of the pallisade defence to secure a firm base and, on the Continent, to what was called the wagonburg defence – a leaguer of baggage wagons from which archers could operate in safety and which was therefore not open to charges by mounted troops. At that time the artillery was of very limited use on the battlefield owing to its lack of mobility – not so much in battle as in the difficulty of getting it to the battle in the first place.

The fifteenth century saw a great improvement in the effectiveness of artillery as a result of the casting of pieces, the introduction of cast iron shot and the appearance of the first movable though not necessarily very mobile carriages. The arm had not yet proved itself in the field, but it was seen to be a promising means of penetrating the pallisade or wagonburg defence and of making the use of large and morally menacing masses of troops unprofitable. Small-arms were also coming into being, though they were still secondary to the bow as missile weapons – their rate of fire being very much slower and their range less than those of the archers. All missile weapons were still auxiliary to the mass of infantry armed with the pike.

By the end of the fifteenth century, armies were maintaining cavalry, infantry and artillery in approximately equal proportions as regards cost. The infantry was concentrated in large square masses, with arquebusiers operating on the flanks; the artillery tended to be widely distributed regarded as a means of extending the range of the infantry's small arms fire rather than as a centrally directed force.

Below: Contemporary sketch of the battle of Lutzen showing the chequerboard pattern of squares referred to on page 75.

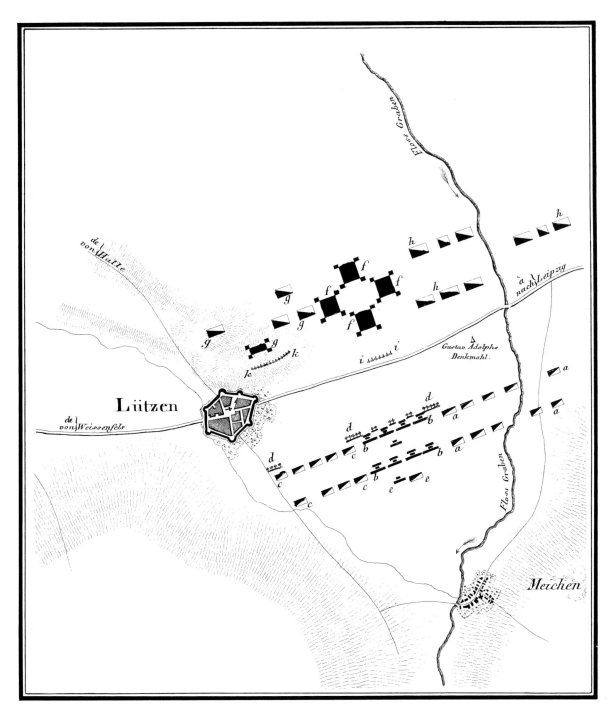

In the sixteenth century the introduction of corned (granulated) powder and the matchlock made small-arms really formidable, though their rate of fire was still slow. The important thing was that they could defeat armour; and they took the place of the bow, which was then abandoned. The deep pike formation remained as the basic component of a force of infantry, but pikes and muskets came to be held in equal proportions. Musketeers, working on the flanks of the pikemen, were vulnerable to cavalry owing to their slow rate of fire; so the earlier solid pike formation was changed to a hollow square within which the musketeers could take refuge when threatened by cavalry. The squares were usually formed by battalions, and often a number of such squares would be arranged in a chequerboard formation in order to support each other by cross-fire.

The improvement of the musket in this period, and the greater reliance placed on it, led to less attention being paid to artillery – which was normally provided on the low scale of one piece to 1,000 men of other arms.

Gustavus Adolphus

In the middle of the seventeenth century Gustavus Adolphus, King of Sweden and Commander of the Swedish Army, directed his wisdom to a complete re-appraisal of the tactics of land warfare and the organisation and equipment of his army. He created a new model army of disciplined regular soldiers; but because his country could support no more than 12,000 to 15,000 of them, he reinforced them with specially selected and trained mercenaries. And he devoted much attention to increasing the rate of fire of the musket, which was the weakest feature of the armoury at that time. This he did by making the weapon lighter and introducing the cartridge. As a result of these improvements, he was able to increase the ratio of muskets to pikes to two to one and reduce to six the number of ranks in which the infantry was deployed.

He then sought to make far more use of his artillery by dividing it into the organic artillery of infantry and cavalry units and the artillery of the park (or artillery of position), which was directed centrally. Each battalion was given two light 4pr guns, and these gave close support under the control of the battalion commander. The artillery of the park was used to prepare the way for an attack by preliminary bombardment,

and its batteries consisted of five 12pr or ten 6pr guns.

As has already been stated, it is difficult to obtain all the information needed to make a quantitative assessment of the effect of the weapons in these early battles; but the battle of Breitenfeld, which Gustavus won conclusively, is worth examining because it gives such a good picture of the way in which battles were fought in the early days of firearms – and it is possible to reach certain conclusions on their performance from its story.

The battle of Breitenfeld was fought on 7th September 1631 between Swedish and Imperial forces, with the initial positions of the two armies as shown in map A. By this time, the increasing power of small-arms had led to the abandonment of the solid mass – or hollow square – of pikemen. The pikemen still formed the foundation of the infantry unit, but for action they were now deployed in lines so that the musketeers, interspersed throughout the front ranks, could develop the whole of their firepower simultaneously. The Swedish pikemen were deployed six ranks deep, though on the Imperial side the battalions of infantry were no less than ten ranks deep and covered a frontage of 50 files each.

The battle began with a preliminary reciprocal bombardment by the artillery of both sides, each of which was divided into the two echelons described above. It would have been the artillery of the park that was chiefly concerned in it. The fire was continued for two hours, and most accounts describe it as 'an artillery duel' – which seems to imply that each was directing it, at least to some extent, at the other's gun positions.

No very precise information is available on the number of guns that took part in this bombardment. The Swedish Army is said to have been supported by one hundred guns, but it is probable that at least half of these were with battalions. And the Imperial Army probably deployed rather fewer guns in its central battery. The restrictions on the permissible rate of fire, already described, would have limited the number of rounds fired to some twenty per gun – so each side might have fired about a thousand rounds at the other. But the range between the opposing armies was 1,800 paces (or 1,500 yards), and even the theoretical estimates of effectiveness that have been given would not claim more than a very low percentage of hits on the target at such long range. It seems likely, indeed, that the effect of this artillery bombardment was more on morale than physical.

The effect of the small-arms is more interesting. The battle, as opposed to the bombardment, began when Comte de Pappenheim's cavalry – on the Imperial left – charged the Swedish right wing. This action was carried out without the authority of the Commander-in-Chief, and it had disastrous results. The Imperial cavalry made no less than seven successive charges, each of which was repulsed in confusion and ruin – shattered, it is said, by the fire of the musketeers.

In contrast to this failure on their left, the Imperial cavalry, under Prince de Furstenburg, then assaulted the Saxons on the opposite flank of the Swedish Army and threw them into confusion. The situation was saved by Gustavus refusing his left flank and stopping Furstenburg's elated cavalry with a well-disciplined wall of pikemen supported, again, by their interspersed musketeers. The battle ended when the whole Swedish line swung forward, pivoting on its left centre, and rolled up the entire Imperial Army.

It is difficult to know how much credit should be given to the firearms, both great and small, at this early stage of their development. A battle was still fought, basically, by 'push of pike'. A line of pikemen could withstand any assault on its front as long as the men not only kept their heads and their will to fight but also maintained their tight formation in which all the weapons supported each other. Their vulnerable flanks were protected by other lines at right angles to the main front. But firearms were beginning to be more than mere useful adjuncts and had, of course, an effect on morale as well as physical effect. Furthermore, a cavalry charge depended for its effectiveness on an initial success or 'break in', and the fire of the muskets probably gave that additional check to the cavalry that prevented it from making use of its daunting mobility.

Firearms were not all-powerful, however, and the result of an action still depended on the ability of the pikemen to stand fast against attack – as the Saxons failed to do on the left flank of the Swedish line. It certainly seems, also, that the small-arms of the time were more effective than the guns, to which no great performance can be attributed.

Above: The column formation used by Gustavus Adolphus at the Battle of Breitenfeld. It consists of three battalions, namely A, B, C, flanked by D and D′. The leading company of pikes (A) is flanked by the fire of musketeers F and F′, whose front is protected by the fire of Company B. The object of this column is to combine shock, fire and movement. Company C is in local reserve.

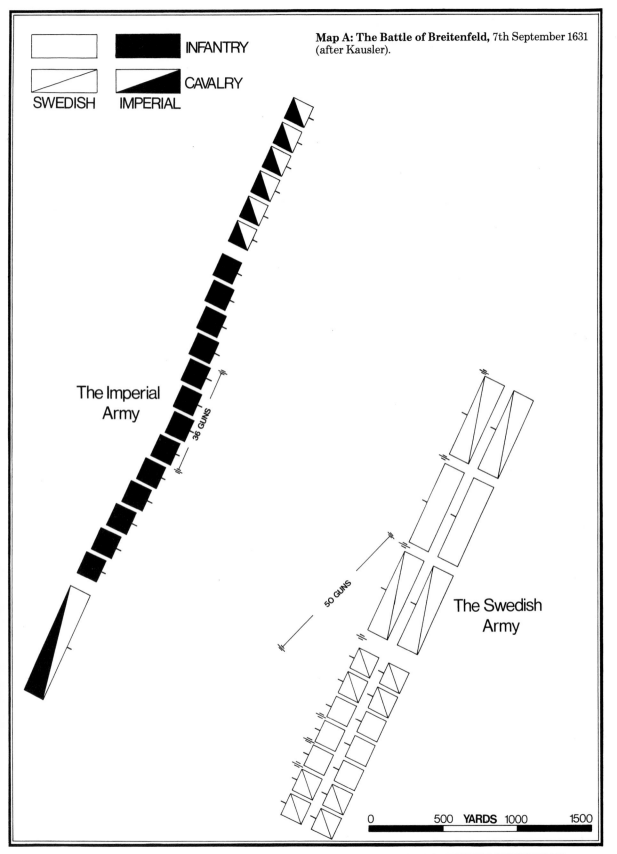

INFANTRY

CAVALRY

SWEDISH   IMPERIAL

Map A: The Battle of Breitenfeld, 7th September 1631 (after Kausler).

The Imperial Army

36 GUNS

The Swedish Army

50 GUNS

0   500   **YARDS** 1000   1500

The attack by Cutts' Division on the fortified village of Blenheim during the opening stages of the battle of that name. The palisades round the village are shown somewhat conventionally, and the defenders seem to be opening fire long before that dramatic moment when they fired their devastating first volley at a range of thirty yards. (By permission of the National Army Museum.)

The early eighteenth century

At this stage the pike finally disappeared, and the infantry was armed with a single dual-purpose weapon in the shape of the flintlock musket to which could be attached the socket bayonet that had superseded the earlier and less satisfactory types. When infantry was well disciplined, unbroken and in a suitable formation, it could use its single weapon either to defend itself against infantry or cavalry or to carry out both the approach to and the assault of a defended position.

The linear formation that Gustavus Adolphus had developed so that the maximum number of muskets could be brought to bear was still in use, but the rate of fire that had now been attained allowed the depth of the lines to be reduced to three ranks. The French and other Continental nations fired their volleys by ranks in succession to produce fire as continuous as possible over the whole front. It was the British custom, however, to fire musket volleys by 'firings' (one-third of the platoon strength). These platoon sub-divisions, firing in succession, produced a slightly different form of continuous fire – and one that was better adapted to take advantage of gaps in the smoke of battle. The front rank knelt, the second rank stood half a pace to one flank and the third rank a full pace to the other flank so that all three ranks could fire at once.

There had been a serious lack of flexibility in the early linear formations of Gustavus, as a result of which his great lines of battle found difficulty in carrying out any manoeuvre on the battlefield other than a straight advance in line. Marlborough was not content with such rigidity and required his troops to move more freely about the battlefield. He therefore introduced drills whereby sub-units could be manoeuvred in any direction.

Guns were still provided in all armies on a scale of from one to three to each battalion. They moved on the flanks of their battalions and were normally propelled by manpower, using drag-ropes. It was Marlborough's custom to 'post' some of these guns himself and encourage their use to provide close support for particular phases of the battle. At the same time, the use of the artillery of the park gradually became more ambitious and more closely directed to the attainment of specific objects rather than indulging in indiscriminate bombardment.

Quantitative evidence on the effect of artillery in Marlborough's wars is very hard to obtain. Concentrations of guns were certainly used by both sides in the War of the Spanish Succession, particularly at Malplaquet, but it is almost impossible to determine their effect in terms of casualties inflicted. Marlborough seems to have devoted more attention to the use of guns in smaller numbers in close support, possibly because he knew that their effect was in inverse proportion to the range at which they were required to fire.

There is, however, one excellent example in Marlborough's wars of the effect of small-arms fire – in the battle of Blenheim in 1704. The battle began with an attack by the Allied force under Marlborough and Eugene on the fortified village of Blenheim, which formed a strong-point on the extreme right of the French position. The attack failed, but enough information is available to enable an assessment of the effect of the fire to be made.

The French, recognising that Blenheim was a key to their position, had fortified it and its surrounding enclosures by erecting palisades and other field works; and it was garrisoned with nine battalions of infantry. This garrison was increased during the battle – ultimately by a further eighteen battalions – but there is some doubt as to when the reinforcement was made. Fortescue states that all twenty-seven battalions were present from the start, but Hilaire Belloc believes that the reinforcement of the original nine battalions was carried out only after the attack. This point, however, does not seem to be really material. The part of the village that was attacked presented a frontage of not more than 900 yards; and even if it is assumed that that frontage was manned by a continuous line of men, three deep, at 22 inches per man – as in the ranks in the open – it would not have been possible to bring more than 4,000 muskets into play at once. Thus it would not have been possible to use more than eight battalions to repel an attack on one face of the village. The presence of a larger garrison would not have increased the firepower available but would have served merely to replace casualties and to guard the other faces of the perimeter.

The attack was made by Colonel Lord John Cutts'

division and was formed in six lines – of which only the first, comprising five British battalions, advanced beyond a sheltered starting line no more than 150 yards from the objective.

A piece of rather doubtful evidence arises at this point. It is generally stated that, as might be expected, some French artillery fired the usual salvoes of case shot at the advancing Allied lines. Indeed, one account asserts that there were four French 24pr guns in front of Blenheim. Had such heavy guns been in action they would certainly have caused losses to the attackers, but they would have been quite immovable in the stress of battle; and it is unlikely that the detachments would have remained exposed in the open when the attack had arrived within 150 yards of its objective. In any case, the figures quoted here relate to casualties from small-arms only – so the effect of the French artillery can be ignored.

Brigadier General Archibald Row's brigade of five British battalions made the attack on a frontage of 750 yards and could therefore have been engaged by all the French muskets on a frontage of 900 yards, which corresponds to the figure of 4,000 muskets already mentioned.

With the superb discipline of those times the British line obeyed its orders not to open fire until its commander touched the palisades with his sword. Such French guns as may have been in action and within range were now either abandoned by their detachments or prevented from firing by the nearness of their own troops. The rigidly-dressed scarlet line moved forward in complete silence until, when it was thirty paces from its objective, a French volley from 4,000 muskets struck it – and one third of its strength fell, killed or wounded.

Whether a single volley achieved this result is not and probably cannot ever be completely clear. It would have been just possible for the French defenders to reload and fire a second volley before the attackers reached the objective, though all accounts of this battle mention only a single devastating volley as having been fired. If a single volley from 4,000 muskets inflicted 800 casualties, it means that 20% of the rounds were effective. It may be, of course, that the number of muskets firing has been exaggerated – there could hardly have been more on that frontage – but it is also possible that the casualty figures in-

cluded some inflicted at other times during the battle. Errors in these two directions would cancel each other; and it seems, on the whole, that there is good evidence for a figure of effectiveness for the musket of the order of 20% at this very short range.

Lest it be thought that this performance was exceptional, it must be recorded that in a second attack the British battalions alone (Row's shattered infantry having been reinforced by a brigade commanded by Brigadier General James Ferguson) suffered a further 1,370 casualties. Even if three defensive volleys are assumed, the result was that over 11% of the shots were effective. In the more likely event of two volleys having been fired, the figure would be 17%.

It may be interesting to compare these figures with those that were suggested on page 64. There, after assuming a realistic misfire rate and a reduction of the theoretical performance to compensate for battle conditions, it was thought that at 100 yards range not more than 15% of the shots fired were likely to be effective. At the very short range at which the battle round Blenheim was fought, it may well be that the effectiveness of the muskets was appreciably higher.

It was the same forty-one years later at Fontenoy, in 1745, where seventeen British battalions marched steadily up the slope in two lines towards the French position while the unsubdued French artillery assailed first their flanks and later even their rear from the Redoubt d'Eu and the village of Fontenoy itself. There, again, musket fire was opened at only thirty paces; but in this case it is the attacker rather than the defender for whose performance some figures of casualties are available. Fortescue wrote, 'Down dropped the whole of the French front rank, blue coats, red coats, and white, before the storm. Nineteen officers and six hundred men of the French and Swiss Guards fell at the first discharge; Regiment Courtin was crushed out of existence; Regiment Aubeterre, striving hard to stem the tide, was swept aside by a single imperious volley which laid half of its men on the ground.' Then, as the battle continued, the British infantry was charged three times by French cavalry – but 'it was like charging two flaming fortresses rather than two columns of infantry'.

This account of Fortescue's states that 600 casualties were suffered by the five battalions of French and

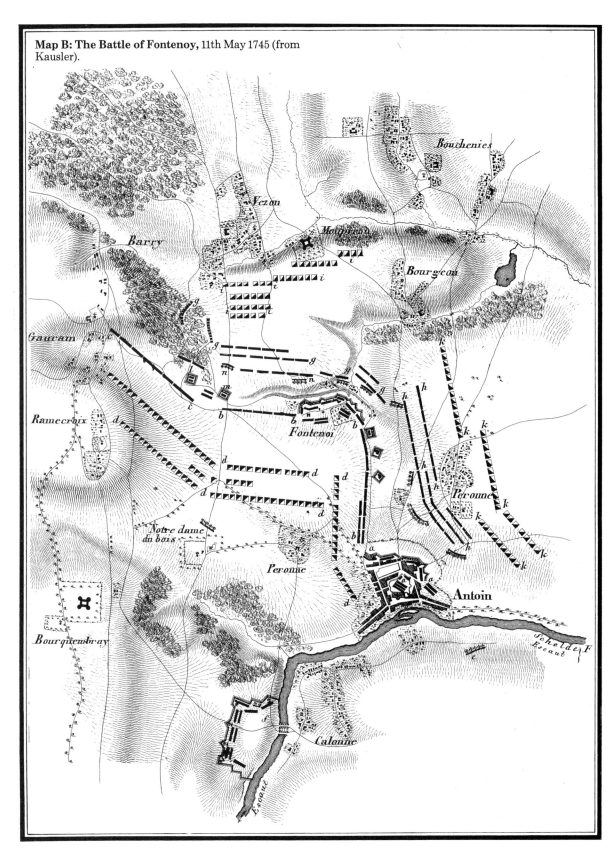

Map B: **The Battle of Fontenoy,** 11th May 1745 (from Kausler).

Swiss Guards. They were caused by the muskets of five British battalions, whose strength at the beginning of the battle would have been about 2,500 men – but all accounts of this battle stress the damage that was done by the French artillery during the infantry's advance, and it must certainly be assumed that it inflicted several hundred casualties.

This would mean that the British muskets were hitting with over 25% of the rounds ordered to be fired.

Turning now to the performance of the artillery in the same period, there is some interesting evidence in the records of the battle of Dettingen – fought on 16th June 1743 and imbued with the glamour of being the last occasion on which an English sovereign commanded his troops in the field. Many historians – not the least of whom was Fortescue – have described in stirring language how the Allied force, penned in Marshal de Noailles' famous 'mouse-trap', fought its way out against a greatly superior French army.

Map C shows the positions of the two forces and the local geography – the first feature of the battle that is always stressed being the presence of a great line of French guns along the west bank of the river Main. The locations of those guns are reliably recorded by the existence of the small knolls on which they would certainly have been sited; and it is clear from the map that guns in those positions could engage the Allied force as it moved northward on Dettingen in full enfilade. It is therefore not surprising that all accounts of the battle tell of the terrible execution wrought by the French artillery, for it would certainly seem that it was presented with a sitting target. There was great confusion and delay as the Allied troops, thoroughly mixed with their baggage wagons, emerged from the village of Klein Ostheim. After moving out of the village in column until the baggage wagons could be extracted and moved away to the right flank, the infantry and cavalry deployed into line, were carefully dressed and then moved slowly forward with further halts to redress the line until the two armies came into contact. A more ideal target for guns in action on the flank of such movements in mass could hardly be imagined, and all experience of the guns of later times suggests that the enfilade fire would have been devastating.

Fortescue states, however, that the four British battalions on the left flank suffered 'not more than 100 casualties each' throughout the whole of this battle. It seems unlikely, then, that more than 100 to 200 casualties at most were inflicted by a number of French guns stated variously to have been between 30 and 40. Looked at superficially, this gives the very low figure of between three and six casualties per gun during a period of at least two hours – which is hard to reconcile with the lurid accounts of the carnage that the guns are said to have caused.

But before the French gunners are condemned too severely, their problems should be examined more closely on map C. The target was admittedly a slowly moving mass and therefore vulnerable to round shot fired from any direction; but the effect of the fire was limited by the range of the guns and their slow rate of fire. The river was 300 yards wide and the guns were sited several hundred yards from the west bank, so they had no great 'reach' beyond the river. Lines indicating ranges of 1,000 yards from the guns, which can be taken as their maximum effective range, are shown on the map. From them it can be seen that the southernmost French battery, deployed for another purpose, could take no part in this stage of the battle; and the one next to it, towards the north, could not have engaged the Allied columns at all after they had emerged from Klein Ostheim. Furthermore, only the flank – and indeed only the extreme flank – of the Allied force would have been within effective range of the French batteries further north for a limited period for each battery. The fire was probably the equivalent of twelve guns firing for a period of about an hour. The guns of that time were capable of a maximum rate of fire of about one round in two or three minutes, allowance being made for the obscuration of the view by smoke and other battle conditions. Some three hundred rounds might therefore have been fired, giving a casualty rate of between one-third and two-thirds for each round. As each round hitting its target usually caused several casualties, this would suggest that from 10% to 20% of the rounds fired were effective.

As regards the small-arms, all accounts agree that the fire discipline of the French infantry was inferior to that of the Allies. This is borne out by the fact that the French losses were twice as high as those of their opponents. It seems that the British platoon firing was very effective when it was well controlled, though there were some units in which the natural tendency

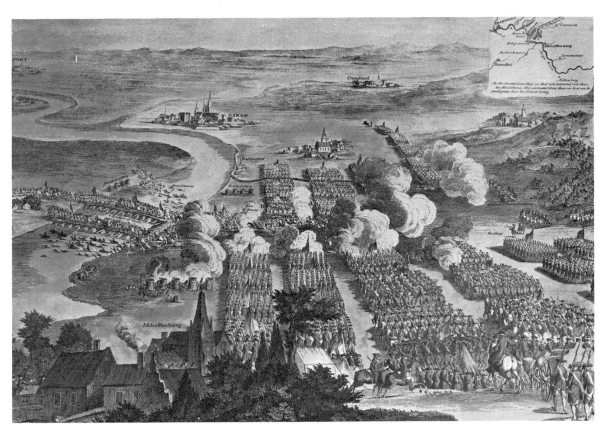

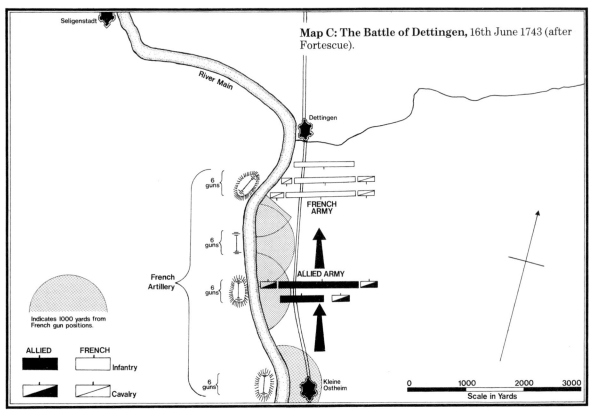

Map C: The Battle of Dettingen, 16th June 1743 (after Fortescue).

Seligenstadt

River Main

Dettingen

6 guns

6 guns

6 guns

French Artillery

FRENCH ARMY

ALLIED ARMY

Indicates 1000 yards from French gun positions.

ALLIED   FRENCH

Infantry

Cavalry

6 guns

Kleine Ostheim

0   1000   2000   3000
Scale in Yards

of the men to fire as often as they could was not properly restrained.

Conclusions

The following conclusions may be drawn on the effectiveness of firearms during this period.

Short range smooth-bore artillery was very sensitive to its siting and to the aspect of its target. It cannot be assumed that a force of x men and y guns was necessarily inferior to one of x men and $2y$ guns. The effectiveness of the artillery support depended entirely on the siting of the guns and, apart from the importance of tactical skill in siting them, the ground rarely permitted the placing of more than a limited number in positions from which they could exert great influence on the battle.

The sighting equipment of guns being less sophisticated than it was about to become, the artillery was of much more use in close support at short range than as artillery of position. Furthermore, the slow rate of fire imposed by clumsy elevating gear and by the weight of the carriages limited the amount of fire that could be provided.

Nevertheless, the persistent reports of heavy casualties caused by guns – even if somewhat picturesquely exaggerated – suggest that their fire had considerable moral effect. Indeed, the sight of the damage caused by a round shot on a closely packed mass of men must have been discouraging to all but the strongest nerves.

The effect of small-arms fire depended entirely on the standard of fire discipline in a unit. When fire could be opened at 60 yards range or less, the effectiveness of the musket could be remarkably high; but any lack of control in this respect led not only to wasted effort but also to muskets often being unloaded when they were most required. And it must not be forgotten that good fire discipline was the result not only of good training but also of the soldier having great confidence in his commanders and in the soundness of their judgment. Nothing discouraged troops more and reduced their confidence in their commanders to a greater extent than having to fire volleys that were obviously ineffective – particularly when it meant that they might be unloaded and unready to fire with effect a few moments later.

It will be noted that the high figures of effectiveness that have been quoted were all achieved by either single volleys or a very small number of volleys fired over a wide frontage at the beginning of a fire fight and at very close range. That was before the smoke of battle began to obscure the view and before the excitement of battle caused discipline to be overridden. There must often have been a great difference between the effectiveness of those closely controlled initial volleys and that of the subsequent exchanges.

Nevertheless – though it may not be possible to attribute to the musket so high an overall performance throughout a battle – it does seem that, with a combination of confidence and discipline, the highly trained professional armies of the eighteenth century could hit with some 10% to 20% of the shots ordered to be fired.

Pictorial section:
Seventeenth century musket drill

Seventeenth-century musket drill, from an English drill
book of 1642.

Order yo Musket

1

Being come to yo first stand hold your
Musket barrell in yo hand about ij high
of yo shoulder w the but end on ij grou
nd. In yo left hand hold ij rest alitle below
the forke, the pike end on the grownd.

Give ij... Rest to ij Musket

2

Sinke downe your right hand not bowing
yo body, then gripe your musket and lift it vp
then bring about the left hand with the rest and
joyne it to your Musket, on ij out side houlding
yo thumb hard against the forke of the rest and so ca
rry both Musket and rest in the left hand only

Open your Pann

3

In the joyning of your Musket and rest t
ether fall back with your right leg, to
your proper stang then hold the thum
of the right hand behind the cutchic
of the pan, and with your two former
fingers draw back the couer of the p

Cast of yo loose Powder

7

Hould your Musket fast with the right
hand att the breech, the lefte as before
turning the Panne downwards that
the loose Powder may fall offe

Blow of ij loose Powder

8

Houla ij Musket in both hands as before, beare it vp towards your mouth
not stoping bloe offe ij loose Pouder

Cast about ij Musk

9

Hould your Musket in both hands as befor
beare it righ vp towards your left side
and with all step forwards the right le
then holding the Musket only in the rig
hand at the breech forsake the rest

Cleare your Pann

4

Bring vp your Musket with the left hand only, towards your mouth and blow your pan stifly not stooping vpon any termes and in the meane time with your right hand take your touch box as in the figure

Prime ye Pann

5

Hould ye touch box betweene ye thumbe and forefinger of the right hand only and soe Prime as in ye figur

Shut ye Pann

6

Lay ye thumbe over the barrell neare the Pann, and with your two formost fingers, shut the Pann

Trayle yr Rest

10

Having forsaken ye rest take ye Musket into ye left hand about ye midle of ye barrell soe as ye butt end touch not the ground trayling your rest beetweene ye Musket and bodie

Open your Charge

11

Take your charge in your right hand with the thumbe and fore finger thereof thrust of the cover

Charge wth Powder

12

Put backe your left hand with the Musket as farr as conveniently you can and with your right hand turne the Powder into ye muzell of ye barrell houlding ye charge beetweene ye thumbe and forefinger only

Charge ... with Bullet

13

Take the Bullet forth of your bag
or out of your mouth and put it
into the muzell of your Musket

*Draw ... forth ỳ scou
ring stick*

14

With your right hand (ỳ Palme turned
from you) draw forth your scouring
stick beating your botle and ỳ left hand
w:th ỳ Musket soe farrbacke as you cann

*Shorten ỳ ... scourin
stick*

15

Having drawne forth ỳ scouri
stick set ỳ Rammer head against ỳ
brest and slip ỳ hand close to ỳ Ramm
ỳ you may the easier put it into ỳ m

*Returne ... ỳ scowring
sticke*

19

Put the scowring sticke to his
place from whence you had it

*Recover ... your
Musket*

20

Bring forward ỳ Musket w:th yo
left hand and beare it right vp
Take it in ỳ right hand at ỳ breech
and soe hold it in ỳ right hand only

*Poize yo ... Musket and
recover ... yo Rest*

21

Fallbacke w:th ỳ right leg to ỳ first
stand hould yo musket in yo right
hand at ỳ breech and recover ỳ
rest in yo left hand holding it
just vnder the forke

Rame home 16

Put your scouring stick downe into your Musket and Ramme home hard twice or thrize

Vdraw yᵗʰ scowring sticke 17

With your right hand turned draw your scowring stick out of your Musket as before

Shorten yᵉ Scowring Sticke 18

Yᵒ Scouring sticke being drawne forth of yᵉ barrell turne it and bring yᵉ Scouringslicke end to yᵉ brest and so slip yᵉ hand wᵗʰ in an handfull of yᵉ end

Giue your Rest to Muskel 22

...ing yᵉ left hand wᵗʰ yᵉ rest towards ...ur right side neere your Musket ...d soe strike yᵉ Musket and hould it wᵗʰ ...rest in yᵉ left hand only the rest bein... the outside of the Musket

Draw foᵗʰ erth your Match 23

Take your match from beetweene your litle finger wᵗʰ the thumb and second finger of your right hand being turned with yᵉ Palme from yᵉ...

Blow your Cole 24

Bring the right hand wᵗʰ the match backward and your left hand wᵗʰ yᵉ muskel and rest forward turning your face somewhat backward blow yoʳ match stiffe

Cocke y^r match

25

Holding your match betweene yor thumb and second finger bring it to the cock and press itt into the cock with the thumb.

Try your match

26

Your thumb and fore finger being upon the cock and the second and third finger under the cocke pull the cock to the pann and with the finger either raise or sinck y^e match.

Gard and blow

27

Lay the two fore fingers of the right hand upon the pan the thumb behind the scutchion of the pan the easier to lift up the musket and see raising up the musket with both hands blow as before in the 12 posture.

Dismount yor musket.

31

Bring your musket and rest to your right side and carry both in the left hand only.

Un cocke yor match

32

Take the match from the coke with the thumb and second finger of yor right hand houlding the musket and rest in the left hand only.

Returne y^r match

33

Put the match betweene the two less fingers of the left hand from whence you had it. No at from henc forward y^u may prime and charg as before fr y^e 8 postur and so forward as in y^e 25 postur

Open your pann

28

With the two forefingers of the right hand open the panne as in the 7 postuer.

Pre= sent

29

Remoue your right hand to your thumbe hale yo' second finger to the tricker w'th your left hand fixe the forke of the rest to your musket and your thumbe against the forke and the pike end of the rest one the ground.

Giue fire

30

Lift up your right elbow and place the but end of yo' musket within y' shoulder neare y' brest the small end appearing a little a boue your shoulder standing with the left leg formost and the knee bent and the right leg standing stiffe.

Shoulder y' musket.

34

...ing y' musket poized hould your rest an d full under y forke then bring your musket ...e y bodie and y rest crose ouer it behind the o hole and soe with both hands lay it gently on shoulder haueing the rest crose your ...e and with all bring your right leg vp to y ... fall backe againe with your right leg.

March with in your your rest right hand

35

First take the match from the left hand betweene the fingers of the right hand then take the string of the rest from the left arme and returne the mach betweene the fingers of the left hand and take the rest in the right hand.

March musket and with y' carrie y' rest.

36

First shift the match as in the former direction then put the string of the rest ouer the left arme and the rest in the hand and soe returne the match and carey y' rest as in the figure.

Vnshoulder your musket

Poyze your musket

Rest y[e] musket

37

38

39

Bring up your right leg to your left sinke
your Musket and carry it right up and with
all turne it that the pike end of your rest
be toward your left side then take the
musket at the breech with your right
hand and slip downe y[e] left wth the y[e] rest.

Hould the musket right up in the right
hand on y[e] right sid raise y[e] left hand to
y[e] forke of y[e] rest and set your thumb
against the forke as in the figuer.

Bring up your left hand wth the fork of
the rest to the musket and soe lett y[e]
musket and rest sinke downe togather
and fall backe with your right
legg to your proper stand

Blow y[r] match

Cocke y[e] match

Trye y[r] match

41

42

4

Beare your musket and rest
forward with y[e] left hand and
y[e] match backward in y[e] right
and blow. as in y[e] 28 posture

Cocke your match as
in the 29th posture.

Trye your match as in
the 30th posture.

Drawe out   your match.

*Take the match betweene the thumb
and the second finger of the right
hand as in the 27 posture and
with the thumbe of your left hand
hould the musket fast on the rest.*

he sentinell   posture.

*ould y̍ ͤ too forfingers of y̍ righthan.
on y̍ pan y̍ thumb behind the
tchin redey upon all ocasions.*

5. Frederick the Great to Napoleon

There were no significant changes in the construction of the musket between 1750 and 1850 – although there may have been some improvement in the composition of the gunpowder, which could have given a better ballistic performance. In general, however, the effectiveness of the weapon remained unchanged throughout this period.

On the other hand, there was a considerable improvement in the performance of artillery from about the middle of the eighteenth century that, although it probably did not affect the artillery of Dettingen and Fontenoy, was certainly apparent in the battles of the second half of the century. It came about, firstly, from the founders' ability to cast more reliable pieces – as a result of which it was no longer necessary to restrict the rate of fire to avoid the risk of burst pieces. But even more significant was the introduction of elevating gear that enabled the gun to be laid more smoothly, more accurately and more quickly than had previously been possible; and the lightening of gun carriages accomplished by Gribeauval in France – and, later, by Congreve in Britain – was another step towards the achievement of a higher rate of fire. There were also improvements in the construction of fuzes and in the composition of the powder used in them; but the most significant practical result of progress was the increased rate of fire, which was at least twice if not four times that obtained in Marlborough's time. Consequently, greater reliance was placed on the artillery and it was required to take a more active part in the fighting and be able to move on the battlefield in order to do so.

Frederick the Great
In the middle of the eighteenth century the tactics of land warfare that Gustavus Adolphus had first developed, and that Marlborough had improved to take advantage of the universal presence of firearms, were developed still further by Frederick the Great. Although Marlborough had demanded battlefield mobility fifty years earlier, the armies of Dettingen and Fontenoy had somewhat fallen back into rigid postures and tended to fling great lines of troops into head-on collisions with each other. But Frederick established a permanent sub-division of his infantry battalions into ten 'pelotons' (platoons) of seventy men each and arrayed each of them in three ranks.

He broke away from the linear rigidity that had come to be imposed on armies and restored the ability to manoeuvre by moving his battalions in column of platoons during the approach to combat. The short range of the small-arms of the day permitted the movement of such a column across the front of an enemy, and when it reached its allotted starting line it was easy to wheel all the platoons into line for the assault. Frederick was thus able to develop his favourite technique of manoeuvring to attack the enemy's weakest flank. Line having been formed for the attack at about two hundred yards from the enemy's position, the infantry was required to fire six volleys at gradually shortening ranges and finally assault from a distance of fifty yards. When volleys were fired, it was done over as wide a frontage as possible – the front rank kneeling and all three ranks firing simultaneously.

The evidence already presented suggests that the opening of fire at such long range was unlikely to have been very effective physically, and it is thought to have been carried out mainly for its moral effect.

Frederick paid little attention to artillery at first; but the effectiveness of the Austrian artillery in the Seven Years' War limited the freedom of manoeuvre that he sought and caused him to develop his own and lay down tactics for it. At that time, the artillery was still divided into that permanently attached to infantry units and that operating under central control as artillery of the park. Frederick increased the scale of the former, giving each battalion in the first line two 6pr guns and a 7pr howitzer. He was the first commander to make regular use of field howitzers, which he considered to be of great value because of their ability to provide overhead covering fire and to fire explosive shells that could deal with field works. The battalion guns of units in the second line were expected to join the fire fight by shooting from eminences in the rear. Heavier artillery was provided on a scale of ten 12pr guns for each brigade, and a further ten heavy guns were allotted to each wing.

Mention has already been made of Frederick's introduction of specially equipped and specially organised mobile artillery, which came to be known as 'horse artillery' and which was used by him to provide a mobile reserve of artillery that could be quickly moved anywhere on the battlefield. It was armed with

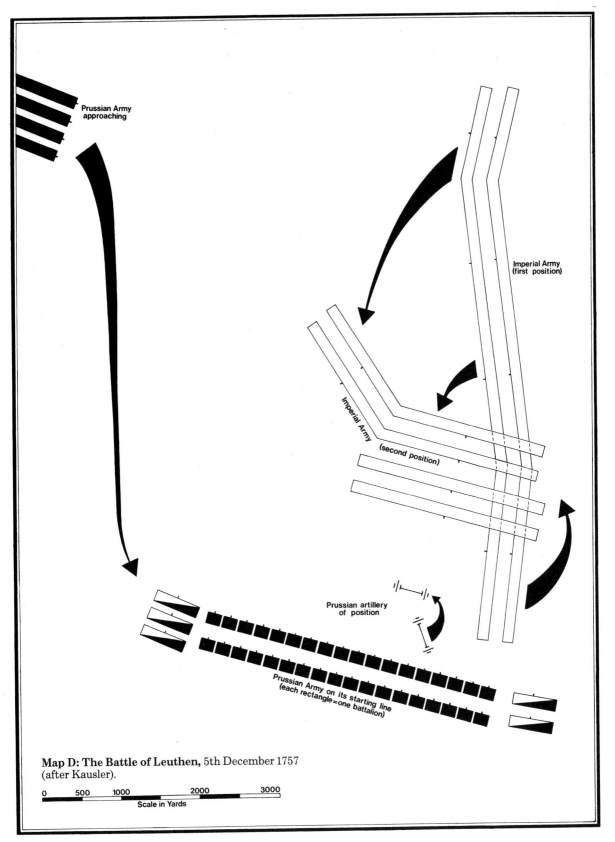

Map D: The Battle of Leuthen, 5th December 1757
(after Kausler).

Prussian Army
approaching

Imperial Army
(first position)

Imperial Army
(second position)

Prussian artillery
of position

Prussian Army on its starting line
(each rectangle=one battalion)

0   500   1000   2000   3000
Scale in Yards

light guns and howitzers and was organised in completely self-contained units – unlike much of the artilleries of most nations, which was held in and detached for service from rather amorphous parks of artillery, its drivers being found from a separate corps.

Thus the essential features of Frederick's tactics were an ability to manoeuvre on the battlefield and the production of overwhelming firepower at the point he had chosen as his objective – usually on a flank. The firepower consisted of the preparatory fire of the artillery of the park, directed at the enemy's infantry rather than his guns, then the covering fire of the battalion guns working forward on the flanks of each infantry unit, and lastly the musketry of the infantry as it moved forward to the assault.

A typical example of Frederick's tactics can be found in the battle of Leuthen, fought on 5th December 1757 and illustrated in map D.

The Imperial Army, 80,000 strong, was drawn up in line in its initial position, as shown on the map, as the Prussian force – numbering only 30,000 – approached in parallel columns. Arriving on the battlefield, Frederick swung all his infantry across the enemy's front, each battalion being in column of sub-units, and established his artillery of the park as shown on the map in order to pave the way for an assault on the enemy's left. At the starting line shown, the infantry wheeled into line by battalions and – its flanks protected by the cavalry and its advance covered by all of the artillery – rolled up the flank of the Imperial Army. That flank was refused, as shown in the sketch; but the movement was carried out under difficulties and under fire. In the ensuing confusion, the Imperial force was routed.

It is extremely hard to find evidence of the relative quantitative effects of artillery and muskets in Frederick's battles, but the battle of Minden – fought in the same period, in 1759 – provides some facts which enable a partial assessment to be made. That battle also illustrates how armies other than Frederick's were beginning to manoeuvre on the battlefield before an assault and how the artillery was starting to be required to make quite ambitious moves during an action.

At Minden, Prince Ferdinand of Brunswick – commanding an Allied force – was confronted by a French army, under Marshal de Contades, encamped outside and to the south-west of Minden as shown in map E (copied from a contemporary print of the battle, Fortescue's map seeming for once to be completely out of scale). The French prepared to move forward to battle, throwing bridges across the Batau stream; and early on 1st August they did, in fact, move to the positions shown. Meanwhile, Ferdinand had entrusted his left wing to General von Wangenheim – commanding an Allied corps – with orders to make a holding attack southward while he moved the whole of the rest of his force round to the west in order to strike at the French left flank.

The Allied troops deployed as shown in the map; but through various mischances it was at first only Major General von Spörcke's column of infantry that actually advanced to the attack – the infantry consisting of three British battalions in the first line, with three more British and three Hanoverian battalions in the second line. It was supported initially by Captain Lieutenant Foy's British brigade of four light 12pr guns, three light 6pr guns and two $5\frac{1}{2}$-inch howitzers that had been purposefully moved to gun positions on the right flank of the advance. Seeing that excellent practice could be and was being developed by the guns in that area, Ferdinand took a step that was far from usual during the battles of the time. He moved virtually the whole of the rest of his artillery of the park to the same area to reinforce Foy's brigade. Captain Forbes Macbean's ten British 12pr guns and Captain Hase's six Hanoverian heavy guns moved across behind the deploying troops and came into action near Hahlen. There were thus twenty-five allied guns in action on the flank of the advance (and some accounts suggest that an additional nine guns under the command of Captain Drummond were also moved to the same area).

The French had adopted a most peculiar formation in which their cavalry was posted in the centre, with infantry on both flanks. They are said to have had at least sixty guns of the park in action on the flanks of the frontage on which von Spörcke's column was attacking, and it is stated that some of these were 18prs.

The ranges at which the guns of both sides were firing can be seen on map E. The guns on the French right flank were further from their target than those

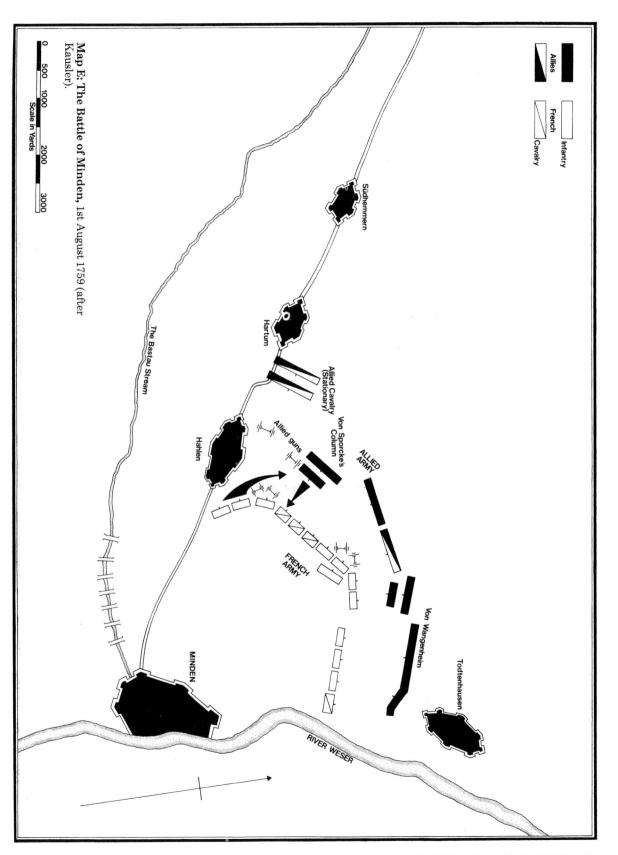

Map E: The Battle of Minden, 1st August 1759 (after Kausler).

Allies
French

Infantry
Cavalry

0   500   1000   2000   3000
Scale in Yards

Südhemmern

Hartum

Hahlen

The Bastau Stream

Allied Cavalry (Stationary)

Von Sporcke's Column

Allied guns

ALLIED ARMY

FRENCH ARMY

Von Wangenheim

Todtenhausen

MINDEN

RIVER WESER

on the left, and it seems likely that it was the latter that played the major part in the action. The French artillery was probably firing at the advancing Allied lines for half an hour before close contact was established, and in that period it would no doubt have been able to fire some 20 rounds per gun from 60 guns – a total of 1,200 rounds.

When the leading Allied infantry arrived at a line 500 yards from the French cavalry, the latter charged and were received – after admirable restraint in holding fire – by a volley at 40 yards range that completely halted and broke them. The charge was repeated, with the same result; and the Allied line resumed its advance. It was then assailed on its right flank by French infantry that had moved forward on the left of the beaten cavalry. That attack was repulsed after a ten-minute fire fight, as was the attack that followed it.

Without going into the details of this battle, it is enough to note that two cavalry charges and two determined infantry attacks were broken by the fire of the Allied guns and muskets. But it is extremely frustating to find – to a greater extent than in many other battles – that though there are many glowing accounts of the efficiency of the Allied artillery, of the then surprising mobility that it displayed on the battlefield and of the solidity and imperturbability of the Allied infantry, it is impossible to make a quantitative assessment of the results of the fire from the available casualty figures. Perhaps this may be a salutary reminder that the number of casualties is not the only criterion of success. It was undoubtedly the bold manner in which the Allied guns were handled and in which their fire was purposefully applied, together with the unshakable efficiency of the Allied infantry, that caused not only casualties but also the breaking of the will to fight of the whole French Army.

Although the French records do not provide the required information, it is possible to use the Allied casualty figures to make some sort of assessment of the performance of the French weapons. The six British battalions went into action 4,434 strong. With the strengths of the three Hanoverian battalions added, the total strength of von Spörcke's column was just under 6,000. It suffered 1,500 casualties, 1,330 of which were in the British battalions on the exposed flank.

It seems unlikely that many Allied casualties were caused during the repulses of the cavalry charges, though the defending ranks were temporarily broken in one or two places. Perhaps 100 might be allowed. Some 1,400 casualties were therefore inflicted by between thirty and sixty French guns and the muskets of the eight battalions that made two attacks on the Allied right flank.

Those 4,000 French muskets can be assumed to have fired a total of ten volleys. If 2% of the shots were effective, the muskets could have claimed 800 of the 1,400 Allied casualties. On the other hand, the three flanking British battalions – HM 12th, 20th, and 37th Foot – suffered a total of about 800 casualties only during the entire battle; so it is possible that this performance is exaggerated.

If 800 casualties are assumed to have been atttributable to small-arms fire, 600 would have been caused by the French guns. Here, again, the records are most frustrating. Rarely, in respect of any battle, has the work of the Allied artillery been so highly praised in purely general terms. Graham, in *The Story of the Royal Regiment of Artillery,* goes so far as to assert that the French artillery was completely silenced as a result of the fire of the Allied guns on the right flank. But in the absence of records of casualties among the French gun detachments it is impossible to say whether the silence was due to losses or to the temporary withdrawal of detachments – which often created the impression that a battery was permanently out of action when it later proved not to be. In any case, if the French guns were silenced it was most likely during the later stages of the battle.

The French artillery must have been firing for at least half an hour and could have fired some twenty rounds per gun. If it is assumed, as is reasonable, that the greater part of this fire was delivered by the 30 guns on the French left flank, 600 casualties would represent a performance of 20 casualties per gun firing – or an average of one casualty per round fired. Most of these casualties would probably have been inflicted while the Allied column was advancing to meet the French cavalry and before the Allied guns began to subdue the French artillery.

It is not pretended that these figures are based on anything more than a series of debatable assumptions; but two general impressions emerge. The first is that – particularly when allowance is made for the depression of the French artillery, of which there is some evidence – the performance of all artillery was improving steadily; and the second is that it seems unlikely that more than about 2% of the musket shots were effective in a somewhat confused attacking battle.

The absence of reliable figures of the casualties caused in this period by guns and muskets separately leads to the exploration of many minor incidents in lesser battles, one of which was the battle of Wandewash in 1760. On that occasion, Colonel Eyre Coote's 500-strong infantry battalion met the 400 men of the French Regiment Lorraine in a conflict that can be separated from the rest of the battle. Coote's battalion first fired two volleys at the advancing French, whereupon the latter formed a column twelve files abreast and assaulted the British line. They were received with musket fire at 50 yards range from the entire frontage of Coote's battalion, and the attack was repulsed. French casualties by the end of the battle were 400, of which one third may have been suffered during this attack. If Coote's battalion fired 10 volleys for 130 casualties, his muskets would have been hitting with $2\frac{1}{2}$% of the rounds ordered to be fired. It is probable, however, that some of the French casualties were caused by the six guns in support – so a figure of no more than 2% seems likely to have been attained.

A cross-check is provided by the figures for the battle as a whole. A total of 1,980 British/European muskets, supported by 14 guns caused 400 French casualties. If 100 casualties were caused by the guns, the overall performance of the muskets would have been $1\frac{1}{2}$% of shots effective. The French, with 2,000 European muskets and 16 guns, caused 187 casualties which, allowing 87 to the guns, gives a figure of $\frac{1}{2}$% of shots effective. Figures for a whole battle always show a lower figure than that achieved in decisive parts of it, but these figures agree reasonably well. It should also be noted that two guns firing a single salvo of case at short range are recorded by Fortescue as having caused 10 to 15 casualties – again a credible performance.

The extremely wide variations in the performance of artillery in the eighteenth century can be illustrated by two more stories of battles. Of these, the battle of Valmy was fought on 20th September 1792 between a Prussian force of 34,000 men with about 200 guns and a French army of 36,000 men with about 160 guns. The Prussians made two attacks, both of which were repulsed with the ludicrously low loss of 184 men, and the battle then became almost entirely an artillery duel at long range. Both sides fired some 20,000 rounds at each other, causing 300 French and 184 Prussian casualties respectively, An appreciable number of these casualties were in the gun detachments, and the Prussian artillery caused some alarm by blowing up several French ammunition wagons. It seems clear, then, that this was mainly an experiment in counter-battery work – and it appears to have been a remarkably inefficient performance at the long range at which it was attempted.

The second example, quoted in order to discourage a natural tendency to disparage the effectiveness of artillery in the eighteenth century, is a famous incident from the battle of Fontenoy. There, before the opposing infantry came within musket range, a French officer – conspicuous on a white horse – was seen to be riding about in front of his own lines. This was taken as a challenge by the British gunners, who started to lay bets on which gun detachment could hit him first despite the fact that the range was about four or five hundred yards. Surprising as it may seem, however, the unfortunate officer was shot and killed by the third round fired.

It is abundantly clear that in this period, as in all others, there was a critical range beyond which the performance of all smooth-bore weapons dropped off so sharply that it became almost entirely unprofitable to fire them. Many were nevertheless fired beyond that range; but the real damage was done by those that were fired under close control by officers who understood the tactical needs of the moment and at ranges at which the weapons were effective.

The turn of the eighteenth century

Towards the end of the eighteenth century and at the beginning of the nineteenth century smooth-bore weapons were at the peak of their performance as pieces of machinery.

The tactics of this period naturally developed during the last fifty years of the eighteenth century, and to understand the battles of the time it is neces-

This picture of a British square at Waterloo gives a good impression of the impregnability of an unbroken square to attack by cavalry. It is of particular interest to note the essential control of fire that is being exercised by the officer and the non-commissioned officer in the centre. The length of time taken in reloading the musket made it essential for small groups of men to be able to fire successive volleys under strict control so that each face of the square could constantly deliver some fire while the remainder presented a wall of bayonets to the attacker. On the other hand, though the square was invulnerable to cavalry attack, it was far more vulnerable to artillery fire than was the line. (By permission of the National Army Museum.)

sary to have some knowledge of the ways in which they were fought at the time of Napoleon and Wellington.

Two new factors had arisen to affect tactics. In the first place, the French armies – so continuously engaged during the Revolutionary and the Napoleonic wars – contained an increasingly large number of conscripts whose state of training could not compare with that of the regular armies of the 1740s and 1750s. French tactics were therefore simplified to meet their needs, particularly where movement was concerned. It is not true, however, that the use of column formations by the French was dictated by the low state of training of their conscripts since such formations had been favoured earlier. A difficulty in manoeuvre certainly did arise in the French armies in the Peninsula, as a result of which it was usually found difficult to deploy from column to line for a final assault – even though there is evidence that the commanders wished to do so. Perhaps the most significant effect of the presence of conscripts in the French armies was their poor state of training in musketry – many having never fired their muskets until they arrived on the battlefield.

The other important change arose from the introduction of skirmishers. The American War of Independence had shown how small numbers of skilled marksmen armed with rifles – which were just becoming available for service – and accustomed by their way of life to make good use of ground could inconvenience the ponderous lines of infantry armed with muskets, which were effective only when fired in their crashing volleys at point-blank range. It was thought at first that a battle might be fought by skirmishers alone, but it was soon realised that armies could produce only a limited number of such specialists; that their firepower was limited, particularly in volume; and that there were distinct limits to the number of such dispersed individualists that could be controlled in battle. So it became the custom to hold a single company of tirailleurs or light infantrymen in each battalion of infantry; and they provided forward elements, for reconnaissance in attack and as outposts in defence – extending by their presence and armament the range and selectivity of the main armament of the battalion and, indeed, of the force as a whole. The skirmishers were supported by the main line of battle – normally consisting of infantry, with cavalry operating on the flanks.

In the nineteenth century the basic infantry unit of all nations was the battalion, the size of which varied between the French establishment of 700 men and the British, which was at times as high as 1,100 men. Battalions were rarely up to establishment, however, and it is more realistic to assume that the battalion strength of all armies was 500 to 600 men.

Battalions were divided into companies. Before 1807 there were nine companies in a French battalion, but after 1807 there were six companies excluding a light company of tirailleurs. A British battalion consisted of a light company, which provided the skirmishers, and nine companies of which one was known as the grenadier company – not meaning to imply that it was armed with grenades, which were no longer used by then: the men in it were picked for their stature and intelligence. For parade and for most kinds of combat, infantry companies were normally formed into bodies three ranks deep in the French and other Continental armies and two ranks deep in the British Army. All the muskets of a company so disposed could be fired simultaneously.

Variations in the layout of a battalion were effected by placing the companies in different positions relative to each other, and a complicated and detailed drill existed whereby they could be manoeuvred into any formation required. The drill could be carried out remarkably smoothly by any well trained unit and was second nature to the trained soldier.

In defence, all armies formed their infantry in line – the companies of each battalion being alongside each other so that the maximum number of muskets could fire simultaneously. There were often reinforcing lines in rear of the first line of defence, but they naturally could not support the front line with fire while the latter remained intact (unless they were on markedly higher ground), though they could counter-attack to restore a situation or act as a long-stop if the front line was overwhelmed.

A line of infantry was admirably fitted to firing to its immediate front, but it could be pierced by a successful attack and it could be rolled up by an attack delivered against its flank – particularly by cavalry. The standard formation adopted in the face of a cavalry attack was therefore one of squares, each usually consisting of a whole battalion. A square of disciplined infantry was impregnable to attack by cavalry as long as it remained unbroken and as long as its volleys were carefully controlled by sub-units or ranks so that no face of the square was ever without some loaded muskets. The attackers found it impossible to force horses into the multiple array of bayonets presented by all faces of the square, and the successive volleys of the muskets could take a steady toll of the cavalry milling about outside it. On the debit side, the square was more vulnerable to artillery fire than the line; and it was often necessary to revert from square to line with some speed if casualties from gunfire were to be avoided.

The line was not the most suitable formation for movement, particularly when the state of training of the men was below standard. It was necessary to maintain the line in its exact alignment in order that its short-ranged firepower might always be available at full strength; but the maintenance of alignment was not easy when moving over broken ground. A third formation was therefore used for movement on a narrower frontage than that of a whole battalion. The simplest form of this was a column of companies – each still formed in its three or two ranks, one behind the other.

Companies could be at 'deploying distance' – which meant that the distance between them was the length of their frontages – so that all could wheel into line to the right or left or could incline outwards to form line to the front: but this naturally led to the column being a long one. Otherwise they could be closed up to half or quarter distance, which shortened the column but made deployment a little more complicated. An alternative to the column of single companies that was much favoured by the French was a column of double companies (or divisions, as they were called); and the British often used a column of half companies.

These formations of French and British battalions are shown in diagrams 11 and 12.

Although a column was well suited to movement to make contact, the firepower it could develop to its front was limited by its narrow frontage and there was therefore much to be said for deployment into line for the actual assault. The well-trained British

1. Jac Weller gives an excellent description, both written and pictorial, of the construction of a square in Part 11 of his *Wellington at Waterloo*.

infantry not only normally attacked in line but also often moved up over considerable distances in line before an assault. The French, for their part, tended to use a series of columns even for an attack – though Napoleon had a personal preference for the 'mixed' formation, in which some battalions were in column and some were fully deployed in line.

In calculating the relative firepower of the front of a column and that of an opposing line, it must not be forgotten that the short range of the musket limited the number of files in the line that could engage the head of the column on either side of the column's direct frontage. Nevertheless, even with this limitation, the firepower developed by a line against an equal number of men in column gave an advantage in firepower to the line; and it was sometimes possible for the extremities of the line to swing forward and enfilade the flanks of the column. On the other hand, the sheer weight of a deep column could be effective and it had the advantage of automatically allowing gaps in its firing-line to be filled from the rear, whereas a line could only shrink inwards as casualties thinned its ranks.

During the Napoleonic wars, the artillery of the French Army was still divided into battalion guns and the artillery of the park, by then known as artillery of position. Battalion guns, permanently attached to infantry units, were usually 4pr but sometimes 8pr – two of which were normally provided for each battalion. The artillery of position consisted of 8pr and 12pr guns, the number of the latter being irregular and small – between two and six per corps. Usually, there was also a small number of field howitzers.

The British Army in Europe had abandoned the provision of battalion guns by 1800. It had been found that greater flexibility and efficiency were attained by keeping the artillery under central command and direction, though batteries were freely placed in support of infantry and cavalry formations during particular battles. Such attachments often became well established and almost permanent. The fact that the British Army in the Peninsula was always weak in artillery led to there rarely being any artillery of position, all the guns normally being placed in direct support of formations of the other arms.

The French used their battalion guns to provide a

Diagram 11. Comparison of British and French infantry disposition in line.

BRITISH

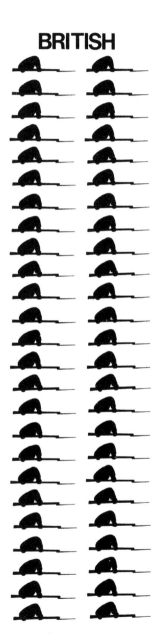

FRENCH

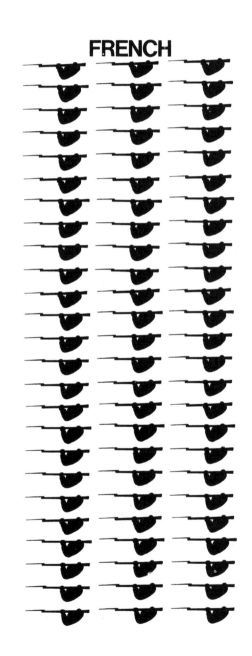

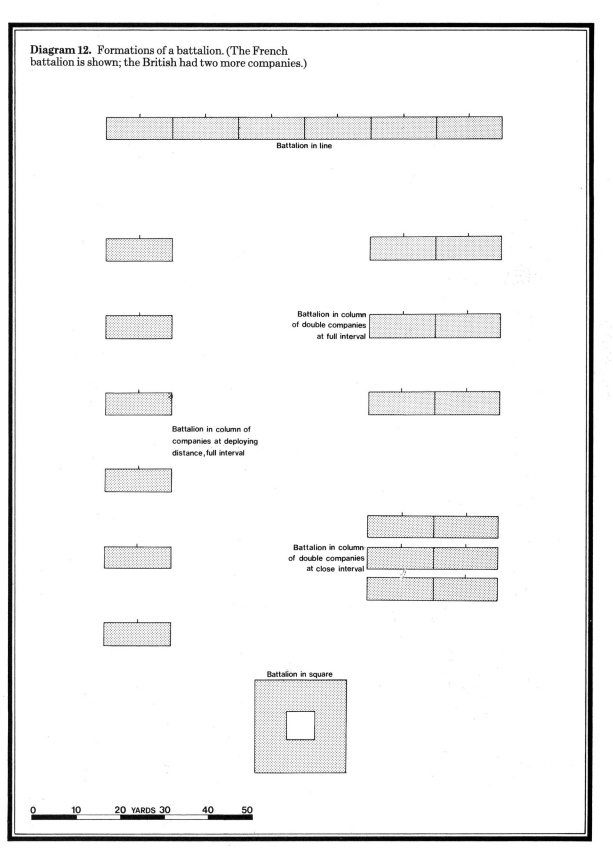

Diagram 12. Formations of a battalion. (The French battalion is shown; the British had two more companies.)

Battalion in line

Battalion in column
of double companies
at full interval

Battalion in column of
companies at deploying
distance, full interval

Battalion in column
of double companies
at close interval

Battalion in square

0   10   20 YARDS 30   40   50

permanent extension of the range of the small-arms of the infantry, and the artillery of position was centralised in large batteries that were used to blast a hole in the objective selected for attack. The British artillery, generally inferior in strength to the French, was usually widely dispersed over the front. Its battery commanders were expected to use their own initiative in the selection of targets and, indeed, change their gun positions if it seemed advantageous to do so. Nonetheless, superior commanders – including the Commander-in-Chief – would often order the occupation of specific positions and direct the engagement of particular targets during a battle.

In defence, it was normally thought unprofitable to indulge in counter-battery fire to any appreciable extent. The small projectiles of field artillery were not very effective against the small targets presented by guns at long range, and it was generally considered better to conserve the ammunition for the carrying out of the guns' primary task. That task was to take toll of the enemy's infantry and cavalry while they were advancing to attack and were still outside the range of the defending small-arms, and it fell into two phases. The first was carried out with round shot and common shell (and, from the British artillery, with shrapnel); and the second was carried out with case shot when the attacker had entered case range. When the attacker had advanced to within small-arms range and the two forces had entered the stage of close combat, it was the task of the defending artillery to harass the flanks of the attack with enfilade fire.

In attack the artillery fire plan was generally developed in three phases, the first of which consisted of a preliminary bombardment on the frontage on which the attack was to be made. This was directed at those parts of the defending forces most likely to defeat the attack. In Europe the French engaged the opposing artillery to a greater extent than the British mainly because they tended to have a larger amount of artillery of position than the British and could more easily spare gun power for that purpose. Napoleon's Grand Battery at Waterloo, for example, inflicted appreciable losses on the Allied artillery before the infantry and cavalry attacks – though not to the extent of preventing the guns from carrying out their defensive tasks. When the defending artillery was particularly menacing, however, as in the Mah-

ratta and Sikh wars in India, the British artillery devoted full attention to counter-battery fire in this first phase.

The second phase of the artillery support was aimed at reducing the firepower of the defending infantry. Because of the flat trajectories of the guns, it was usually necessary for them to fire from the flanks – the artillery moving forward on the flanks of the infantry and producing cross-fire over their front. This was the only supporting fire that could be applied until the infantry had advanced to within 100 yards of their objective.

With the opposing infantry within small-arms range, the guns could no longer fire on the frontage of attack because they were masked by their own infantry. Their task in this third phase was to seize every opportunity of intervening and to guard the flanks.

In order to obtain a picture of the firepower that could be developed in a nineteenth-century battle it is necessary first to visualise the ranges within which the weapons could act and then the period of time during which they were able to fire. A purely diagrammatic and purposely over-simplified example illustrates these points and is shown in diagram 13.

It is assumed that a force of, say, four battalions – A – is attacking another – B – of the same strength, both formations being disposed in line and each numbering 2,000 men. Each force is supported by the normal scale of artillery – that is, one battery of six light guns. The artillery is deployed by half batteries on the flanks of the infantry, and that of the attacking force moves forward on the flanks of the line as the attack progresses.

The two forces are initially 1,000 yards apart and, until A advances to reach a line 800 yards from its objective, artillery fire will have a very limited effect and may well not even be attempted. As soon as A arrives within 800 yards of B, however, both artilleries open fire and seek to take toll of the opposing infantry. This position and that of the subsequent phase are shown in diagram 13, letter A.

It takes force A 4½ minutes to move from its last position to one 350 yards from the objective – assuming the new position to be the maximum range of case shot. During this time both the attacking and the defending artilleries have fired 9 rounds of round shot, common shell or shrapnel per gun – that is, a total of

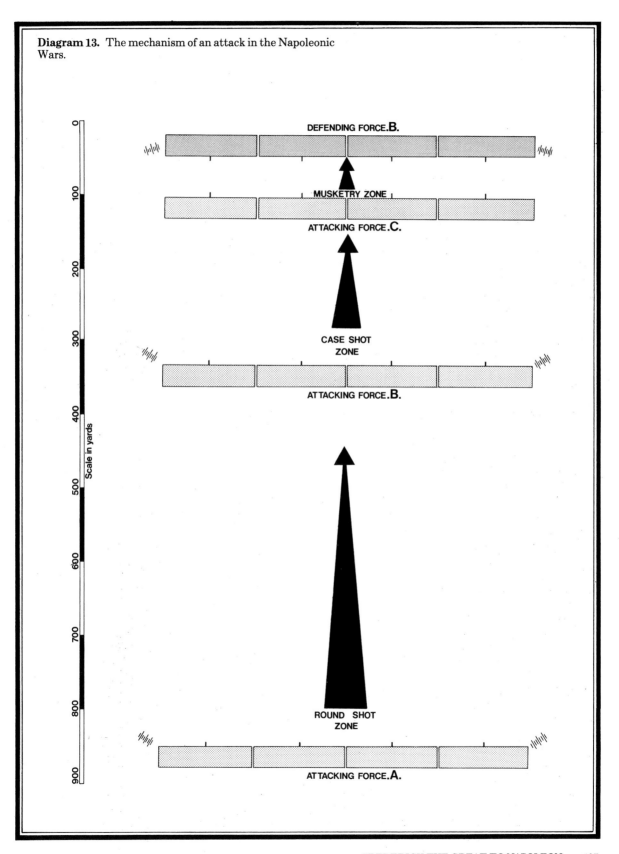

Diagram 13. The mechanism of an attack in the Napoleonic Wars.

Scale in yards

0
100
200
300
400
500
600
700
800
900

DEFENDING FORCE.**B.**

MUSKETRY ZONE

ATTACKING FORCE.**C.**

CASE SHOT ZONE

ATTACKING FORCE.**B.**

ROUND SHOT ZONE

ATTACKING FORCE.**A.**

54 rounds. According to the calculations made in Chapter 3, some 40% of these rounds can be expected to have hit the target; and at three casualties per hit, they would have caused 66 casualties – a toll of 3.3%.

When force A reaches the position 350 yards from the objective, as in diagram 13, letter B, the defending artillery begins to fire case shot. From this point until force A reaches a position 100 yards from the objective salvoes of case are fired for $2\frac{1}{2}$ minutes. The guns fire a theoretical maximum of 45 rounds containing 3,825 bullets in all, assuming the guns are 6prs.

Finally, as in diagram 13, letter C, force A covers the last 100 yards of its advance, taking one minute to do so; and the defending infantry is able to fire at least two, possibly three, volleys – a theoretical total of 4,000 to 6,000 bullets. The defending artillery can contribute by firing case shot from the flanks but is not able to engage the attackers' front.

The attacking artillery has not been able to fire so effectively as its range has remained a long one; nor has it been able to fire so continuously since its guns were masked by its own infantry as the two sides closed.

This contrived example assumed that the two forces were of exactly equal strength, were deployed on identical frontages and possessed equal resources – conditions unlikely to be found on any battlefield. It does show, however, how the two weapons – the gun and the musket – operated in depth. Beyond case shot range the guns could be expected to inflict a certain toll which, allowing for the limitations imposed by battle conditions, might account for rather more than 3% of the attacking force. Within the range of case shot and musket bullets, in theory and under perfect conditions, the whole force could have fired some 6,000 to 10,000 bullets – the muskets firing about twice as many as the guns. When allowance has been made for the impedences to fire, the misfiring of the muskets and the other factors affecting firepower described earlier, it must be concluded that the number of bullets reaching the target area is unlikely to have been more than 3,000 to 4,000. If 5% of them took effect, about 150 to 200 casualties might be expected – a not unreasonable figure in an engagement of this kind.

As this example has been so much over-simplified, however, it is desirable to introduce a more realistic picture of events as they were seen and heard by soldiers in battle. Few attacks were as simple as that just described, and the attacker rarely moved smoothly forward to take the objective in one bound without a check. A more accurate description would be as follows.

The preliminary action of the artilleries of both sides would have been much as described above – but one would have to take into account the ensuing great clouds of white smoke that enveloped the gun positions and then drifted over the battlefield, often causing the whole action to be conducted in a haze of smoke. Nor should one forget the daunting sight of whole files of men mown down by round shot, which appeared as black dots boring their way through the haze as they flew towards the closely packed ranks of the infantry, while the gun flashes in the distance announced the departure of yet another salvo.

During the preliminary bombardment the defending infantry might have been lying down or concealed behind a crest; but before long, the coloured uniforms of the attackers would be seen through the smoke in the distance and the defenders would take post in their solid line. (When the British were defending, their scarlet line stood silent, motionless and menacing, as many have recorded, while the more volatile French infantry surged forward with encouraging cries.)

As the distance between two sides decreased, the guns would increase their rate of fire and begin pouring in salvoes of case – which were more deadly at short range than round shot; but as the space between the two infantries was reduced, the attention of the guns would be transferred to the flanks and the battle of the muskets would begin.

When the attacking infantry arrived within musket shot of its opponents – and with well-disciplined infantry this would have been well within 100 yards – its line would be halted, a volley would be fired over the whole front, and the whole line would be obscured by smoke. Then, as soon as the smoke cleared, the defending line would probably come to life and reply; and thereafter the space between the two forces would become a swirling mass of smoke, through the gaps and clearances of which volleys would be exchanged. This fire fight would continue for a period of between twenty minutes and perhaps as much as an hour. Casualties in the shallow British line would be replaced by the men in each battalion moving inwards on the colours, as a result of which gaps would develop between battalions; and casualties in the deeper French formation would be replaced by men moving forward from the rear ranks.

It was difficult for any individual – commander or soldier – to see what was happening. The task was simply to maintain formation, in spite of losses, and fire apparently endless series of volleys through gaps in the smoke. There was little scope for any tactical manoeuvre, though it was sometimes possible for the flanks of the British line to move forward to overlap and enfilade the French columns; and though the bayonet was sometimes used in individual combat, a concerted bayonet attack was rarely carried out until the fire fight had been won. That fire fight was, in fact, a groping half-blind affair – a battle of endurance that, apart from skill at arms, could be won only by superbly well-disciplined troops. It ended only when the spirit of one side or the other was broken and that side quitted the field.

The evidence of the effectiveness of firearms in the battles that have already been discussed was, of necessity, drawn from a number of isolated incidents for which there was insufficient data; and the conclusions arrived at were largely based on reasonable assumptions and calculated guesses. But there were a few battles in the Peninsular War from which, rather exceptionally, there exists concrete evidence for a much wider quantitative assessment of the effect of firepower. The number and the locations of the weapons are known, their expenditure of ammunition can be accurately worked out, and the casualties inflicted by guns and muskets are recorded separately.

For each of these battles, again exceptionally, not only are the exact initial positions of the guns known but also – thanks to Lieutenant Unger's detailed sketches – there is reliable evidence of the moves made by the artillery. Precise graphical information on such moves – which would have affected the support given by the guns to a very great extent – is very rarely available.

In the following chapters the battles of Albuera, Talavera, and Bussaco (for each of which one of Unger's maps is available) are examined. And though it is out of its chronological context, Albuera is dealt with first because the evidence from that battle is the most complete.

Musket drill in the early nineteenth century, from *The New Manual of Platoon Exercises as Practised by His Majesty's Army*, current at the time of the Peninsular war. The copy of the manual from which these

reproductions were made was picked up on the battlefield of Waterloo and is now in the library of the Royal Artillery Institution.

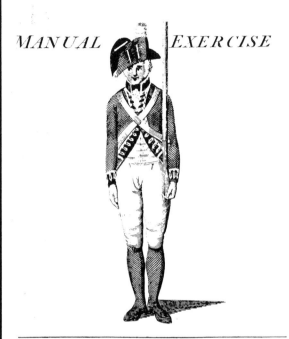

MANUAL EXERCISE

Pofition of the Soldier under Arms

I   *3 Motions*

Order Arms

IV   *3 Motions*

Prefent Arms

V   *2 Motions*

Shoulder Arms

II   *3 Motions*   III   *2 Motions*

Fix Bayonets   Shoulder Arms

VI   *2 Motions*   VII   *2 Motions*

Charge Bayonets   Shoulder Arms

3 Motions

Support Arms

1
2

I

2 Motions

Under Arms

Make Ready

1
2

V

3 Motions

Prime

1
2
3

VI

3 Motions

Load

1
2
3

II , III   *2 Motions*

Prefent   Fire

IV   *2 Motions*

1   2

Handle Cartridge

VII   *2 Motions*

1   2

Draw Ramrods

VIII   *4 Motions*

1   3   2

Ram down Cartridge

IX  *2 Motions*

X

1

2

Return Ramrods

Shoulder Arms

3 Ranks. Make Ready

3 Ranks. Prefent — Fire

6. Albuera

The battle of Albuera was fought on 16th May 1811 between a French army under the command of Marshal Nicholas Soult, Duke of Dalmatia, and an Allied force of Spanish, Portugese and British troops under Marshal William Cass Beresford. The French army consisted of 18,000 well-trained and disciplined infantry, 3,700 cavalry and 48 guns. It was opposed by one of about 31,000 infantry (some of whom were not well-trained or organised), 3,700 cavalry and 38 pieces of artillery.

Albuera was an untidy battle, involving a considerable amount of movement on the battlefield and a major change of front during the engagement. But only two phases of the rather complicated manoeuvres that took place are relevant. Those two phases can be fairly isolated from the rest of the story, and they provide one of the clearest pictures now available of the firepower of the Napoleonic wars. The elements of the battle are shown here:

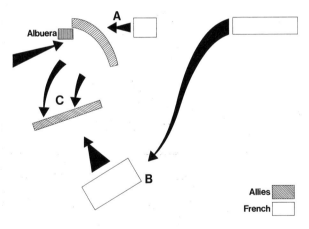

When the two forces met, the French put in a holding attack – A – on the bridge and village of Albuera. They then swung their main force round to the south to outflank the Allies, who then had to re-deploy to a flank at C, where the main battle took place. Although considering only those two phases of the battle on which the necessary information is available, a brief summary of the sequence of events throughout the whole engagement is necessary in order that the locations of the troops and their relative strengths and purposes can be visualised.

There was considerable confusion on the Allied

right flank at first – partly, at least, because the French flanking movement was concealed by the ground during its opening stages and caught the Allied commander off his guard – and the Allied line at C was built up piecemeal as troops were able to be transferred from the left to the right flank, where a low ridge cut across the gentle slope that ran generally from west to east and provided a defensive position of sorts. It was held at first by four battalions of Spanish infantry, which were reinforced somewhat confusedly by other Spanish units during the battle.

The French attack was made by their V Corps of two divisions. General Jean Baptiste Girard's 1st Division led, having adopted the French 'mixed' formation as shown in map F. In the centre was a column of four battalions, one behind the other, each in column of double companies. The strength of each of the six companies of these battalions was about 75 men, and they were formed three deep. The frontage of a company was therefore 25 files, and that of a battalion in column of double companies was 50 files. On each flank of the centre column was a battalion in line, three deep, with 150 men in each rank. Still further to each flank were two more battalions, probably in column of single companies with 25 men in each rank. The flanking battalions were formed in that way so that they could easily form squares if a flank attack was made by cavalry. There were thus three ranks of 400 men each to form the firing line of the French formation.

That is how the attack began. But later in the battle – after the leading division had failed to take its objective – the infantry of General Honoré Gazan's 2nd Division, which was following the 1st, pushed forward and became mixed with the division in front. The French V Corps then formed a solid rectangular mass, still with a frontage of 400 men and some 20 ranks deep.

The V Corps was supported by three field batteries and one horse battery – a total of 24 guns. Fortescue's map shows all the French guns deployed on their left flank; but Unger, whose sketch map confirms Fortescue's infantry dispositions, shows two French gun positions – one on each flank. Though it would not have been impossible for all the guns of position (hitherto called guns or artillery of the park) to have been in action as one large battery, as was often the

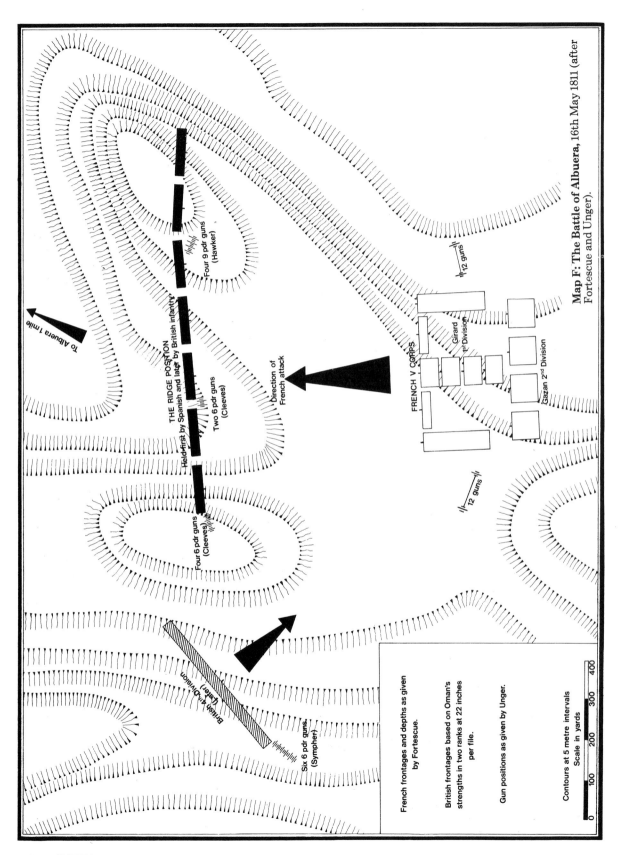

Map F: The Battle of Albuera, 16th May 1811 (after Fortescue and Unger).

To Albuera 1 mile

THE RIDGE POSITION
Held first by Spanish and later by British infantry

Four 9 pdr guns
(Hawker)

Two 6 pdr guns
(Cleeves)

Direction of
French attack

Four 6 pdr guns
(Cleeves)

FRENCH V CORPS

Girard
1st Division

Gazan 2nd Division

12 guns

12 guns

British 4th Division
(later)

Six 6 pdr guns
(Sympher)

French frontages and depths as given
by Fortescue.

British frontages based on Oman's
strengths in two ranks at 22 inches
per file.

Gun positions as given by Unger.

Contours at 5 metre intervals
Scale in yards

0   100   200   300   400

French custom, it is more likely that they were divided into two, as shown in map F, since better support could be provided from both flanks. However, the fire support given by this artillery before the infantries came into contact does not need to be described in detail. It is sufficient to note that both French batteries were within some 500 yards of the objective and therefore, although fire on the frontage of attack would have been masked as the infantry moved forward, they would still have been in a position to fire on the flanks and may well have moved forward in order to do so more effectively.

The battle on what is known as the Ridge began when the French V Corps advanced to within 60 yards of the Spanish infantry and opened fire with its 400 files of 3 ranks of muskets – a total of 1,200. The Spanish troops held their ground stoutly while reinforcements, in the shape of Major John Colborne's leading brigade of the British 2nd Division, moved across behind them and deployed into line on their right flank. This brigade extended outside the frontage of the V Corps and so swung in to engage it from its left front. The battalion on the left flank of the French formation faced outwards to meet this threat, and their rectangular mass was therefore firing from both its front and its left flank.

At this point, artillery support for the Allied line was provided by Captain Hawker's brigade of four 9pr guns on the left, two 6pr guns of Captain Cleeves' King's German Legion brigade in the centre, and three 6pr guns and a 5½-inch howitzer of Cleeves' brigade on the right flank.

The intervention of Colborne's brigade had thrown the French attack into some confusion when, taking advantage not only of a heavy rainstorm that masked their movement but also of their enemy's concentration on the affairs on their front, the French cavalry charged the British line from the flank. In a few disastrous moments, the three right-hand battalions of Colborne's brigade were virtually annihilated and three of Cleeves' guns were captured. The fourth battalion of the British brigade had time to form square and repulse the cavalry; but the promising counter-attack of the 2nd Division had collapsed.

It is salutary, in studying the effects of firearms, to mark this incident in which the firepower of 1,500 muskets proved to be totally ineffective. Indeed, it is a perfect example of the way in which cavalry could be used decisively when given the right conditions in which to exploit its special characteristics. Complete surprise was achieved by virtue of the cover from view providentially provided by the blinding rainstorm; and the charge was delivered at right-angles to the front on which every slow-firing musket was aligned. The infantry was thus caught completely off balance and incapable of any defence against the long lances of the Polish cavalry. This is an entirely different picture from that seen when the French made their series of tremendous charges at Waterloo. Then, preparation for the charges could be seen a thousand yards away and there was enough time for the infantry to form its impregnable squares from which every musket could take its toll and which could be relied upon in the last resort to present a wall of bayonets that no horse would face. In this incident of the battle of Albuera, indeed, the rearmost battalion of Colborne's brigade had enough warning and time to form such squares and defeated the attack.

There was then a lull while the surviving battalion of Colborne's brigade (His Majesty's 31st Foot), the three battalions of Major General Daniel Houghton's brigade (His Majesty's 29th, 57th, and 48th Foot) and the three of Colonel the Hon. Alexander Abercrombie's brigade (His Majesty's 28th, 39th, and 34th Foot) moved up in succession to form line on the Ridge behind and to the right of the Spanish troops, who then retired through them. The left-hand battalion of Abercrombie's brigade was displaced too far to a flank to have taken part in the next phase of the battle,[1] which was fought by the six battalions on the right of the line opposite the French V Corps – His Majesty's 31st, 29th, 57th, 48th, 28th and 39th Foot, in that order from the right.

Thus a French mass of 8,000 soldiers opposed a thin British line of, at most, 3,000 men. However unmanoeuvrable the former was as a whole, it would have aligned its front on this fresh British line and would still have been presenting a frontage of 400 files and a firing line of 1,200 muskets. Its opponent was that part of the British line that was within mus-

1. There is some difference of opinion on the extent to which Abercombie's brigade took part in the first part of the battle on the Ridge; but it does not affect the argument, which is based on a number of muskets that could have operated regardless of the particular units firing them.

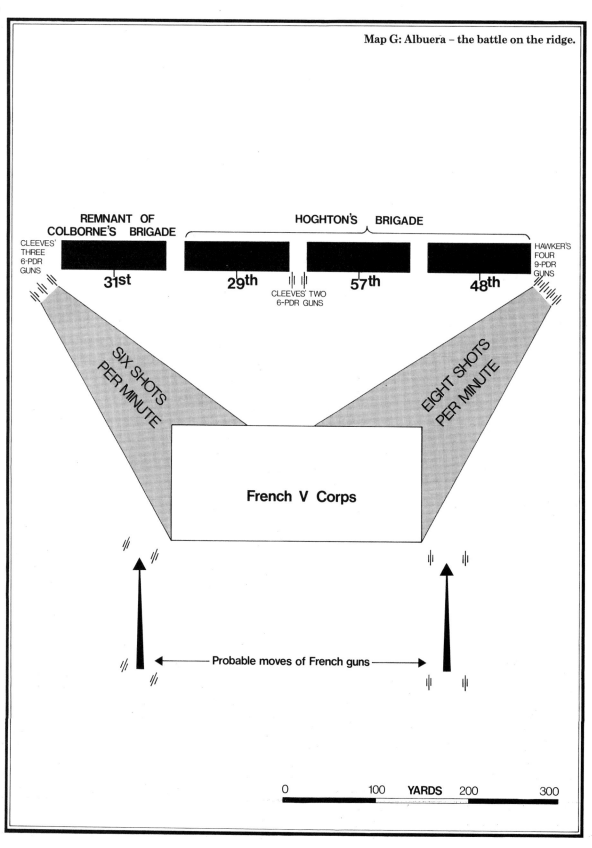

Map G: Albuera – the battle on the ridge.

REMNANT OF
COLBORNE'S BRIGADE

HOGHTON'S BRIGADE

CLEEVES'
THREE
6-PDR
GUNS

31st

29th

CLEEVES' TWO
6-PDR GUNS

57th

48th

HAWKER'S
FOUR
9-PDR
GUNS

SIX SHOTS
PER MINUTE

EIGHT SHOTS
PER MINUTE

French V Corps

◄── Probable moves of French guns ──►

0   100   **YARDS**   200   300

ket range of its frontage. This comprised the 400 files directly in front of the French firing line, whose musket-power was two-thirds that of the French by reason of the British two-rank formation, and the files on both flanks whose muskets could reach far enough to engage the French target.

Clearly, the number of flanking files that could engage with effective fire in any battle was determined by the maximum effective range of the musket. At the same time, the number of files that actually did fire may often have been greater; for although firing at excessive range was sometimes the result of poor fire discipline, there were undoubtedly occasions when fire was ordered in an understandable attempt to provide some help, however small, to hard pressed comrades – or when a unit on the flank of the main attack was galled by the fire of the enemy's artillery and it was thought better to give the men something to do than to accept punishment without any retaliation.

The relationship between assumed maximum effective range and the number of flanking files that could have engaged when 100 yards or less separated the two sides is shown in the following table. It assumes that each man occupied 22 inches of lateral space and that the overlap was on both sides of the column's frontage.

Maximum effective range of musket	Number of flanking files that could engage
100 yards	330
150 yards	480
200 yards	650
250 yards	800

The definition of maximum effective range of the musket is controversial. As was stated in Chapter 2 some would put it as no more than 100 yards and other reputable authorities – remembering that in cases such as this the target was a dense mass of men in close order – would claim that effective fire could be delivered from 250 yards. There was, indeed, no hard-and-fast dividing line within which fire was effective and beyond which it was not. There was a gradual decrease in accuracy and lethality as the range increased, and there was an area where a curve plotting this would begin to fall so steeply that fire beyond that range would be ineffective. The consensus of technical opinion suggests that it would

not be unreasonable to assume a maximum effective range of 200 yards. This is the range at which a trained marksman could expect no more than 30% of his shots to hit a target, as was shown in Chapter 2.

Though a round figure of 200 yards is assumed in the following calculations, it is not suggested that the muskets outside that range would not have been firing. Furthermore, though the maintenance of an unbroken line was often of importance, there were occasions when the defending units on the flank of an attacking column moved forward and inwards to develop enfilade fire – as happened in a later stage of this battle. Some reasonably accurate figure of maximum range must be assumed, however, if the resulting estimate of the performance of the musket is not to be degraded by the inclusion of muskets that, though they might quite properly have been firing, were contributing nothing but noise and smoke to the result.

According to this calculation, the French firing line of 1,200 muskets was initially opposed by a British musket strength of 800 on the frontage of attack plus 1,300 (650 files of 2 ranks) on the flanks – a total of 2,100.

From the gun positions occupied by the superior French artillery, shown in map F, the fire of twelve light guns could be applied to both flanks of the British force; but it would have been barely possible to fire on the actual frontage of the struggle as friendly troops would have masked the fire. Oman mentions the casualties inflicted upon the British infantry by what he calls grape shot (probably heavy case), which the French were accustomed to fire at rather longer ranges than those thought profitable by the Allied artillery.

Reviewing the Allied gun positions shown in map G, there is little doubt that Hawker's brigade of four 9pr guns was extremely well sited and could have developed very effective enfilade fire against the deep right flank of the French corps. But the two guns of Cleeves' brigade, in the centre, would have been hard put to it to provide more than momentary bursts of fire whenever they were not masked by their own infantry. Cleeves' other guns, on the right flank, could barely have recovered from their trouble with the French cavalry. One howitzer had been carried away by the enemy, and there is some doubt as to whether

This print of Bussaco, like that on page 146, depicts one of the moments when the British line met the heads of the French columns climbing the hill from the right. It also gives a good impression of the dense clouds of white smoke that enveloped the battlefield. (By permission of the National Army Museum).

the remaining three guns could have been brought back into action by the beginning of this phase of the battle. It seems likely that not more than seven guns were capable of supporting this action, and it may well be that it was only the four 9prs that could do so effectively.

Insofar as the infantry was concerned, this phase of the battle consisted of a head-on collision between a British force that initially deployed 2,100 muskets and a French force that brought 1,200 muskets to bear. Both sides became locked together, enveloped in the smoke of their own and each other's volleys and encumbered by the dead and wounded as the British force slowly pushed forward and the guns flailed the flanks of their opponents. The French suffered 3,000 casualties as opposed to British casualties numbering 1,500.

It must be remembered that, apart from the results of confusion in the struggling ranks, the French column formation enabled the strength of their firing line to be maintained at 1,200 muskets. Casualties in the British line, on the other hand, could not be replaced from the rear. As the British musket strength was reduced to 600 by the end of this engagement, the average number of British muskets available throughout the battle can be taken as 1,350.

The final picture, therefore, is one of 1,350 British muskets, supported by between four and seven guns, inflicting 3,000 casualties on the French while very much the same number of French muskets, supported by 24 guns, caused only half that number of casualties in the British line. Thus it seems clear that the overall performance of the British weapons was superior to that of their enemy. Out of this particular phase of the battle, however, comes one of the rare records of the relative number of casualties caused by guns and muskets, providing an equally rare and valuable chance of analysing their performance in detail.

Fortescue and Oman both state that of the 3,000 casualties suffered by the French 1,000 were caused by the guns and 2,000 by the British muskets; and though these are round figures, they provide a good enough basis for analysis.

The 1,000 casualties caused by the Allied artillery were inflicted by an absolute maximum of seven guns, giving a casualty rate of 140 per gun. But it is almost

certain that the number of guns in action – and even more, the number that could provide continuous and effective fire – was less than this and that the four 9prs, which must have done most of the work, may well have caused casualties at a rate of more than 200 per gun.

The maximum number of rounds that could possibly have been fired by all seven guns was the total held in their firing battery wagons – 1,000 rounds.[1] This would give a casualty rate of one for every round fired. The firing of the whole echelon, however, would have taken from 60 to 90 minutes of uninterrupted firing at the highest possible rate. But the whole of this phase of the battle lasted only some 45 minutes, and the inevitable impedence of firing by smoke and confusion would also have made it quite impossible to fire so many rounds. It is far more likely that not more than half the echelon was fired – or, say, 500 rounds as a maximum. This would give a casualty rate of two per round fired. But as each round finding its target in these circumstances could have been expected to cause three or four casualties, it may be concluded that in this case some 50% to 60% of the rounds fired were effective. If it is assumed, however, that the greater part of the artillery support was provided by the four 9pr guns, with a corresponding reduction in the amount of ammunition fired, it may well be that the percentage of effective rounds was appreciably higher.

These figures may be compared with the theoretical estimates that were given in Chapter 2. The guns would mostly have been firing round shot, for only eight rounds of heavy case and eight rounds of light case were held by each 9pr gun. The theoretical estimate of performance at a range of 300 yards gave 70% of the shot as effective against a screen target. When allowance is made for battle conditions, it would seem reasonable to claim that between 50% and 60% of the shot could be expected to take effect. The performance suggested to have been achieved by the Allied guns on this occasion would therefore seem to be credible in view of the short range and the vulnerability of the deep French formation to enfilade fire from a particularly well-chosen gun position.

If the Allied fire was as damaging as it appears to

have been, it may seem strange that the strong French artillery made little attempt to neutralise the powerful 9pr battery – which, since it incurred only some ten casualties during the battle, was clearly not under heavy fire. During the Peninsular War, however, it was not the custom of either side to carry out counter-battery fire to any considerable extent – or with any great success. Gun positions did not present particularly vulnerable targets to the projectiles of light guns, and it was generally thought that the guns could be better employed in giving direct support to their own infantry. Nor did a communications system exist whereby the infantry, harassed by particular guns, could call for retaliation from their supporting artillery.

As far as British small-arms fire was concerned, an average of 1,350 muskets inflicted 2,000 casualties – at a rate, therefore, of $1\frac{1}{2}$ for each musket operating at reasonable efficiency within a range of 200 yards or less. The inclusion of muskets firing outside this range would naturally have reduced the figure; but provided that the basis of the calculation is known, it seems fair to consider only those muskets that were really affecting the issue.

Rather unusually, it is known that in this battle more than one British battalion fired all or nearly all of its ammunition. If each man fired an average of 50 rounds, this would mean that just over 2% of the rounds ordered to be fired were effective.

The effect of the French fire is more difficult to assess as there appears to be no record of the proportions attributable to guns and muskets. The 3,000 British soldiers on the Ridge suffered 1,500 casualties caused by 24 guns and a firing line which, apart from the results of confusion, would have remained constant at 1,200 muskets. The French artillery was certainly presented with a less rewarding target than were the Allied guns, but it must have accounted for some part of the Allied losses. It is unlikely that 24 French guns could have failed to exact a toll of three or four hundred casualties – in which case it would be impossible to attribute a higher performance to the French muskets than rather less than one casualty per musket. This would mean that only about $1\frac{1}{3}$% of the rounds ordered to be fired were effective.

It is not possible, in any account of this battle, to completely discount the supreme discipline, endur-

1. 6pr: 180 rounds per gun; 9pr: 116 rounds per gun.

ance and devotion that enabled four of those six British battalions so admirably to endure 60% casualties and still prove the victors. But from the viewpoint of firepower alone, based on the calculations given above, it does appear that gun for gun and musket for musket the Allied force was capable of applying more effective fire than its opponents and that this factor played a considerable part in the defeat of an enemy force that outnumbered it by more than $2\frac{1}{2}$ to 1.

After both contestants in this appalling struggle had endured casualties on the scale described, it is not surprising that there was a lull in the fighting.

The next stage of the battle can be regarded as a separate operation, consisting of an attack by a brigade of nine fresh battalions under the command of General Werlé that was countered by the British Fusilier Brigade of three battalions reinforced by 3,000 Portugese infantry.

The Fusilier Brigade of the British 4th Division had moved forward on the right but somewhat in the rear of the 2nd Division. Its commander was without orders, but when he saw Werlé's brigade moving forward through the smoke he took it upon himself to launch a counter-attack. At that moment, the French cavalry charged the Allied right flank again. This time, however, there was no surprise: the Portugese infantry guarding that flank were properly formed to meet the cavalry with fully deployed musket-power, and their disciplined volleys threw the cavalry back in confusion.

The three Fusilier battalions were formed in line as shown in map H, having a total strength of 1,900 and deployed on a frontage of 660 yards. The Portugese guarded the flanks and were not engaged in this part of the battle. Werlé's brigade, 5,400 strong, was formed in three columns – each comprising three battalions, one behind the other, in column of double companies. All nine battalions were exceptionally strong, and the frontage of each battalion column was 60 files wide so that each column could bring 180 muskets (60 files of 3 ranks) to bear. The total French musket-power was thus 540 against the British 1,900.

This is an extreme case of the advantage in firepower of the line over the column. The distribution of the two forces enabled each British battalion to con-

front one of the French columns, and the British frontage of 250 files was short enough to put every one of its 500 muskets within range of the front of the opposing columns. Thus the line – at less than half the column's strength – could engage with nearly four times as many muskets. The column, however, possessed more brute strength and had a greater ability to reinforce its firing line.

History was to give the battle of Albuera a reputation for carnage – a reputation now being earned. In the head-on collision that followed, the British brigade suffered 50% casualties (1,045) and the French lost 1,800 men.

A King's German Legion brigade of six 6prs commanded by Captain Sympher supported the Fusilier brigade from a gun position on the right flank. Cleeves' brigade is said to have done so from the left, but it is not clear to what extent his two divisions on the right had recovered from their losses during the French cavalry attack. His division of two guns on the extreme left could probably have fired in support. A troop of Horse Artillery under Captain Lefebure was also in action on the extreme right and could have supported at somewhat long range. This gave eight guns for certain and seven or eight more that may have taken part. The French were supported by the same twelve guns that had been in action throughout in support of V Corps, on the left rear and flank of that formation.

At this point there is no indication of how many of the known casualties were attributable to the guns and how many were due to the muskets, but it is possible to make a conservative allowance for the action of the artillery on both sides in order to arrive at the relative performance of the muskets. It is known that of the 1,045 British casualties an appreciable number were caused by the French artillery when the Fusiliers were pursuing the defeated French infantry; and it may be assumed that 700 or 800 casualties were inflicted during the battle itself and that at least some of these must have resulted from gun fire. This would put the performance of the French muskets at just over one casualty per musket.

The French casualties amounted to 1,800 for certain, and some authorities put them as high as 2,000. These were caused by a combination of at least six guns (Sympher's, whose brigade cannot have failed to take a toll of the French left flank) and a number of muskets – originally, 1,900 but reduced to 900 by the end of the action. Taking a mean of 1,500 muskets, and making an allowance of two or three hundred casualties caused by the guns, it seems that for the British the performance was also slightly over one casualty per musket.

In this instance, however, there is accurate information on the length of the engagement to provide a further check. The battle lasted for 20 minutes, most of the fighting being at 30 to 40 yards range. The absolute maximum number of musket shots that could have been fired in that time by men doing nothing but loading and firing was 40. But in confused conditions and poor visibility it is much more likely that not more than 20 rounds per man would have been fired. If this figure is assumed for both sides, the French fired 20 by 540, equalling 10,800 rounds for 600 casualties, and the British fired 20 by 1,500 equalling 30,000 for 1,700 casualties. Thus about $5\frac{1}{2}\%$ of the rounds ordered to be fired were effective on both sides.

These figures should not be pressed too far; but they seem to indicate that during this phase of the battle the standard of musketry was much the same on both sides and that the infantry were hitting with rather more than 5% of the bullets that they were ordered to fire. The plain fact is that in this particular engagement more muskets killed more men. Superb courage, endurance and discipline on both sides enabled daunting casualties to be endured; but in the end, the troops that had killed more men than their opponents won the day.

When the analysis of these two phases of the battle are compared, it becomes immediately apparent that the percentage of musket shots stated to be effective varies greatly between the two. This discrepancy certainly demands an explanation, a search for which reveals several interesting points – both of fact and of theory – that can be of value in a study of other battles.

It is suggested that there were two reasons for the greater effectiveness of the muskets in the Fusiliers' battle than in that on the Ridge. In the first place, the Fusiliers' battle was a simpler affair in which a superior number of muskets blasted the enemy from the field in less than half the time that the Ridge

battle lasted. The men, though tired, were working at full efficiency throughout, whereas towards the end of 45 minutes of desperate struggle the musketry of the defenders of the Ridge could be expected to have deteriorated. Furthermore, the very heavy casualties among officers and senior non-commissioned officers must inevitably have led to a reduction in the standard of fire control.

More significant still – and a point of considerable importance in the studying of other actions – was the disparity between the number of muskets available to both sides as they were disposed on the ground. In the second action, every British musket was within 100 yards of some part of the French columns and was therefore operating at full efficiency. On the other hand, it will be remembered that flanking muskets up to a range of 200 yards were included in the calculation for the Ridge. Whatever maximum effective range is assumed, there can be no doubt that there was a falling off in effectiveness between 100 and 200 yards. The calculation therefore included some muskets that were operating below their maximum efficiency, with overall performance degraded as a result.

Acknowledging that some of the British muskets on the Ridge must have been shooting outside their effective range, but without contending that they were wrong to do so, it is interesting to repeat the calculation taking into account only those that were fired at 100 yards or less. There were 1,460 of them at the start – an average musket strength of, say, 1,000 throughout the battle. This would give a casualty rate of two per musket and a percentage of effective rounds of 4%. Such a figure of performance approaches that attained by the Fusilier Brigade and suggests that the superiority of the British musketry over that of the French on the immediate frontage of the action was more marked than was stated earlier.

Summary

These two phases of the battle of Albuera were chosen for study because they present the simplest possible picture of the actions and effect of the firearms of the Peninsular War during periods when all arms were in close contact. They were not deliberately staged attacks delivered from a distant starting line, pre-

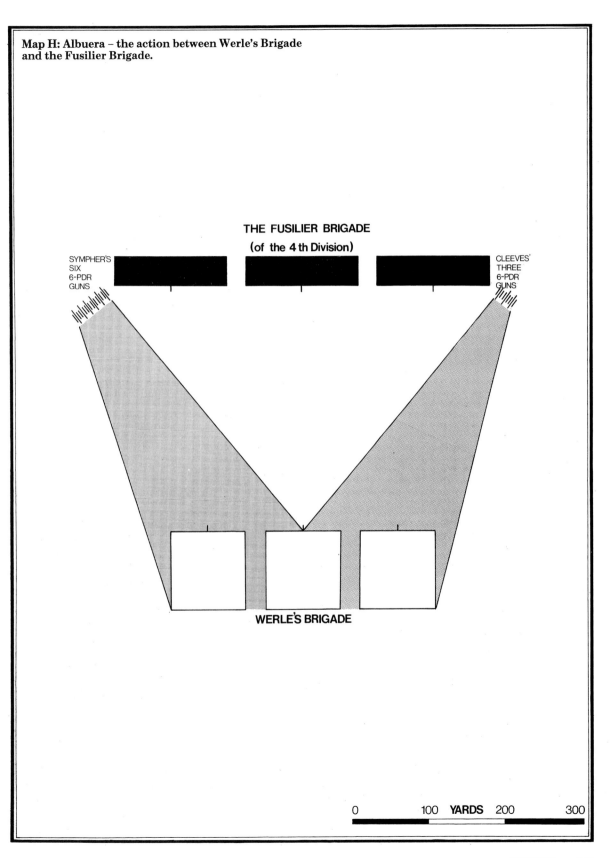

Map H: Albuera – the action between Werle's Brigade and the Fusilier Brigade.

THE FUSILIER BRIGADE

(of the 4th Division)

SYMPHER'S
SIX
6-PDR
GUNS

CLEEVES'
THREE
6-PDR
GUNS

WERLE'S BRIGADE

0   100   **YARDS**   200   300

ceded by preliminary bombardment and provided with continuous covering fire from the artillery. The two sides moved into musket range and began the fire fight immediately; and the artilleries could provide no more than close support to the mêlée once it had been joined.

Artillery performance

As regards the artillery of this period, it must be remembered that the capabilities of its equipments had been still further improved since the middle of the previous century. The increased rate of fire and the greater accuracy of laying meant that a larger number of well calculated rounds were finding the target. In full visibility, the rate of fire could be two rounds a minute – three or four times as fast as it had been in Marlborough's time; and guns could provide continuous support during periods of activity, totalling as much as two hours without replenishing their firing battery wagons.

An all-round improvement in the effect of artillery fire was therefore to be expected, and the records of Albuera show that it had certainly been attained. But it must be remembered that all short-range firearms are naturally very sensitive to their siting and, in the case of artillery, to the aspect presented by their target. There may often have been a considerable difference, therefore, between what the whole of the artillery of a force achieved and what was carried out by the batteries that had the best gun positions. In other words, a distinction must be made between the potential under the best conditions and the average performance of all the guns spread over the whole battlefield.

The British line was less vulnerable to gunfire than was the French mass. A line of infantry in close contact with the enemy could not be easily engaged to any effect by guns firing from positions alongside their own infantry. In contrast, the deep French mass presented in its closely packed rearward parts a good target for guns similarly sited. This difference in vulnerability is reflected in the figures of gun performance given above.

Therefore, although it cannot be claimed that all the artillery of a force operated with an equally high efficiency, it does seem that in this period the part of the artillery that was supporting infantry continuously and from a well-chosen position during a major phase of a battle could expect to inflict a hundred or more casualties per gun firing. This can be translated into a casualty rate of between one and two casualties for each round fired. As most effective rounds caused several casualties, it follows that some 60% of the rounds fired at normal fighting ranges took effect.

It must be borne in mind, however, that the task of artillery was usually easier in defence than in attack. When an artillery brigade was well placed in defence, as was Hawker's at Albuera, the number of casualties inflicted may have been appreciably higher than 100 per gun.

Musket performance

In the sense that its casualties could not be so easily replaced, the British line was more vulnerable to musket fire in a prolonged fight than was the French mass. Rear ranks could replace casualties in the French firing line as it became depleted; and the front ranks, alive or dead, provided some protection to those in the rear. The French could, in fact, take advantage of a superiority in numbers by using the column as a battering ram; but the line could only shrink inwards, unit by unit, as casualties reduced its strength.

How, then, did the markedly inferior British force defeat the French V Corps in the battle on the Ridge? Without in any way minimising the superb discipline and endurance of the British, it is suggested that there were two other important reasons.

One of these was that the British line could initially bring more muskets to bear. This superiority in firepower checked the momentum of the attacking columns and threw them into a posture which, while it could not be strictly described as defensive, was much less offensive than it was intended to be.

More significant, however, is the evidence that British firepower was more effective than that of the French. It would seem that the muskets of the British infantry inflicted a higher casualty rate than those of their enemy and that this, coupled with the support of more effective artillery, enabled the weaker force to wear down the resistance of its enemy and eventually emerge victorious.

Regarding the second phase of the battle, between the Fusilier brigade and Werlé's brigade, it does not seem possible to assert that there was any obvious difference between the effectiveness of the musketry of both sides. There, the British infantry was disposed so that more muskets could engage the French than could be fired back at them. As a result, more French soldiers than British soldiers were killed.

It appears, from the figures presented above, that when muskets of this time were firing at ranges of 100 yards or less over the full period of an engagement casualties were caused by some $5\frac{1}{2}\%$ of the bullets ordered to be fired. When other muskets firing from up to 200 yards also delivered fire, that figure might drop to 2% or $2\frac{1}{2}\%$.

These figures are not necessarily inconsistent with those quoted from earlier battles. They do not refer solely to those crashing opening volleys at thirty paces that swept away whole ranks; they also include all the fire delivered in twenty to forty-five minutes of desperate hand-to-hand fighting, when the enemy could barely be seen through the smoke and when fire control was necessarily less efficient in the turmoil of battle.

It is interesting to note how the percentage of effective rounds dropped as the range was increased from 30 to 200 yards. The musket had not changed during the previous hundred years. It was the way in which a battle was conducted that determined its casualty rate.

Musket power and infantry formations

It is never wise to assume that a line formation was always superior in firepower to a column by some constant factor; and it is always worth while to examine the exact number of muskets available to both sides. The figures for the battle of Albuera are illuminating, as follows:

	Total infantry strength	Number of muskets firing	Remarks
First attack French	8,000	1,200	Constant as casualties replaced.
Allied	3,000	2,100–600	Reduced by casualties to a greater extent than in column.
Second attack French	5,400	540	Constant.
Allied	1,900	1,900–900	Reducing.

It may perhaps be argued that no account has been taken of the casualties inflicted by rifles and bayonets. These have been ignored for two reasons. Firstly, it was quite impossible to obtain any reliable figures on the number of casualties caused by those weapons and it was therefore thought better to avoid what could only be pure speculation. But secondly, and more importantly, it seems clear that the number of casualties inflicted by rifle and bayonet was small in comparison with those caused by musket and gun. Riflemen acted as skirmishers and undoubtedly killed and wounded a certain number of the enemy as they fell back on the main line in defence or probed the enemy's defences in attack. Their numbers were small, however, and their opportunities were limited. The bayonet, also, was used to a limited extent – chiefly when musketry had broken down the enemy's will to resist.

In the absence of any indication of the number of casualties attributable to rifles and bayonets, it is thought best to remember that the performance claimed for muskets should be slightly reduced: and the small reduction should be applied to both sides in all cases. An exception must naturally be made if an engagement ended in the pursuit of a beaten force; but efforts have been made to exclude the results of such fighting from the assessments made here.

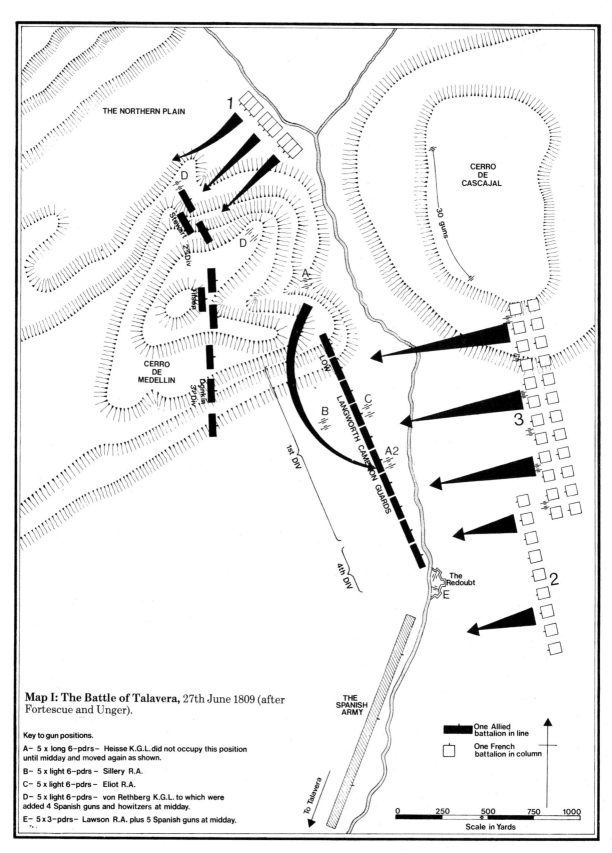

THE NORTHERN PLAIN

1

CERRO
DE
CASCAJAL

30 guns

D

Stewart
2nd Div

D

A

Hill
1st Div

Donkin
3rd Div

CERRO
DE
MEDELLIN

Low

LANGWORTH CAMERON GUARDS

C

B

A2

3

1st DIV

4th DIV

The
Redoubt

E

2

Map I: The Battle of Talavera, 27th June 1809 (after
Fortescue and Unger).

Key to gun positions.

A– 5 x long 6–pdrs– Heisse K.G.L. did not occupy this position
until midday and moved again as shown.

B– 5 x light 6–pdrs – Sillery R.A.

C– 5 x light 6–pdrs – Eliot R.A.

D– 5 x light 6–pdrs – von Rethberg K.G.L. to which were
added 4 Spanish guns and howitzers at midday.

E– 5 x 3–pdrs – Lawson R.A. plus 5 Spanish guns at midday.

THE
SPANISH
ARMY

To Talavera

■ One Allied
battalion in line

□ One French
battalion in column

0   250   500   750   1000

Scale in Yards

7. Talavera

The battle of Talavera presents an entirely different picture from that of Albuera. Here it is possible to study the whole sequence of events in a deliberate attack from the time that the attacking force left its starting line; and it is possible to do this three times over during the course of the battle – under rather different conditions each time. The initial artillery bombardment, the reaction of the defending artillery, the medium–range battle with case shot and the final clash of musket power happened in orderly sequence, and it is possible to determine the effectiveness of the weapons collectively if not individually.

Talavera was chosen for examination partly because there is an accurate record of the precise locations of the artilleries in one of Unger's maps, together with his notes on some very significant artillery moves during the battle. This information is not available from any other source. In addition, although there is not such a specific record of the division of casualty figures between guns and muskets as there is for Albuera, there is evidence that the majority of British casualties were caused by gunfire and that the majority of French losses were the result of musket bullets. Bearing in mind the proportions in which casualties were inflicted by guns and muskets at Albuera, it is assumed that at Talavera one-third of the French casualties were caused by guns and two-thirds were caused by muskets, and that these proportions were reversed in respect of the casualties to the Allied troops. This is admittedly an assumption, but it should be possible to test it by considering what the two arms should have been able to achieve.

On 27th June 1809 a British force, reinforced by units of the King's German Legion and commanded by Sir Arthur Wellesley, moved out of Portugal and into Spain. It was shortly afterwards to retreat into Portugal again; but this was the first forward movement of a campaign that, after four more years, would result in the French armies being finally driven out of the Peninsula.

Wellesley's army consisted of the 1st, 2nd, 3rd and 4th Divisions, comprising ten infantry brigades, three cavalry brigades and six batteries (then called brigades) of light artillery. Its total strength was just over 20,000 men with 30 guns, the howitzers of each battery having been left behind for lack of horses.

Acting rather capriciously in collaboration with Wellesley was the Spanish General Don Gregorio de la Cuesta, who was in command of a force of some 38,000 men and who, full of optimism and confidence, pushed on ahead in an attempt to storm his way into Madrid.

These forces were opposed by a French army numbering about 50,000 men under Marshal Victor; but another French army, under Marshal Soult, was menacing the left flank of any advance – and that threat imposed caution on a commander as realistic as Wellesley.

Sir Arthur's force reached Placentia on 10th July, Cuesta having by then reached Almaraz and Victor being at Talavera. Victor then moved down to a position between Wellesley and Cuesta and might well have tried to defeat the Allied forces in detail had he not been ordered by the king, Joseph, to retire to Oropesa, north of Talavera. Some very uneasy co-operation between the British and Spanish commanders resulted in agreement that both forces should pursue Victor; but the British troops were much impeded by the inability of the Spanish authorities to provide transport and supplies on the scales that had been promised, and Cuesta rushed on ahead and was flung into confusion when he met Victor in battle beyond Talavera.

It was mainly to save this situation that Wellesley brought his army forward and decided to oppose Victor's elated troops on a selected defensive position north of Talavera. The parts of the defeated Spanish army that could be rallied were to take post on the right of the British line – so that, on paper at least, the opposing armies were about equal in strength, though not necessarily equal in fighting ability.

The left or northern half of the position occupied by the Allied armies is shown in map I. The small stream running north and south led down from the range of high hills north of the position, through the 'Northern Plain', to the river Tagus, which it entered at the town of Talavera (about 1,200 yards beyond the bottom edge of the map). The main features on the battlefield were the two hills shown – that on the west side of the stream, the Cerro de Medellin, being higher and steeper on its eastern face than the Cerro de Cascajal on the French side. The stream

A reproduction from a French print of the battle of Talavera that, rather surprisingly, depicts the battle as seen from the Allied side. The town of Talavera can be seen on the right and the Cerro de Cascajal, on which the French artillery of position was sited, dominates the battlefield on the left.

The scene is probably intended to be that of the last great French attack over the whole front, and it may be

was no obstacle, and the ground was generally open and unobstructed.

From the redoubt shown on the right of the British line to the town of Talavera, however, the front was strongly protected by ditches, enclosures, walls and breastworks of felled trees. That part of the front was held by the Spanish army and was, in fact, virtually impregnable. Since the Spanish troops took little part in the battle and suffered no appreciable casualties, their actions need not be considered further.

The occupation of the northern half of the position by the Anglo-German troops was not accomplished without some confusion, due partly to the shortage of transport animals and partly to the exhaustion of the underfed men and horses. That part of the position lying between the redoubt and the Cerro de Medellin was manned in an orderly line; but though the hill was clearly the key to the whole position, it was not firmly occupied when the troops first deployed on the afternoon of the 27th. It was then held by a brigade of only three battalions of the 3rd Division commanded by Colonel Donkin, and they were not on the summit of the hill.

The French army moved forward on that same afternoon, and Victor decided to try to take the ill-guarded Cerro de Medellin by an evening attack that came in from the north-east. Confused fighting for the hill took place, at the end of which the French were finally ejected. The reinforcing Allied troops then took up the positions shown on map H. Throughout the subsequent operation, this flank was refused somewhat in view of the possibility of further French attacks from the left flank.

The night of the 27th/28th having put an end to this preliminary encounter, both sides prepared for the main battle that was to take place on the 28th. The main part of the Allied line was held by ten battalions in two ranks, each of rather over 200 files – that is, on a frontage of about 150 yards per battalion. Reinforcing them in the rear of the front line were Donkin's three battalions; and the six battalions of the 2nd Division held the top of the Cerro de Medellin. These positions are as shown and accurately plotted by Fortescue. The British and King's German Legion gun positions are those given by Unger, the most reliable authority and the only one giving these in detail.

that it is intended to depict its failure and the beginnings of retreat since various guns and wagons seem to be moving to the rear.

A good picture is given of the appearance of a line of French battalions, each in column of double companies with each column fifty files wide; and it can be seen that the formation was more linear than the use of the word 'column' might suggest.

The gun position in the foreground is probably Captain Sillery's, which was sited, rather exceptionally, on a piece of rising ground from which it was possible to shoot over the heads of the infantry it was supporting. The French artist has made the gunners and their guns entirely French in appearance. (By permission of the National Army Museum).

It must be assumed that the siting of Captain Sillery's brigade on the lower slopes of the Cerro de Medellin allowed it to shoot, exceptionally, over the heads of the infantry in front. At this time the brigade of long 6prs shown at A was on the extreme right of the line and was not moved to the position shown until after the first French attack, now to be described. It also seems clear that the Spanish guns and howitzers shown as reinforcing the brigades of Captain Lawson and Captain von Rettberg did not come into action until after midday, when Sir Arthur asked Cuesta for help. When these Spanish guns did arrive, they were not only well manned but also they were 12prs and thus more powerful than any others on the Allied side.

The French artillery was initially brought into action as shown in map J, the layout being in accordance with normal French practice whereby the guns of position were concentrated in a single battery – in this case, on the commanding height of the Cerro de Cascajal. According to Fortescue, there were 30 guns on the Cerro de Cascajal and a further 36 in support of the columns attacking in the centre. The rest of the total of 80 guns known to have been with this French army were in reserve in the rear.

Three successive attacks were made by the French during the 28th, each shown – numbered 1, 2 and 3 respectively – in map I. Each presents a different aspect of the influence of firepower and is described in its turn.

Soon after dawn on the 28th, it became clear that the French formation that had failed to capture the Cerro de Medellin on the previous evening was about to try again. The great battery of 30 guns on the Cerro de Cascajal began a bombardment of the Allied left, and a division of three regiments (nine battalions) under the command of General Ruffin moved forward to attack from somewhat north of east.

It is difficult to evaluate the effect of this preliminary bombardment, made in pursuance of the customary French practice of trying to blast a hole in the objective selected for attack. The French battery was well placed on the flank of the axis of this first attack and could provide flanking fire to some effect. But it can be seen from the sketch that – if the positions of the British infantry were accurately plotted by Fortescue – the French guns were firing at a range of at least 1,000 yards, at which even Müller's estimate claims only 20% hits on a line of infantry. It is true that the French battery contained some 12pr and 8pr guns, which were of heavier metal and longer range than the Allied 6prs, and it was impossible for von Rettberg's five guns to make an adequate reply. Possibly, the British infantry were initially somewhat further forward than is shown on Fortescue's map; but Sir Arthur did, in fact, withdraw them behind the crest during the bombardment. Nevertheless, there seems to be little doubt that appreciable casualties were inflicted, Fortescue stating that the fire 'tore great gaps in the ranks of the right of Stewart's brigade'. This is strong commendation of the efficiency of the French artillery, and it suggests a higher performance at long range than is generally assumed.

One other significant event occurred at this stage. The light easterly wind caused the smoke from the French guns to drift over the battlefield, and this continuous smoke-screen tended to conceal the French columns during the whole of the battle.

It was a pity that the brigade of long 6prs commanded by Captain Heisse was away on the right flank at this time. If it had occupied the position to which it was moved later, it could have engaged the French artillery to some effect at the very reasonable range of 600 yards – though Sir Arthur might well have prohibited such a possible waste of ammunition.

Ruffin's nine battalions were all formed in column of double companies. Each of the six companies of a battalion was about 75 men strong and was formed in three ranks with a frontage of 25 files. The frontage of each battalion was therefore 50 files and its depth was nine ranks. All nine battalions were in line alongside each other, so the firing line consisted of 50 (each battalion) by 9 (battalions) by 3 (ranks), equalling 1,350 muskets. This was a formidable amount of firepower; but unfortunately the 9th Light Regiment, on the right, swung well out to the north of the Cerro de Medellin and took little or no part in this battle. The actual musket power available was thus reduced to 900 and was distributed over a frontage of about 200 yards.

The men carrying those muskets laboured up the steep side of the hill and had reached a position beyond which their own guns could no longer give them frontal support when the five guns of von Rettberg's brigade, in action on both flanks of the British infantry, began to take their toll with salvoes of case. It would have taken the French infantry three or four minutes to climb the slope between 350 and 100 yards from their objective; and in that time nine to twelve salvoes would have been fired, assuming no impedence or obscuration of the target. Ten salvoes from five guns would have discharged 4,250 bullets – the equivalent of, say, eight battalion volleys. By Müller's estimate, modified to conform to British ranges and rates of fire, this would have claimed 100 killed and 400 wounded. It is not suggested that this fire would have had an overwhelming effect, but there can be little doubt that it was a useful contribution that reduced the musket power the infantry had yet to face.

Eventually, the opposing infantries came within musket range of each other. Again, as with the battle of Albuera, it is important to examine the exact frontages in order to determine the number of muskets that were engaged on both sides. On the exact frontage of the narrow French formation, their three ranks of muskets were naturally 50% more powerful than those of the same number of files in two ranks that faced them. It was the addition of the flanking British files that could turn the scales. The number of flanking files that can be assumed to have taken part was discussed on page 119, and on that basis some 650 could have done so. In this case, the 900 French muskets were confronted by 300 files (the frontage of the French formation) plus 650 (flanking British files), equalling 950 files firing 1,900 muskets initially. Fortescue's account and map suggests that the battalion in second line, being further up the slope, could have fired over the heads of the units in front. He certainly writes of the French being engaged by three battalions – which would have increased the disparity in musket power even more. Oman goes further and talks of engagement by all six battalions of the 2nd Division; but this would not have been possible on the frontage of the attack. Be that as it may, the admirably controlled volleys of the British muskets brought the attack to a standstill. Flailed by over three thousand shots a minute from their front, and lashed by von Rettberg's case on their flanks, the French infantry retired defeated.

This phase of the battle lasted for about half an hour, during which Ruffin's force lost rather more than 1,500 men. As has been shown, the guns might have fired some 4,000 bullets of case in the approach to the objective and an unknown number of additional rounds in the subsequent fighting. The British infantry could have fired between fifteen and thirty volleys – a total of 22,500 to 45,000 shots, allowing for a reduction in musket strength through casualties. It seems likely that the guns – being less powerful and perhaps less well sited than at Albuera – caused about a quarter of the 1,500 French casualties, the remaining three-quarters attributable to muskets.

Five guns firing continuously for half an hour could have fired a maximum of 300 rounds. But it is much more likely that no more than 200 were fired; and these could have claimed 200 to 250 casualties at 1 to $1\frac{1}{2}$ per shot. This would have been a good and credible standard of shooting, leaving 1,250 to 1,300 casualties to be accounted for by musket fire. Twenty volleys, totalling 30,000 shots, would give a figure of effectiveness of about 4% of the shots ordered to be fired; thirty volleys would give 3%.

The battalions of the British 2nd Division suffered 835 casualties during the battle, but a considerable number of these were caused by the French artillery later in the afternoon. Ruffin's infantry may have inflicted 600 casualties with their 900 muskets – so their standard of musketry seems to have been inferior to that of the British infantry.

These figures bear out the conclusion that between 3% and 5% of the shots of well-trained infantry could be expected to be effective and that well-sited and properly-handled artillery could inflict 1 to $1\frac{1}{2}$ casualties per round fired at close or medium range. It will be noticed that, as in the battle of the Ridge at Albuera, the maximum effective range of muskets has been taken as 200 yards. Those fired at 100 yards or less would probably have attained a figure of 5%.

After the unsuccessful attack on the Cerro de Medellin there was a lull in the battle until about midday, when the French began their final series of attacks – delivered in a slightly disjointed manner. An assault on the extreme right of the British part of the Allied line came first and can be described separately. It was made by General Jean Leval with a German division of nine battalions in line, each

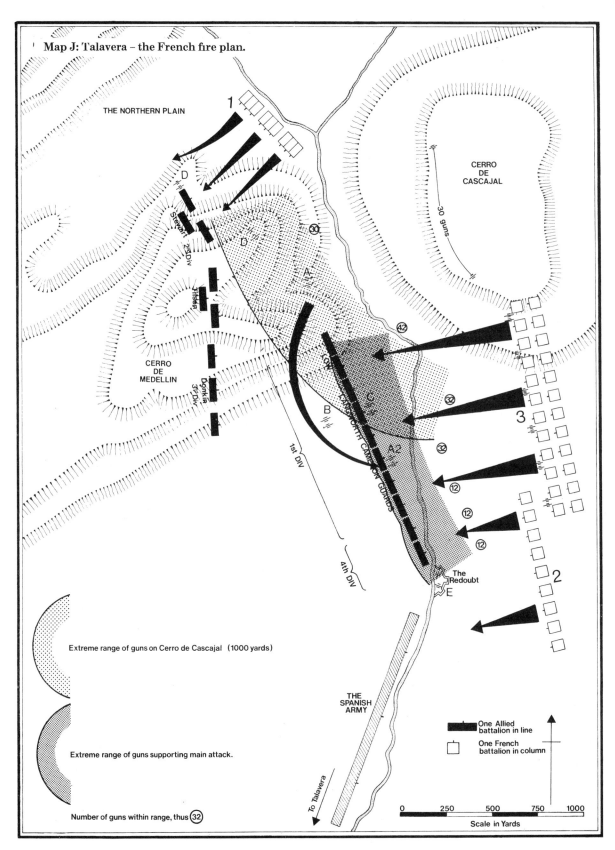

Map J: Talavera – the French fire plan.

THE NORTHERN PLAIN

1

D

Stewart 2nd Div

Tilson

D

30

A

CERRO
DE
CASCAJAL

30 guns

42

CERRO
DE
MEDELLIN

Donkin 3rd Div

B

C

32

A2

3

32

1st DIV

12

12

4th DIV

12

2

The
Redoubt

E

THE
SPANISH
ARMY

Extreme range of guns on Cerro de Cascajal (1000 yards)

Extreme range of guns supporting main attack.

One Allied
battalion in line

One French
battalion in column

Number of guns within range, thus 32

To Talavera

0   250   500   750   1000

Scale in Yards

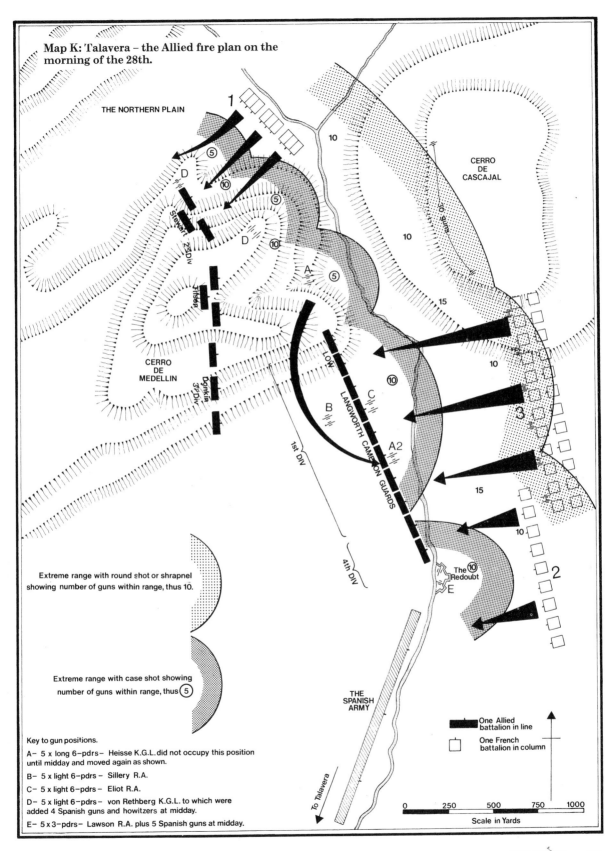

Map K: Talavera – the Allied fire plan on the morning of the 28th.

THE NORTHERN PLAIN

1

10

CERRO
DE
CASCAJAL

30 guns

10

D

Steven
2nd Div

D

10

A

5

15

Fitzer

3

10

CERRO
DE
MEDELLIN

Donkin
3rd Div

LOW

LANGWORTH CAMERON GUARDS

C

10

B

A2

1st DIV

15

10

Extreme range with round shot or shrapnel
showing number of guns within range, thus 10.

4th DIV

2

The
Redoubt

10

E

Extreme range with case shot showing
number of guns within range, thus 5

Key to gun positions.

A– 5 x long 6–pdrs– Heisse K.G.L.did not occupy this position
until midday and moved again as shown.

B– 5 x light 6–pdrs – Sillery R.A.

C– 5 x light 6–pdrs – Eliot R.A.

D– 5 x light 6–pdrs– von Rethberg K.G.L. to which were
added 4 Spanish guns and howitzers at midday.

E– 5 x 3–pdrs– Lawson R.A. plus 5 Spanish guns at midday.

THE
SPANISH
ARMY

One Allied
battalion in line

One French
battalion in column

To Talavera

0   250   500   750   1000

Scale in Yards

battalion being in column of double companies. The frontage of the attack overlapped the redoubt to the south and threatened the Spanish troops beyond it, but its main impact was on two battalions commanded by Brigadier General Henry Campbell. The French, with a firing line of 9 (battalions) by 50 (files) by 3 (ranks) equalling 1,350 muskets, would seem to have had an appreciable advantage over the British 2 (battalions) by 225 (files) by 2 (ranks) equalling 900 muskets: but three factors countered this disparity.

In the first place, part of the French frontage was south of the redoubt. Secondly, the orderly array of the French was greatly disturbed by their passage over some much broken and obstructed ground on the way to their objective. Lastly – and of particular significance here – the redoubt on the right of the British line was occupied by Lawson's five 3pr guns, which had just been reinforced by four Spanish 12prs. Most accounts refer to this redoubt as 'unfinished', but there is little doubt that it provided the field works that gave considerable protection against the small projectiles of field artillery and probably complete protection against small-arms fire. Protected from fire from the front by the wall of the redoubt, Lawson's guns continued to fire at point-blank range throughout the engagement, even when the infantries were locked in battle. It would normally have been difficult for a battery to remain in action in the open in such an advantageous flanking position throughout a battle, but the existence of the protective field works made it possible in this case. As was seen at Albuera, the massed French columns were particularly vulnerable to such fire from a flank; and there can be little doubt that this skilful siting of Lawson's guns must have enabled them to provide an effective contribution to the firepower that helped to defeat this attack.

The actual figures of performance are interesting. Leval's attack lasted for three-quarters of an hour, and his division suffered 1,007 casualties from a strength of 4,500. Remembering that Captain Hawker's four 9pr guns caused 1,000 casualties at Albuera, it would seem that Lawson's five little 3prs, even when reinforced by the Spanish 12prs, could hardly have equalled such a performance. Lawson is likely to have fired some 300 rounds in all – that is,

about one round a minute through visibility that was more restricted by smoke than usual. It would be reasonable to assume that his guns inflicted 300 casualties, representing one casualty per round and also one third of the total casualties – both of which conditions have emerged from previous analyses. Thus the remaining 700 casualties would have been due to the fire of 900 muskets, giving a casualty rate of rather less than one per musket. The French musket performance was of a considerably lower standard, 1,350 muskets causing only 236 casualties.

Shortly after this repulse, the main French attack was made on the centre of the Allied line. As is shown in map J, 24 French battalions moved forward in two great lines – each battalion in column of double companies with a frontage of 50 files and a depth of nine ranks. They were opposed by a line of ten Anglo-German battalions supported by nine more that could not take part in the fire fight without moving up into the firing line.

Maps J and K show the artillery firepower available to both sides. The French artillery was greatly superior in numbers to that of the Allies: but it must be remembered that a gun is of value in battle only if its trail is on the ground and it is sited in a position from which it can influence the fighting. Even if a maximum effective range of 1,000 yards is assumed for the French 12pr and 8pr guns on the Cerro de Cascajal, an examination of the French fire plan will show that those guns were displaced too far to a flank to be able to engage more than about half the Allied line. And although the 36 guns that were providing close support to the French columns could, in theory, concentrate the whole of their fire on any point on the front, in practice there were not the communications whereby such a concentration could be ordered and put into effect. The six French batteries were distributed over the whole front, each battery supporting two battalions and moving in the intervals between the infantry units. The maximum amount of fire that could normally have been applied to any one target was that of six guns. At the same time, the capacity of the French artillery to engage more than one target at a time was clearly greater than that of their opponents simply because they had more guns in action.

Although it is hard to see how the limited amount of Allied artillery could have been better deployed initially to provide coverage over the whole front – particularly when the previous threats had been aimed at the vulnerable Cerro de Medellin – the diagrams show that there was necessarily a weakness in the case shot coverage in the right centre of the line. Furthermore, although the effectiveness of fire from a flank has been mentioned several times, such fire would be less effective when an attack was made on a very broad front since the columns on the flanks shielded those in the centre.

Fortunately, this is one of the all too rare occasions when accurate information is available regarding artillery moves during a battle. Thanks to Unger's careful notes it is known that, as soon as it became clear that the third and final French attack was about to be delivered on the centre and right of the Anglo-German line, the most powerful fire unit in the Allied artillery – Heisse's brigade of long 6prs – was moved from its position on the left flank to one on the left of the two battalions of Guards. This move greatly improved the firepower that could be applied to the centre of the French attack. Map L shows how this closed the gap in short-range coverage that had previously existed there.

No matter how actively and intelligently the Allied artillery may have been handled, the fact remained that the French had more guns in the field: and though their guns of position were not well sited, they could put more shot into their enemy than could the Allies. A different picture emerges, however, when the musket power is examined. The French columns were on a frontage of 12 battalions of 50 three-deep files each, giving a total musket strength of 1,800; and the 8 Allied battalions, at an initial strength of 5,964 men, could develop at least $2\frac{1}{2}$ times that firepower. The number of muskets firing would be reduced by casualties – perhaps more so on the Allied side as a result of the heavier artillery support available to the French – but the disparity in musket power was caused by the wide frontage over which the French force was deployed, making its entire front vulnerable to small-arms fire.

With such a preponderance of musket power on the Allied side, it would seem that the result must have been beyond doubt. But that was not the case. An extremely hard-fought battle took place; and at one moment, disaster to the Allied force was averted

only by Sir Arthur's incredibly keen perception. That was when the Guards – galled beyond measure by their ordeal – charged forward into the French mass, leaving a gap in the Allied line. It was the ever-watchful Commander-in-Chief who instantly ordered up the 48th Foot to close the gap and preserve the line at that critical moment.

Why, then, did superior musket power not prevail more certainly? It seems that there are three possible answers. The first is that the column formation used by the French, although deficient in frontal firepower, contained large reserves of manpower. The rear ranks, protected by those in front of them, could move forward to replace casualties: and though the larger number of muskets in the line inflicted more casualties, it must have been discouraging indeed to find reinforcements springing up like dragons' teeth after every volley.

The second reason may well have been simply that the musket was a very inefficient performer: and when machinery is operating inefficiently, an increase in the number of machines may not be as significant as it appears on paper. The standards of musketry exhibited by both sides bear examination here. The number of casualties caused by 1,800 French muskets must have been appreciably lower than the total of 2,249, for the French guns are known to have exacted a considerable toll. It seems likely that the French muskets could have claimed about one casualty per musket. The 5,000 Allied muskets were reduced to about 2,700 by the end of the battle, giving a mean of 4,000 muskets in action. These caused 2,200 French casualties; so it certainly seems that on this occasion the Allied performance was inferior to that of the French.

Lastly, there is the fact – never ignored in any sound study of warfare – that battles are not won by weapon power alone. But without going into the morale factors that must have affected the issue, it can be said here that in this particular battle the side bringing the greater firepower to bear ultimately won it.

When the battle is surveyed as a whole, it is interesting to look a little more closely at the actions of the two artilleries. It is generally asserted that the Allied army won in spite of having to face a greatly superior French artillery – and 66 guns to 30 is certainly a formidable disparity. If it is assumed, however, that one-third of the French casualties and two-thirds of the Allied losses were due to gunfire, 3,600 Allied casualties were caused by 66 French guns. This gives a casualty rate of 55 per French gun. On the other side, 30 Allied guns caused 2,400 casualties at a rate of 80 per gun. Although this is a generalisation, it does seem to indicate that the numerically inferior Allied artillery may well have operated more effectively than that of the enemy.

It is also worth noting that, on all three occasions when the Allied small-arms fire had stopped the French attacks, the British infantry charged with the bayonet and pursued the enemy up to the muzzles of the French guns. During those rather uncontrolled forward rushes they came within point-blank range of the French guns and suffered heavy casualties then and in their subsequent withdrawal. When allowance is made for the occasions on which the French artillery was presented with easy targets, it may be that the overall effectiveness of the French guns during the main battle will prove to have been as little as half that of the Allies.

There is no doubt that the artilleries of the two sides were handled in very different ways. The French had a permanent and rigid decentralisation of more than half their artillery to infantry battalions, as a result of which those guns could be used only as local extensions of the firepower of the infantry's muskets. As a counter to this dispersal of their resources, they used their artillery of the park as an independent battering ram. At Talavera, however, the specious attractions of a commanding feature led to the siting of that powerful weapon in a place from which it was not well placed to exert its full influence.

The Allied artillery, on the other hand, seems to have been more actively and intelligently handled – the greatest possible use having been made of it in each of the three situations that arose. It is hard to fault the locations of the various gun positions and the changes made to them during the battle. They seem to have been well designed to make the best possible use of a limited number of guns: and although there is no definite evidence on the point, it is more than likely that the siting and moves of the guns were directed by the commander himself.

In this connection, there is one very significant record regarding the artillery at Talavera. None of the great historians mention it and even the meticulous Unger is silent on the matter, but it appears in a source that can be expected to be entirely reliable, All editions of *The Bombardier and Pocket Gunner*, published after 1809, contain a short description of the action of the artillery in certain battles. One of the battles so described is Talavera, and it is worth reproducing here the diagram of it that illustrates the text (map M). This shows Lawson's brigade in the redoubt and the positions of the infantry and the rest of the artillery in diagrammatic form. The accompanying text states that, as the French columns closed for their final attack, the guns on the left were moved forward into positions from which they could engage the right flank of the French columns in enfilade. This would certainly have been possible, and it seems very unlikely that a statement of this sort would have been made in what was the standard training manual of the Royal Artillery without foundation. The story is made even more convincing by the inclusion of a caution on the danger of such a move making the artillery vulnerable to enfilade fire from hostile guns on their outer flank, which certainly seems to be a reference to the French gun positions on the Cerro de Cascajal.

There is no doubt that many minor moves of artillery were made in battle and that these are seldom recorded other than in personal papers. It is inconceivable that from time to time a battery commander in action would not have appreciated that a short move of his guns would improve the fire support that he could give in an action that was never completely stationary. Such a move, over a short distance, would not have demanded the presence of vulnerable teams of horses since equipments could be moved by gun detachments using drag-ropes.

It does seem that the Allied artillery was directed and operated more efficiently than that of the French at Talavera. It is likely that its weakness in numbers encouraged its active direction and that its organisation permitted this to a greater extent than would have been possible in the French army. Once more, as at Albuera, the power of a well placed battery – in this case Lawson's – applying enfilade fire from a flank is seen to have been extremely effective against the rearward parts of the French mass.

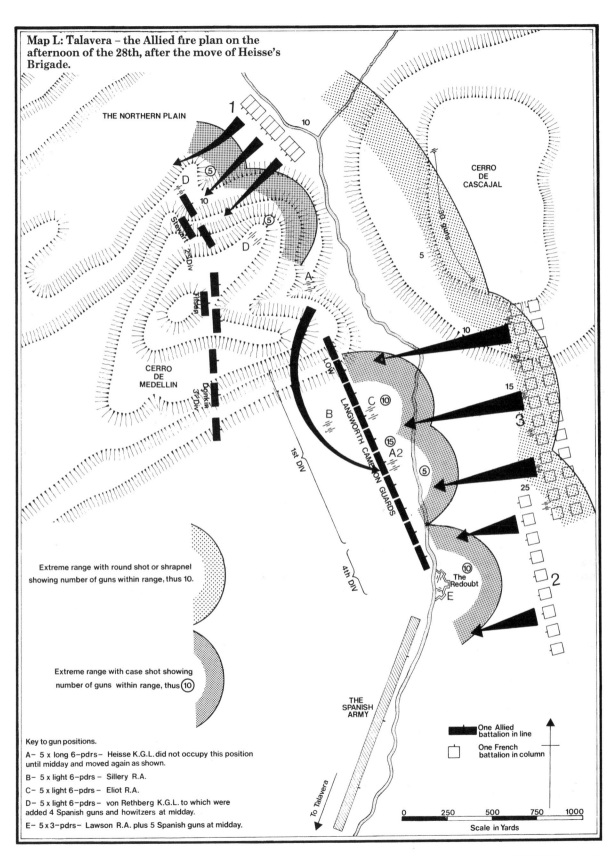

Map L: Talavera – the Allied fire plan on the afternoon of the 28th, after the move of Heisse's Brigade.

THE NORTHERN PLAIN

1

10

D

5

10

D

5

A

CERRO DE CASCAJAL

36 guns

5

10

Stewart 2 Div

Tilson

Donkin 3 Div

CERRO DE MEDELLIN

LOW

LANGWORTH CAMERON GUARDS

C 10

B

15

A2

5

1st DIV

6

4th DIV

15

3

25

10

The Redoubt

E

2

Extreme range with round shot or shrapnel showing number of guns within range, thus 10.

Extreme range with case shot showing number of guns within range, thus ⑩

THE SPANISH ARMY

To Talavera

One Allied battalion in line

One French battalion in column

Key to gun positions.

A– 5 x long 6–pdrs– Heisse K.G.L. did not occupy this position until midday and moved again as shown.

B– 5 x light 6–pdrs – Sillery R.A.

C– 5 x light 6–pdrs – Eliot R.A.

D– 5 x light 6–pdrs – von Rethberg K.G.L. to which were added 4 Spanish guns and howitzers at midday.

E– 5 x 3–pdrs – Lawson R.A. plus 5 Spanish guns at midday.

| 0 | 250 | 500 | 750 | 1000 |

Scale in Yards

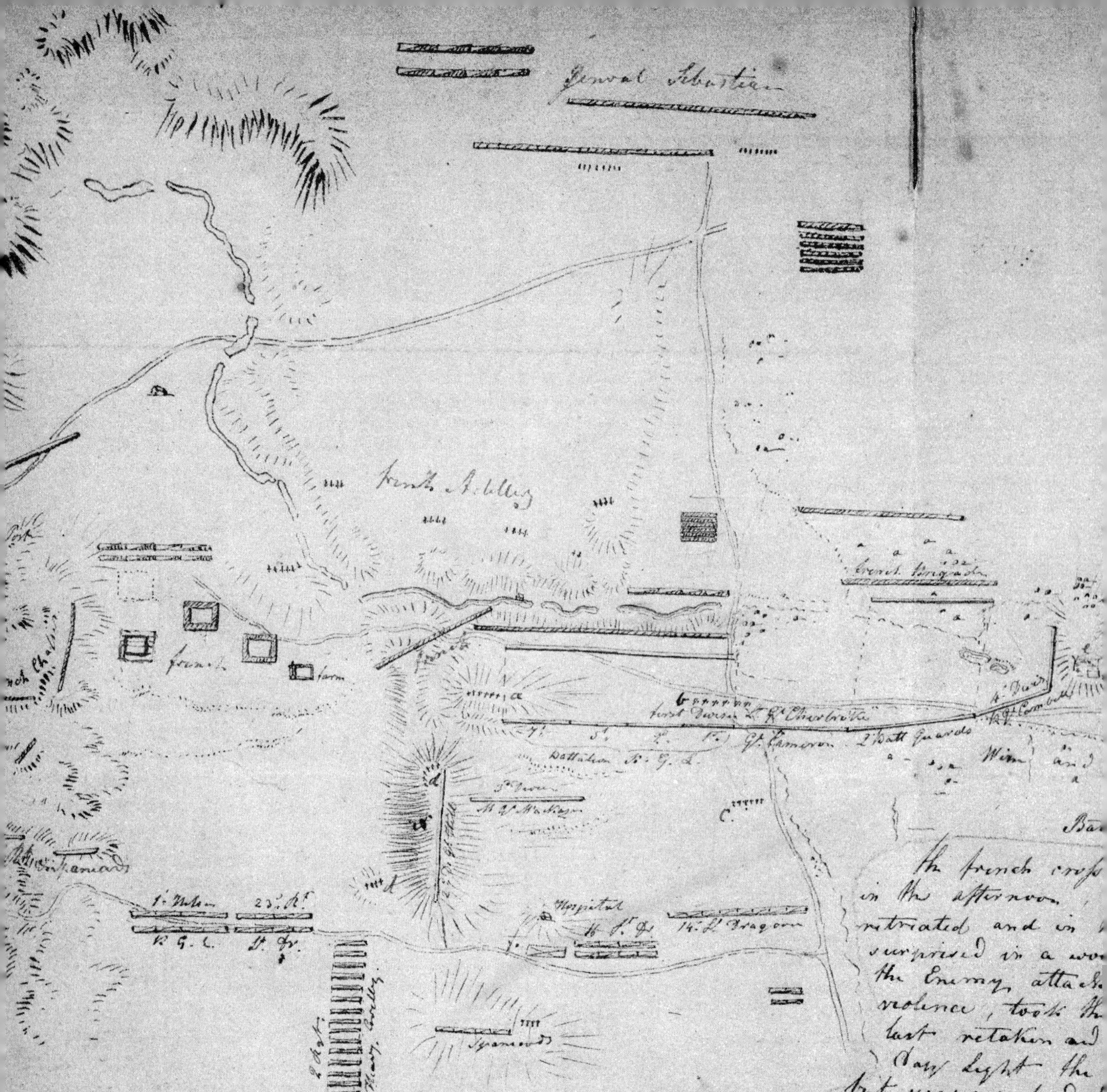

General Sebastiani

French Artillery

French

French Brigade

first Divisn L.G. Charlotte

Lt. Cameron 2 Battn Guards

Battalion K.G.L.

1st Divn M.G. Mackenzie

Hospital H.F.G.

14th L. Dragoons

Spaniards

French Infantry

1 Batln K.G.L.   2 Br. K.G.L.

Shot

Heavy Cavalry

Spaniards

A Division of about 20,000 best troops
under the command of King Joseph did not take
part of the Enemys attacks but kept
the Spaniards (by a distance of aby 2500 Yds)
in tranquility.

Remarks

a, Brigade Maj Bt C. Thier
b, — Light Br. C. Elliot
c, — Light Br. C. Pellew
d, — Light Br. C. Buckley & hussars G. & Hoy
e, — Light Dr. C. Lawson
f, — Reserve Ammunition

The french cross
in the afternoon
retreated and
surprised in a wood
the Enemy, attacked
violence, took the
last retaken and
Day light the
but was repulsed
the 4th Division to the
till about 12 oClock when
At 2 oClock a very heavy
heavy Brigade Ok was
in half an hour's time
the with the Bayonett
ted to attack the Hill again
& ... KGL charging the
Viles the steadiness of the
ted the surrounding of this
with 15,000 infantry &
the whole charged them
of the 7th Battn the G
No further attack took
french retire being the

Unger's sketch map and notes
of the Battle of Talavera.

Although the guns undoubtedly took considerable toll of the attacking columns and continued to harass them when they were in contact with the Allied line, it was ultimately the musket and bayonet power of the infantry that decided the issue. Talavera provides good examples of the ways in which their firepower could be applied by various formations. Where well-trained and well-disciplined troops were concerned, however, it will be seen that even a considerable numerical superiority in musket power did not always sweep all before it. This seems to have been due, in part, to the small percentage of bullets ordered to be fired that found their mark. It was also certainly due to the strength of the deep French columns, in which casualties in front were replaced from behind and which possessed a considerable weight of struggling manpower effective in a hand-to-hand struggle.

If one assumes the same ratio of casualties attributable to guns and muskets as was mentioned earlier, the overall picture appears to be that some 4,000 French muskets inflicted perhaps 1,300 casualties and 7,000 Allied muskets accounted for 3,600 men. This certainly seems to indicate that the Allied musketry was of a somewhat higher overall standard than that of the French; but it is probably best to draw no more than a general conclusion from such figures. Indeed, it has been shown that during part of the battle the reverse was the case. Perhaps, therefore, it is best to merely say that the side deploying the greater amount of firepower won. Even so, as a reminder that not even superior firepower can always win battles, it is worth noting that critical moment during the last French attack when the Guards had surged forward with the bayonet and the resulting gap in the Allied line was closed only by the Commander-in-Chief's inspired calling forward of the 48th Foot to close the breach.

Again, as at Albuera, the small number of casualties in the artilleries show that counter-battery fire was either hardly attempted or remarkably unsuccessful. With the exception of the large French battery on the Cerro de Cascajal, however, the artilleries of both sides did not present concentrated, and therefore profitable, targets; and the large French battery was a long way from any Allied guns. Certainly, as far as the Allied artillery was concerned, the French infantry was a better and more menacing target.

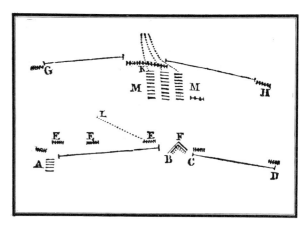

Map M: Talavera (reproduced from *The Bombardier and Pocket Gunner*).

8. Bussaco

The battle of Bussaco is the third battle of the Peninsular war of which Lieutenant Unger produced one of his valuable sketch maps. It was an action of an entirely different character from that of either Albuera or Talavera, and it presents a number of interesting points in the matter of firepower.

In the first place, the steep hillsides and broken ground over which it was fought had a considerable effect on the way in which it was staged and on the minor tactics that had to be adopted. This was no clash of great lines of infantry advancing on a wide front. Instead, narrow-fronted French columns clambered up steep hillsides and had to negotiate boulder-strewn ravines while the extended Allied line waited behind the crest to give them a rough reception. There was more scope, too, for minor manoeuvre than was possible when both forces were rigidly deployed on a wide front. Consequently, there was a great deal of movement of units and sub-units of all arms during the battle.

Insofar as it concerned the artilleries, the battle of Bussaco is of exceptional interest. The nature of the ground presented a number of technical difficulties that affected each side in different ways. Furthermore, it was a battle in which the Allied artillery was handled personally and in detail by the Commander-in-Chief; and there is a very full record of how he did this. The fact that the battle consisted of a number of separate engagements of parts of a somewhat dispersed pair of forces on broken ground meant that it was necessary to use the guns in small packets, and this demanded continuous direction and redirection of their efforts. The way in which this was done shows the value that was placed on their fire in what would now be called the 'close support' role.

Just over a year after the battle of Talavera, in the late summer of 1810, Wellington was being driven back into Portugal by the French armies and was fighting a series of delaying actions before making his final stand in the lines of Torres Vedras. The French Marshal André Massena, Prince of Essling, had been sent to command the Army of Portugal in April 1810, and it was he who was in command of the French forces when Wellington, perceiving the strength of a position on the Serra do Bussaco, decided to give battle to the invading army there.

The physical features of the battlefield and the initial positions of the two armies are shown in map N. The Serra, or ridge, was a steep-sided hog's-back along the crest of which was a series of hillocks. On the eastern (or French) side the ground fell steeply into a ravine, the bottom of which was over a thousand feet below the top of the Serra at a distance from it of less than a mile. Beyond the ravine, the ground rose again more gently and less regularly but never attained the height of the Serra. Only two indifferent roads and one or two rough tracks crossed the Serra from east to west; and its eastern slope was cut up by many minor ravines and watercourses, most of which were choked with boulders and heather.

The French seem to have carried out a most perfunctory reconnaissance of the Allied position. Their efforts to discover where and how it was being held were not helped by the deliberate concealment of the Allied troops behind the crest, but they seem to have assumed that the Allied right did not extend much south of a convent at the north end of the Allied position. Their plan of attack was therefore designed to roll up the Allied line from the south. A corps commanded by General Jean Reynier was ordered to attack astride and somewhat to the north of the track leading to Palheiros and, having gained the crest of the Serra, to swing northwards while a corps under Marshal Michel Ney assaulted the convent from the east. The attacks of these two French corps were, in fact, delivered quite separately and can be described in turn.

Reynier's corps consisted of two divisions – General Pierre Merle's of eleven battalions, and General Étienne Heudelet's of fifteen battalions. Merle's division advanced to the right, or north, of the Palheiros track and Heudelet's moved astride the track itself. Each infantry regiment of both divisions appears to have been in a single column of companies on a frontage of fifty men. Furthermore, the columns seem to have been echeloned from the right. The advance began at about 5.30 a.m.

Wellington, anticipating the attack from observations made the previous evening, had strengthened this part of his front – in particular, by bringing in Major General Stafford Lightburne's brigade. And when, in due course, a swarm of skirmishers announced the imminent arrival of the French infantry behind them, the Allied light companies moved down

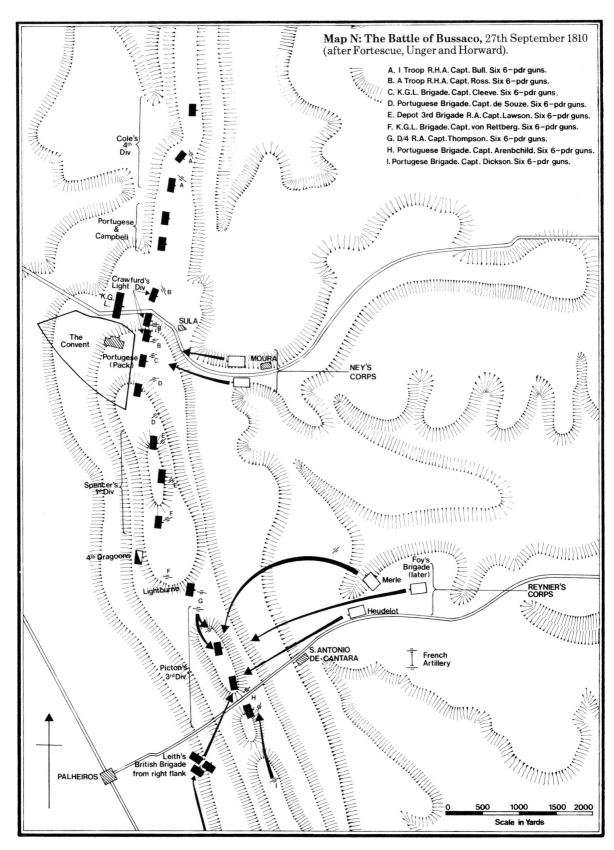

Map N: The Battle of Bussaco, 27th September 1810
(after Fortescue, Unger and Horward).

A. I Troop R.H.A. Capt. Bull. Six 6–pdr guns.
B. A Troop R.H.A. Capt. Ross. Six 6–pdr guns.
C. K.G.L. Brigade. Capt. Cleeve. Six 6–pdr guns.
D. Portuguese Brigade. Capt. de Souze. Six 6–pdr guns.
E. Depot 3rd Brigade R.A. Capt. Lawson. Six 6–pdr guns.
F. K.G.L. Brigade. Capt. von Rettberg. Six 6–pdr guns.
G. D/4 R.A. Capt. Thompson. Six 6–pdr guns.
H. Portuguese Brigade. Capt. Arenbchild. Six 6–pdr guns.
I. Portugese Brigade. Capt. Dickson. Six 6–pdr guns.

Cole's
4th
Div

Portugese
&
Campbell

Crawfurd's
Light Div

K.G.
L.

The
Convent

Portugese
(Pack)

SULA

MOURA

NEY'S
CORPS

Spencer's
1st Div

4th Dragoons

Lightburne

Foy's
Brigade
(later)

Merle

REYNIER'S
CORPS

Heudelot

S. ANTONIO
DE CANTARA

French
Artillery

Picton's
3rd Div

Leith's
British Brigade
from right flank

PALHEIROS

0   500   1000   1500   2000

Scale in Yards

to meet them and a fire fight began among the rocks and undergrowth. Wellington then arrived on the scene in person, withdrew the main body of the infantry behind the crest and ordered two of the guns commanded by Captain George Thompson forward into action on a knoll from which the French advance could be engaged advantageously.

It will be seen from map N that Merle's division had inclined to its right. This was caused by the natural effect of a steep slope on heavily laden men trying to climb it. But faced by the fire of the Allied skirmishers and the British guns, the whole division swung sharply to its left – and Lightburne's brigade was left holding its original position.

This attack seems to have been deflected solely by the fire of two light companies (according to Fortescue, only the 83rd and the 5th) and, at most, six 6pr guns firing at about 400 yards range. The broken nature of the ground and the amount of cover available would have made the French troops a difficult target, but it does seem that this was an occasion on which the fire of the guns at short range was exceptionally effective.

Meanwhile, Heudelet's division was advancing up the track leading over the pass to Palheiros. His 31st Regiment was in front and was, indeed, the only part of the division to make this attack: General Maximilian Foy's 1st Brigade was held back for a later assault, and the other regiment of General Joseph Arnaud's Brigade did not take part.

It is interesting to examine here the firepower that was available to both sides in the resulting action. Unger shows Lieutenant Colonel Frederick de Arentschild's Portuguese battery of six 6pr guns in action at the top of the pass; and though Unger shows Major Alexander Dickson's Portuguese battery as initially further south, Fortescue states that it was moved to join Arentschild's before the attack came within range. There were thus twelve Allied guns capable of firing down the slope.

It was impossible for the French artillery to provide any sort of effective support. Gun positions at reasonable ranges would have been in the bottom of the ravine, from which it would have been impossible to shoot at the Serra nearly a thousand feet above them. The best that could be done was to occupy the gun positions shown on map N, which were 1,800 yards from the French objective. Even so, the guns would have been firing at an angle of sight of nearly ten degrees – and an examination of the Gribeauval carriage suggests that it would have been impossible to apply the thirteen degrees of quadrant elevation that would have been needed without digging in the trail. In any event, the effect of round shot fired at such an exaggerated angle of elevation, and with a resulting much larger angle of descent, would have been almost negligible. Therefore, in spite of there being 14 French guns in action – including seven 8prs – it is not surprising to find Fortescue recording that their fire, though heavy, was ineffective.

The defending artillery was also not without difficulties arising from the conformation of the ground. The slope in front of the gun positions was slightly concave, so there would have been no dead ground other than that provided by its broken nature; but the guns would have been firing at an angle of sight of perhaps as much as 14 degrees of depression. It would have been difficult to apply so much depression to the Congreve block trail carriage, and it would probably have been necessary to raise the trail to get the guns to bear. A worse trouble no doubt arose from the tendency of the whole carriage to overturn backwards on firing when the recoil thrust was directed upwards. There is, indeed, a record of two of Arentschild's guns having been 'dismounted' by the French guns.[1] It is almost inconceivable that this feat could have been achieved by 8pr guns firing at 1,800 yards range. If the report is correct, it can only be regarded as one of the flukes of the battlefield. It seems likelier that these guns were overthrown by their own recoil – a much more credible explanation when they were firing at extreme depression.

Another interesting circumstance of this battle is that it was one of the first occasions on which the British artillery fired the new shrapnel shell. Its initial appearance in the Peninsula, at Rolica on 17th August 1808, had surprised the French and impressed Wellesley.[2] It could be expected to have been a useful projectile for the engagement of troops in broken ground as at Bussaco, and a Captain Guingret wrote

1. *Supplementary Dispatches of the Duke of Wellington,* 16th June 1809, to Colonel Robe.
2. Wellington's dispatches, to Liverpool, 12th March 1812, Vol. VIII, p. 658.

Below: This view of the battle of Bussaco shows the
British infantry appearing in line over the crest to meet
the French columns as they struggled up the steep slope
to be thrown back in confusion. (By permission of the
National Army Museum).

of its use there: '. . . despite the shrapnel shells that wiped out entire companies.' There is, however, a celebrated record of the British Commander-in-Chief personally examining the wounds of General Simon, who had been captured at Bussaco after having been hit by the new shell. Wellesley was disappointed at the result and described the wounds inflicted as 'very trifling'.[1] He then went on to make some penetrating remarks on the application of fire with shrapnel [2] pointing out that the shell was effective only if the fuzes were correctly set and that it was often very hard to judge whether they were so set by observing from the gun position. He thought that in many cases fire was continued with an inaccurate fuze simply because the officer directing the fire was unable to detect errors in his initial rounds. This difficulty faced gunners throughout the whole period that shrapnel shell was in service, even when observation was helped by the use of binoculars and when the fuzes were more reliable and functioned more consistently.

Even when it is admitted that shrapnel was always a somewhat fickle projectile, and in spite of the Commander's strictures, it does seem to have proved of value in this battle. It was likely to be a great deal more effective in broken ground than the round shot, which would tend to riccochet wildly, or the common shell – the bursts of which could be smothered by rocks and undergrowth.

Whatever projectile was used, the steep slope on which the battle of Bussaco was fought made the task of the Allied guns easier than that of the French; and though the defenders were not without their technical problems, the action was one in which the effect of the Allied artillery was greater than it was in many other battles of this period.

Heudelet's column is said to have taken the astonishingly short time of half an hour to climb the slope. During that time the 12 guns at the top of the pass could, in theory, have fired over 60 rounds per gun. Taking into account the usual impedences already discussed, it can be assumed that they probably fired a total of some 360 rounds.

Though all accounts stress the damaging effect of that fire, it was not in itself capable of stopping the

1. Ibid, p. 659–660.
2. *Supplementary Dispatches of the Duke of Wellington,* Vol. VI, pp. 636–639.

attack of the gallant French column. It was the muskets of the infantry that finally turned the scale, showing how the gun and the musket could best be used together in depth.

So Heudelet's attack failed, with a loss of some 300 casualties from a strength of 1,700 – a loss of 18%. The attack had been opposed by three battalions (the British 74th Foot and two Portuguese battalions) with a total of 1,500 muskets. Of these, not more than 500 could have engaged the narrow-fronted French column at any one time – allowance being made for the flanking fire that the skilful manoeuvre of units and sub-units produced on this occasion. If each group of 500 muskets fired 5 volleys during this action, with a 5% rate of effectiveness they would have caused 370 casualties.

The 360 rounds that were probably fired by the guns would have been capable of inflicting about the same number of casualties in open ground. But the unfavourable nature of the ground, which gave more cover than was usual, would have reduced the performance of both guns and muskets. In the absence of any evidence on the ratio in which casualties were caused by guns and muskets, it is impossible to offer proof; but the inference from all reports of this action is that about half of the 300 French casualties were inflicted by each weapon. This would represent a halving of the normal performance of each – attributable in these circumstances to the difficult nature of the ground.

In returning now to Merle's division, which had swung aside from the front of Lightburne's brigade and sought to gain the ridge further to the south, it is unnecessary to follow the story of the confused fighting that took place before the French were finally ejected from the ridge and driven back down the hill. There was a great deal more movement in every direction than took place in the more rigidly organised battles of the time, and the majority of Merle's 1,000 casualties were probably caused by muskets and bayonets in the hand-to-hand fighting that took place among the rocks and bushes. It should be noted that during this engagement Wellington again ordered two of Thompson's guns to occupy a particular position from which they could bring flanking fire to bear on the mêlée. Insofar as Merle's attack is concerned, it is useful to remember the way in which the fire of

two companies of riflemen and, at most, six 6pr guns turned aside the attack of a very determined French column at the beginning of the action, before they could get to grips with the defending muskets. No quantitative assessment of the results of this fire can be made, but it seems clear that the guns were making a considerable contribution to the combined casualty rate.

The attacks by Merle and Heudelet having failed, Reynier put in yet a third with Foy's brigade. The 17th Léger led with the 70th Line echeloned back on its left, both formations being in column of companies. There is a little doubt on the exact objective chosen by Foy, some accounts saying that he tried to avoid the fire of Arentschild's guns by swinging somewhat to the right. In fact, it can have made little difference: the whole of the slope leading up to the pass was swept by all the guns at a comfortable range.

Those guns took their toll once more; but again it was not enough to stop the attack, and Foy's columns pressed on to overwhelm the 8th and 9th Portuguese regiments and actually establish themselves on the summit of the ridge in a position that was a serious danger to the Allied force. Slightly earlier, however, the Duke had anticipated this danger and had ordered Major General Sir James Leith, commanding the 5th Division, to move up from the south to reinforce the troops at the head of the pass. Leith, moving ahead of his troops, found that one of Arentschild's batteries was short of ammunition and ordered one of his own 6pr batteries to take its place. Hurrying his British brigade up the road that ran along behind the crest of the Serra, he launched it into a charge that caught the triumphant French troops off balance and hurled them back down the hill. This was largely a matter of bayonet work – although the guns, the 74th Foot and the 8th Portuguese Infantry co-operated with fire from the flanks. Foy's division lost 670 men in the attack, but a large proportion became casualties during the pursuit that followed.

When allowance has been made for the several hundred casualties that must have been caused by the guns, it seems clear that the Allied small-arms must have inflicted less casualties than was usual in the battles of this time. The counter-attacking troops carried 1000 muskets, but there is a record of some controversy as to whether the attack of Leith's 9th and 38th Foot was preceded by a volley at close range or whether the charge was made with the bayonet alone. Leith's clear intention was to apply brute force to the incompletely-organised mass in front of him and start a movement down the slope that could throw the whole French column into confusion; and it would probably have been better to make the bayonet charge with the muskets loaded rather than enter the mêlée unable to fire later. This action seems certainly to have been decided more by the bayonet than the musket. At the same time, it can be noted that of the counter-attacking British battalions the 9th lost only 38 men and the 38th lost 23 men – so the French musketry must have been even less effective.

Meanwhile, on the northern flank of the battlefield, Ney – commanding the French VI Corps – was waiting to launch an attack on the convent, which he had been ordered to do as soon as Reynier's troops had established themselves on the ridge. Thinking that the movements he saw on the skyline were indications that Reynier was succeeding, he gave the order to move at about 6.30 in the morning; and the corps advanced astride the road leading from Moura to the convent enclosure. A division commanded by General Louis Loison was on the right, and one commanded by General Jean Marchand was on the left.

Before the advance began, Ney's corps artillery had started a heavy bombardment of the Allied position – again ineffective. That artillery consisted of twelve 8pr guns, six 4pr guns and six 6-inch howitzers, giving a total of 24 pieces. It had an easier task than that which had faced Reynier's guns since the ground between the two armies fell far less steeply and the selection of gun positions would have been a great deal easier. Unfortunately, there seems to be no exact record of where these French guns were brought into action apart from a rather unsatisfactory sketch in Alison's *Atlas* that puts them about 1,000 yards from their objective. Wherever they were, however, they would not have had to fire at any extreme elevation; but the steepness of the slope near the target would have diminished the effect of their shot. All accounts agree that the fire was ineffective, the most likely cause being that they were firing at extreme range.

The Allied artillery, on the other hand, was extremely well sited; and the direction of the Commander-in-Chief can be discerned in this matter. Unger shows I Troop, Royal Horse Artillery, under Captain Robert Bull, as considerably displaced to a flank where it would have been out of range of the action that followed, but A Troop, Royal Horse Artillery, under Captain Hew Ross, Cleeves' battery, a Portugese battery and a battery under Captain Lawson – each armed with six 6pr guns – would have been able to cover the approaches to the convent not only by frontal fire but also by most effective fire in enfilade. The Allied artillery was very much better placed to provide effective fire on the area in which the two infantries were about to meet than was the French.

The assaults on the heights round the convent, made first by Loison's division and then by Marchand's, followed exactly the same pattern. The French columns were preceded by a large number of skirmishers, and as soon as these appeared the Allied force pushed forward its own light companies – here numbering about a thousand men – to delay the French advance as much as possible, though it was unlikely that they could stop it. Meanwhile, the Allied artillery sought to inflict such casualties as it could, although the mixing of the skirmishers of both sides must have made it risky to shoot into their midst. In fact, the artillery would normally have been shooting at the massed infantry columns that were following the skirmishers. On this occasion, Loison's skirmishers had a brisk bout of street fighting in the hamlet of Sula and eventually captured it, pressing on until they reached a position just below the crest from which their following infantry would make their final assault. It was then that the Allied infantry, so far sheltering behind the crest, rose to its feet and delivered a devastating charge that carried all before it. The effect of that charge was increased not only by the temporary exhaustion of troops who had just climbed a steep hill but also by the fact that the French column, on its narrow front, was deficient in firepower. It was the official French policy to deploy into line for these final assaults, but the attempt to do so in the confusion of battle nearly always led to difficulty in meeting an immediate counter-attack by fresh troops.

So both of Ney's two leading divisions recoiled from the ridge and accepted defeat; and a reinforcing brigade, under General Marcognet, that tried to support Marchand's halted front line was actually prevented from moving forward by the fire of the Allied guns alone. Loison's division suffered 1,255 casualties and Marchand's 1,173 for the loss of under 500 Allied troops. The French losses were caused firstly by the fire of 24 Allied guns, then by three volleys fired by the 52nd and 43rd as they counter-attacked from behind the crest, and lastly as the result of hand-to-hand fighting during the pursuit down the hill. The three volleys contained a potential total of 3,000 bullets of which, at that very short range, it might be reasonable to assume some 300 hits. Perhaps as many as half the total 2,400 casualties were brought about during the pursuit, but it certainly seems that a very large number – perhaps as many as 1,000 – were inflicted by the guns. If those guns were in action for half an hour they could probably have fired some 700 rounds, and it may well be that the expenditure of ammunition was appreciably lower. It does seem possible to assert with some confidence, however, that both the guns and the muskets were operating at a higher degree of effectiveness than has been shown to be normal in the other engagements described.

The first general feature of the battle of Bussaco that attracts attention is the wide disparity in the number of casualties suffered by the two forces. A force of 26,000 French soldiers lost 4,480 of its number, and an Allied force of 17,800 lost 1,252 men. Was this solely due to superior firepower, or did some other factors affect the issue?

The nature of the ground undoubtedly had a great effect. Brave and determined though the French troops were, they arrived at their objective under considerable physical stress as a result of their climb of 1,000 feet over broken ground. The Allied counter-attacks were delivered by fresh troops with the force of gravity in their favour; and once a determined and initially successful counter-attack had begun and had attained impetus, the deep French column tended to be thrown into confusion that became chaos as the struggling mass was forced down the steep slope. It seems clear that in this battle a very large proportion of the casualties were caused by the bayonet in hand-to-hand fighting.

The battle provides several instances of the difficulty of completely stopping an attack by fire alone. The plain fact is that the slow rate of fire of smooth-bore weapons of all kinds, coupled with the inefficiencies already discussed, made it difficult to produce a sufficient volume of effective fire to halt determined troops. This does not mean that a daunting toll could not be taken of an enemy. On the occasion of each separate attack during this battle, the effect of a larger number of supporting guns than was usual in the battles of the Peninsular war was most marked.

It has been shown that the support provided by the French artillery was almost entirely ineffective as a result of the difficulty in finding suitable gun positions. The Allied guns, however, were not only admirably sited but were also available at the decisive points in larger numbers than was usually found. After the battle there was some criticism of Wellington's failure to concentrate his artillery to a greater extent than he did. But it is difficult to see how a better initial distribution of the artillery could have been devised to defend a ridge ten miles long; and it has been shown that guns were moved on several occasions to improve the fire support as the battle developed. It is true that there was no battery of guns of position, but the nature of the ground made it impossible to establish one. Furthermore, the nature of the fighting – a succession of small battles on narrow frontages – made it far more important to use the guns in close support as extensions of the range of the infantry's small-arms. That task appears to have been carried out with more effect than usual, and the story of Bussaco suggests that the casualty rate inflicted by the guns may well have been appreciably higher than the average of one casualty per round fired that has been seen elsewhere.

The effect of musketry is even harder to determine in this battle than in others. However, the general impression gained is that in the battle as a whole not more than 5% – and sometimes less – of the bullets fired were effective but that this figure may have risen to 10% under favourable circumstances at close range.

9. Ferozeshah and the Sikh Wars

The battle of Ferozeshah in the first Sikh war, concerning which there is an exact record of the positions and moves of all arms, was one in which the Bengal Army was on the offensive; and the tactics employed were appreciably different from those used in the Napoleonic wars.

In the wars of the 1840s, the Bengal Army of the Honourable East India Company was opposed first by the Mahratta army of Gwalior in 1843 and then by the army of the Sikhs in 1845–6 and 1848–9. Both armies were not only numerically superior to the Company's forces but also well disciplined, well trained, well equipped and possessed of fanatical courage in all but the last stages of defeat. In these campaigns – and, indeed, in all the previous ones in which the Company's armies had become involved in order to secure its interests – it had been consistently proved that the best tactic was always that of the boldest possible offensive, using the few British troops that were usually available to provide an example to the Indian soldiers supporting them. General Sir Hugh Gough, who commanded the Bengal Army in the Gwalior and in both Sikh wars and was in direct command in six of the eight major battles that were fought in them (becoming Lord Gough after the first Sikh war), was a firm believer in getting to grips with the enemy with as little delay as possible. Consequently, although there were variations in the amount and quality of the preparations made for each of the attacks and a corresponding difference in the losses incurred during them, all of the battles took the form of an all-out attack by the Bengal force.

The artilleries of the Company's enemies were well armed with ordnance made to very high standards by Indian gunmakers. As a weapon, the gun was held in high esteem by Indian soldiers; and their artillery units were well and most courageously manned and competently directed. On the field of battle, the Mahratta and Sikh artilleries – apart from their numerical superiority – had pieces that were generally heavier and discharged a heavier weight of metal to longer ranges than the Company's. The resulting disparity in the amount of artillery support available to both sides therefore forced the Bengal Army to devote very much more attention to counter-battery work than was carried out in the Peninsula.

That such counter-battery tasks were necessary became evident in the first battle in the series, at Maharajpur. There it was clear that it was highly undesirable to launch infantry over open ground without first subduing the defending guns and preventing them from taking a heavy toll of the attackers with their devastating salvoes of case shot.

Another difference between the Indian battles and those of the Napoleonic wars already described – and this is connected with counter-battery fire – was that it was the normal custom of the Bengal Army to take into the field what was called heavy field artillery. Armed with iron 18pr guns and 8-inch howitzers, it was not usually provided on a large scale and its movements were slower than those of the light artillery – the impetuous General Gough finding himself unable to wait for its arrival in some of the earlier battles – but it was able to play a considerable part in the subjugation of the enemy's powerful artillery.

A further peculiarity of the wars in India was the extensive use of entrenchments and field works by the Mahrattas and the Sikhs. Indian villages were normally walled and capable of defence against marauders; for although the walls were usually made of mud, they gave complete protection from view and often provided appreciable resistance to bullets and small shot. Villages were therefore often used as strong-points in defensive positions, as at Maharajpur. The Sikhs, for their part, were fond of occupying what were called entrenchments – easy to construct in the soft alluvial soil of the Punjab and also giving much protection against small projectiles.

These conditions were somewhat different from those that had obtained in the Peninsula, so the battles fought under them naturally tell a rather different story. All of the battles give a great deal of information about the effects of firepower, and at least one other than Ferozeshah is mentioned to illustrate various points. But Ferozeshah – the second battle of the first Sikh war – is the one yielding the most complete information on the positions of the troops and it is therefore the first to be described.

After the death of the great Ranjit Singh, who had ruled the Punjab with stability for thirty years, the Sikh kingdom was torn with internal strife and its powerful army sought to rule the state. Up to that time the Sikh kingdom had maintained friendly

This contemporary print of the opening stages of the battle of Chillianwala in the second Sikh war gives a good idea of the way in which the great line of battle of the Bengal Army was formed. The infantry battalions can be seen in line, their colours marking the centre of each unit. The Horse Artillery and Field Artillery, not yet in action, are moving forward on the flanks of formations and in the intervals between them. Heavy artillery armed with iron 18pr guns appears in the foreground; but it took little part in this battle as the enemy was concealed in the jungle, which is seen in the distance. This was not the most successful of General Gough's battles. The wooded nature of the country and the impetuosity with which the attack was delivered, without effective artillery support, led to confusion and heavy casualties.

relations with the East India Company and had, indeed, provided a reliable buffer state on its northwest frontier. Now, however, the kingdom's less reputable elements saw profit in attacking the Company, and its weak nominal rulers sought to stabilise their position by giving the army its head and supporting an invasion of the Company's neighbouring territory.

This danger had been foreseen, but the Governor General was most reluctant to take any step that might precipitate a war, and military preparations were somewhat retarded as a result. Nevertheless, a suitable proportion of the Bengal Army was eventually mobilised and moved up towards the frontier that ran along the river Sutlej. Meanwhile, the small garrison of the frontier post at Ferozepur made a bold show despite its obvious weakness.

The Bengal Army had a long way to march from its cantonments down-country, and it arrived at the scene of operations in instalments. But Sir Hugh Gough was naturally concerned to seize the initiative and relieve the garrison of Ferozepur, so he pressed forward with as much of his army as had managed to arrive. He met part of the Sikh forces at Mudki; and there, in a late evening battle, he discomfited them sufficiently to cause them to withdraw on their main prepared position near Ferozeshah.

It is worth looking now at the conditions under which the Bengal Army was operating. Its units had been hurriedly thrown together into formations in which they had not worked before. In many cases, commanders were unknown to their subordinates and the staffs were not used to working together. Most units had made a series of forced marches over long distances from their peacetime stations. The army had started on the last stage before Mudki early in the morning without any breakfast, and it had marched all day in great heat and clouds of choking dust. It had bivouacked and started to cook its first meal since the previous evening when the alarm was raised and a great dust cloud rising above the surrounding jungle showed that part of the Sikh army was bearing down on it. Within moments, orderlies were galloping through the camp shouting 'Tayari ka hukm hai' ('Take post' or 'Prepare to move') – and the already exhausted men and horses were plunged into battle without food, water or rest.

Some accounts of these battles suggest that the Indian sepoys showed a tendency to hold back in action, and it is probably true that they were a little apprehensive in fighting such formidable enemies as the Sikhs. But it is also fair to remember that the Indian soldier did not have the physique of the European: under physical trials as severe as were imposed on this army, the sepoy might well have been expected to feel the strain.

The day after the battle of Mudki was spent in resting and tending the wounded. Some reinforcements reached the army, including a pair of 8-inch howitzers as heavy field artillery. Ammunition was replenished and men and horses were, at least, fed. But no more rest could be allowed, and on 21st December the Bengal Army moved forward again to attack the main Sikh position at Ferozeshah.

Two Sikh armies were in the field. One, under the command of Sardar Tej Singh, was containing the garrison of Ferozepur. The other, commanded by Sardar Lal Singh, was holding the entrenched position at Ferozeshah. Lal Singh's force, consisting of 17,000 infantry and cavalry, was holding a perimeter that was oval in shape.

A contemporary sketch map drawn immediately after the battle by Captain C. R. Sackville-West of the 62nd Foot, one of the Commander-in-Chief's ADCs, is reproduced as map O. Much of the following account is based on the information given in it, but as it covers all the movements made during the two days of the battle it is a little difficult to grasp in its original form. Simplified sketches on a rather larger scale are therefore provided to illustrate later parts of the text.

Very detailed information regarding the Sikh armies is contained in a modern work, *The Military System of the Sikhs* by Fauja Singh Bajwa, from which it appears that in 1845 the Sikh Army possessed a total of 381 field guns and 104 garrison guns, howitzers and mortars. A high proportion of the field guns could be expected to have been in support of the field army. A large number of different calibres were used, and these were nearly always slightly larger than those of the corresponding British equipments. Moreover, as previously noted, the Sikh pieces were generally heavier – which meant that they could use heavier charges and thus range farther than the

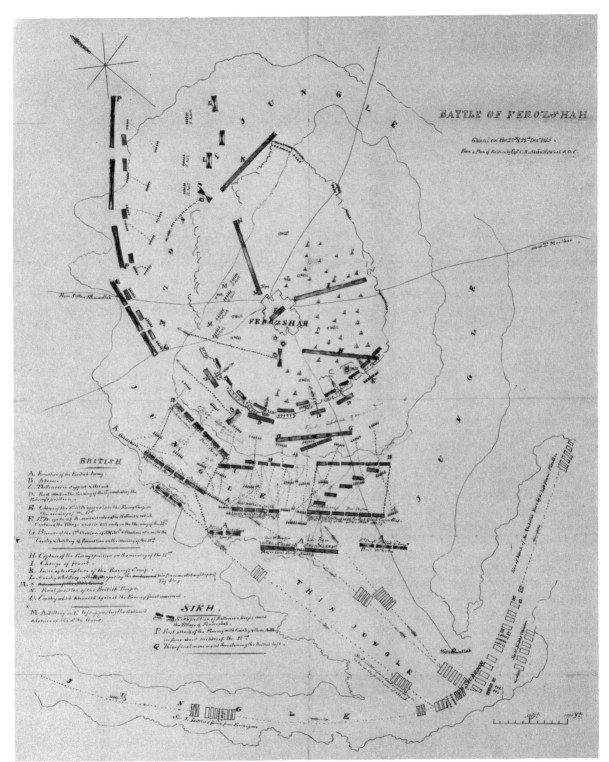

Map O: The Battle of Ferozeshah, 21st–22nd December 1845. This sketch map, which is reproduced by kind permission of the owners – the Trustees of the Museum of the Wiltshire Regiment (previously HM 62nd Foot) – was drawn by Captain C. R. Sackville-West, 62nd Foot, who was acting as A.D.C. during the battle of Ferozeshah. It is not entirely easy to follow since it shows all the movements made during both of the days on which the battle was fought. But it provides valuable evidence on a number of points concerning the battle, though it is more probable that Littler's Division was on a one-brigade front.

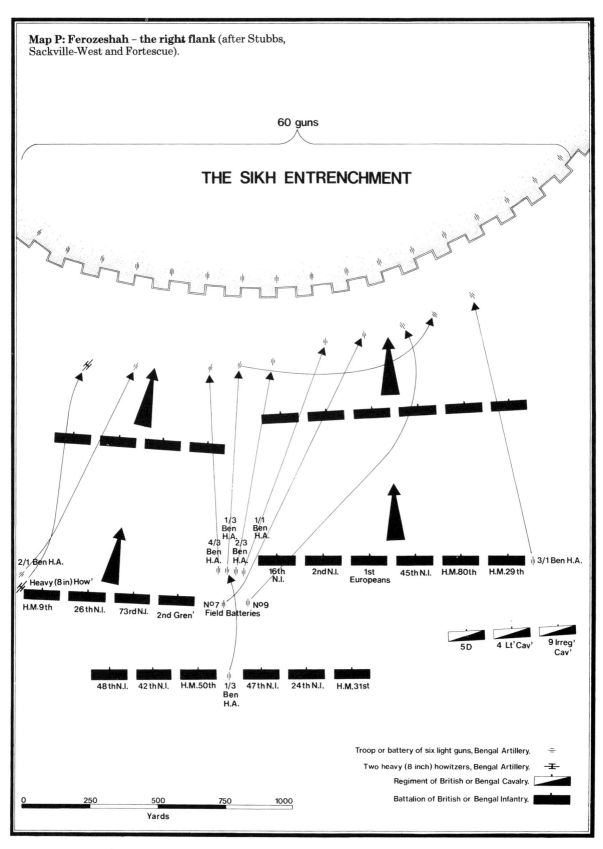

Map P: Ferozeshah – the right flank (after Stubbs, Sackville-West and Fortescue).

60 guns

THE SIKH ENTRENCHMENT

1/3 Ben H.A.

1/1 Ben H.A.

4/3 Ben H.A. 2/3 Ben H.A.

2/1 Ben H.A.

Heavy (8 in) How'

H.M.9th   26th N.I.   73rd N.I.   2nd Gren'

Nº7   Nº9
Field Batteries

16th N.I.   2nd N.I.   1st Europeans   45th N.I.   H.M.80th   H.M.29th   3/1 Ben H.A.

5D   4 Lt'Cav'   9 Irreg' Cav'

48th N.I.   42th N.I.   H.M.50th   1/3 Ben H.A.   47th N.I.   24th N.I.   H.M.31st

Troop or battery of six light guns, Bengal Artillery.
Two heavy (8 inch) howitzers, Bengal Artillery.
Regiment of British or Bengal Cavalry.
Battalion of British or Bengal Infantry.

0   250   500   750   1000
Yards

guns of the Bengal army. This is confirmed by an album of drawings of Sikh ordnance captured during the first Sikh war and now in the library of the Royal Artillery Institution. It shows a total of 261 pieces, all of which are distinctly heavier than the corresponding British/Indian equipments.

Stubbs records that 68 guns, 3 howitzers and 2 mortars were captured at Ferozeshah. Buckle estimates the number of guns in action as 'above 100'. It therefore seems likely that the Sikhs were supported by at least 120 guns at Ferozeshah. And those guns were undoubtedly distributed in batteries of about six or eight guns spaced evenly over the frontage of attack. The total frontage held – and attacked – was about 3,000 yards, so there was one gun to every 25 yards of frontage. This was formidable firepower from which the assaulting infantry would suffer severely over the last few hundred yards in front of their objective unless the Bengal artillery could develop effective counter-battery fire.

On 20th December Sir Hugh sent orders to Major General Sir John Littler, commanding the garrison of Ferozepur, to march out on the following day to join the main army. Littler did so – leaving his piquets in position and thereby deluding Tej Singh into continuing to watch the deserted garrison – and formed up on the left of the Bengal Army. His division consisted of two brigades, each of three battalions of which only one was British (His Majesty's 62nd Foot). All six battalions were formed in line, two deep, each covering a frontage of about 150 yards. Sackville-West's map shows the two brigades in line side by side; but both Stubbs and Fortescue state that the attack was made on a one-brigade front – Colonel Thomas Reed's brigade, which contained the British battalion, leading – and that Lieutenant Colonel the Hon. Thomas Ashburnham's brigade, in support, took no part in the attack. The noteworthy point is that the attack was made on a very narrow front, and this was accentuated by the 62nd pressing forward in advance of the two Indian battalions.

The attack was supported by two six-gun troops of the Bengal Horse Artillery (5/1 and 3/3), each armed with five light 6pr guns and one 12pr howitzer, and by one and a half batteries of field artillery armed with 9pr guns and 24pr howitzers – the other half battery having been left in Ferozepur. According to Stubbs,

the whole field battery – which was drawn by bullocks – seems to have failed to keep up with the advance.

The Bengal Army deployed its artillery in two ways, the object in both cases being to provide as continuous support as possible taking into account that initial gun positions would be too far from the objective to permit the most effective fire and that the guns could not fire through or over their own infantry. In this instance, the attack being made on a narrow front, the artillery moved on the flanks of the infantry line and occupied a succession of positions until the guns were finally in action within 250 yards of the objective in positions from which they could continue to fire across the front of the infantry until the last possible moment. (The alternative method of deployment was carried out in the second phase of this battle.)

There are some discrepancies between the layout of units shown in map O and those given by Stubbs, and it is probably safer to follow Stubbs' description of the actions and locations of the artillery since he was himself a gunner. The two troops of Horse Artillery certainly bounded forward, one on each flank, as was their normal drill – all moves being carried out at the gallop – their main object being to get into point-blank range as quickly as possible. The half field battery seems to have followed the right-hand horse artillery troop, though it could not move so fast. As General Stubbs put it, 'Captains Campbell and Day with their Troops went rapidly forward to cover the advance; opening a cross-fire at intermediate distances, at first with round shot, then with grape (sic).[1] till about 200 yards from the enemy, where they kept it up till the infantry got too close.'

It seems that in these attacks on Indian enemies it was not the custom to engage them with small-arms fire but rather to get to close quarters with the bayonet as quickly as possible. The fire support of the artillery was therefore of particular importance. Map P shows the artillery firepower available to both sides in this battle, and it will be seen that that of the attackers was markedly inferior to that of the defence even on a basis of the relative number of guns. When it is remembered that the Sikh guns were generally heavier than those of the Bengal light artillery and that they were entrenched in such a way that the

1. It was probably case shot.

little 6pr shot could do little damage to them, the disparity becomes more marked. Nevertheless, Buckle records that the Bengal guns 'had for a time completely silenced the batteries opposite to them'.

This was, indeed, a common occurrence in the warfare of those times. Under effective preliminary bombardment, the detachments of the defending guns would be withdrawn under cover, creating the impression that they had been silenced. Light shot would have done little or no damage to the equipments themselves, however. As soon as the fire of the attacking artillery was masked by the advance of their infantry, the gun detachments of the defenders would take post again and be able to fire those few killing salvoes of case during the last hundred yards of the assault.

That is exactly what happened on this occasion. Concentrating their fire on the one British battalion, the Sikhs inflicted 260 casualties and the attack failed.

Meanwhile, somewhat belatedly, the remainder of the Bengal Army was preparing to assault the eastern half of the Sikh position. This attack was made by nine battalions in first line, as shown in map Q; but here the artillery was deployed somewhat differently from Littler's division in a way better suited to the support of a large force deployed on a wide front than moving the guns on the flanks of infantry formations.

The method was as follows. As the infantry formed its line of battle at 1,500 yards or more from its objective, the whole of the artillery would be sent forward to come into action in a great line within long range of the enemy's guns. From there, it would engage the enemy's gun positions with round shot and shrapnel while the infantry moved up behind the guns. As the advancing line approached the gun positions, the guns would be limbered up and moved forward to a second line of positions closer to the enemy. This process would be continued until the guns were often within 200 yards of the objective, their fire becoming more effective as the range was shortened. When the advancing infantry masked the frontal fire of the guns, some would usually be pushed out to the flanks to positions from which they could continue to fire on the objective in enfilade.

The fire plan to support this attack is shown in map Q, upon which the fire support provided by the 8-inch howitzers – which eventually got within 400 yards of the objective – can be noted. It will be seen, too, that the disparity between the gunpower of both sides was considerably less than in the case of Littler's attack. This was not only because there was more Bengal artillery supporting this attack but also because Littler's attack, made prematurely on a narrow front, attracted the fire of at least a third if not nearly a half of the Sikh artillery. The subsequent attack, made on twice the frontage, faced a diluted concentration of not more than half the Sikh guns.

The battle did not begin until 3.30 p.m. on the shortest day of the year, and darkness, smoke and confusion brought it to an end by 4.30 p.m. – but not before the infantry had broken into the Sikh entrenchments and the famous charge of the 5th Light Dragoons into the Sikh camp itself had added to the discomfiture of the enemy. What took place on the following day, when the remnants of the Sikh army were finally dispersed, does not need to be detailed here since the events of the 21st provide so much information in themselves on the effects of firepower. It is clear that Littler's attack – made in advance of that of the rest of the force, on a narrow front and with inadequate artillery support – received the full weight of nearly half the Sikh artillery and suffered intolerable casualties as a result. This attack, incidentally, was renewed later by His Majesty's 9th Foot in conjunction with the advance of the rest of the force and with no stronger artillery support; and it succeeded, though with even more casualties. On that occasion, however, some of the effort of the defending artillery was distracted to deal with the remainder of the Bengal attack.

It has been shown that the fire support provided for the main attack on the right was comparable, at least in the number of guns employed, to that of the defenders. Furthermore, the attack was made on a broad front and the Sikh artillery was therefore forced to distribute its fire and reduce the concentration that could be applied to any one unit.

It is not easy to produce a quantitative estimate of the results of firepower at Ferozeshah. During the two attacks on the left (by His Majesty's 62nd and 9th Foot) 540 casualties were inflicted by, say, 50 Sikh guns. At first sight, this does not seem a very high figure; but it must be remembered that the two at-

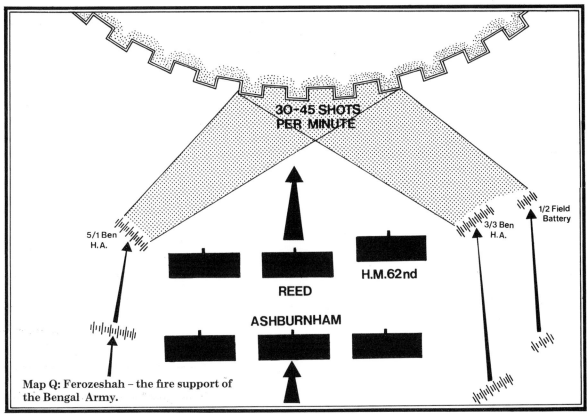

30-45 SHOTS
PER MINUTE

5/1 Ben
H.A.

3/3 Ben
H.A.

1/2 Field
Battery

H.M. 62nd

REED

ASHBURNHAM

Map Q: Ferozeshah – the fire support of
the Bengal Army.

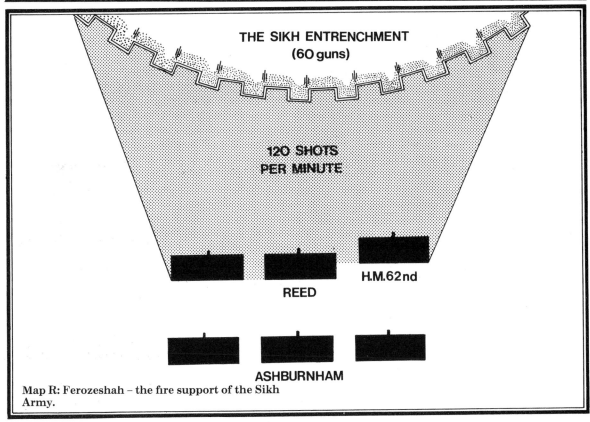

THE SIKH ENTRENCHMENT
(60 guns)

120 SHOTS
PER MINUTE

H.M. 62nd

REED

ASHBURNHAM

Map R: Ferozeshah – the fire support of the Sikh
Army.

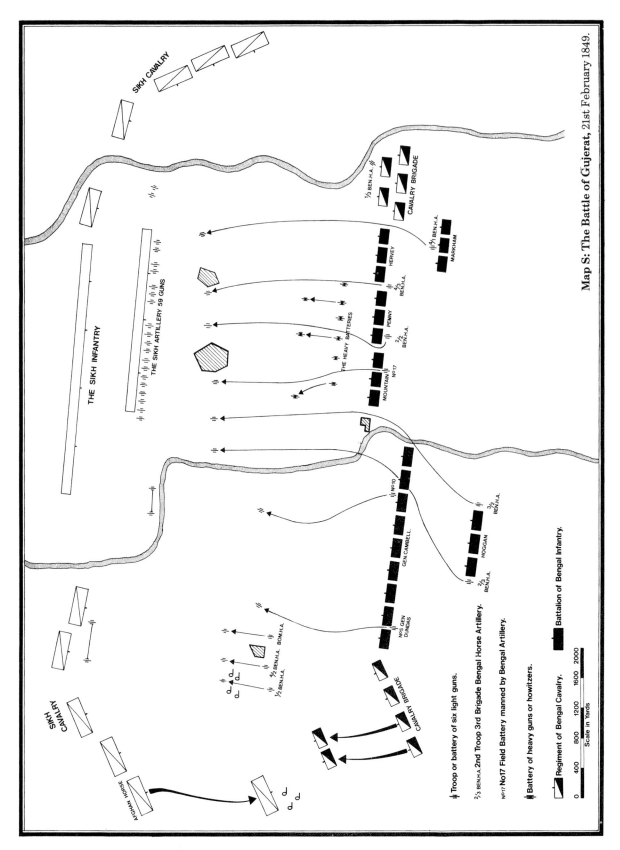

SIKH CAVALRY

SIKH CAVALRY

THE SIKH INFANTRY

THE SIKH ARTILLERY 59 GUNS

HERVEY

MARKHAM

⅓ BEN.H.A.

CAVALRY BRIGADE

¼/21 BEN.H.A.

4/3 BEN.H.A.

PENNY

2/2 BEN.H.A.

THE HEAVY BATTERIES

MOUNTAIN
Nº17

Nº10

3/2 BEN.H.A.

GEN CAMBELL.

HOGGAN

2/3 BEN.H.A.

Nº5 GEN DUNDAS

½ BEN.H.A. BOM.H.A.

⅓ BEN.H.A.

½ BEN.H.A.

CAVALRY BRIGADE

CAVALRY BRIGADE

SIKH CAVALRY

AFGHAN HORSE

Map S: The Battle of Gujerat, 21st February 1849.

⫶ Troop or battery of six light guns.

⅔ BEN.H.A. 2nd Troop 3rd Brigade Bengal Horse Artillery.

Nº17 Nº17 Field Battery manned by Bengal Artillery.

⫴ Battery of heavy guns or howitzers.

▨ Regiment of Bengal Cavalry.

■ Battalion of Bengal Infantry.

Scale in Yards

0   400   800   1200   1600   2000

tacks could not have exposed the infantry to fire for more than a total of about half an hour, and there must have been considerable obscuration of view by smoke and dust during much of that period. In any event, the infliction of nearly 50% casualties on an attacking unit cannot be regarded as a mean performance.

Nevertheless, the overall performance of the powerful Sikh artillery seems to have been disappointing. The Bengal Army suffered 2,415 casualties during the fighting on the 21st and 22nd, a proportion of which were inflicted by muskets and bayonets – leaving a very low figure attributable to over a hundred guns. Stubbs and certain other sources suggest that the laying of the Sikh guns was not accurate at long range; and there is little doubt that the majority of the casualties were caused at short or point-blank range, when less accurate laying was called for. In this connection, it is interesting to note that in trying to subdue the Sikh artillery the Bengal artillery suffered 213 casualties among the men and no less than 323 among the horses. This represents about 18% of men and 19% of horses. Losses among horses were partly the result of teams remaining on the gun position during action instead of being withdrawn to covered wagon lines. These comparatively heavy artillery casualties arose largely because, in the earlier battles of these wars, the artillery tended to push right forward into musketry range of the enemy. In later battles it was found that no less effective support could be provided, with less casualties among gunners, if the most forward gun positions were kept outside the range of the enemy's small-arms fire but still at short range for the guns.

Ferozeshah is also of interest because it was one of the few battles in which the artillery ran out of ammunition – although that did not take place until the second day of the fighting. Indeed, it would be surprising if there had been a shortage of ammunition after a battle on the 21st that lasted for not more than an hour. The trouble arose, however, from the destruction of at least 500 rounds of ammunition when whole wagons were blown up during the close-range confusion of that evening's fighting; for the Sikhs had left a quantity of loose powder lying about in their entrenchment and the ignition of this increased the risk to the wagons, whose highly explosive contents were always vulnerable in battle.

Ferozeshah has been described in order to take advantage of the sketch map reproduced. It was only the second battle in the two Sikh wars, and it was one which Sir Hugh was forced to fight before the whole army – and particularly its supporting artillery – had been fully concentrated. Hence there was less careful preparation, especially regarding artillery support, than appeared in his later battles. And there was a tendency on the part of the whole army to rush forward into close contact and suffer unnecessary casualties as a result. It is therefore worth while examining the last of this series of actions, in which the tactics of the period may be expected – with justification – to have been perfected.

The battle of Gujerat, fought on 21st February 1849, was the crowning victory of the second Sikh war. Once again the Sikhs occupied an entrenched position, as is shown in map S, this time held by 60,000 infantry and cavalry with 59 guns in support. The Bengal Army was to attack in two great lines on a frontage of nearly three miles over country that was open and unobstructed and presented no difficulty in maintaining the direction and alignment of the whole force. But before the infantry was launched to the assault, a carefully designed plan of artillery preparation was put into effect. And never before in India – even at Sobraon, final victory of the first Sikh war – had such powerful and well directed artillery been used to prepare the way for the other arms.

The first move was to establish a large battery of heavy guns and howitzers opposite the centre of the Sikh position and about 1200 yards from it. It consisted of ten 18pr guns and ten 8-inch howitzers and its fire was distributed carefully over the front, directed and corrected by artillery commanders observing from near the gun positions. At the same time, the whole of the light artillery of the force came into action rather further forward and added its fire to the bombardment. There were thus 10 heavy guns, 10 heavy howitzers and 66 light guns and howitzers taking part in a single fire plan; and they were all controlled by a continuous chain of command so that the fire plan could be adjusted to suit the needs of the moment. The artillery plan also allowed for the allocation of two troops or batteries of light artillery to each infantry division or cavalry brigade during the ultimate assault of the objective.

The preliminary bombardment was carried out for three hours, from 9.0 a.m. until noon. And unlike the fire plans in other battles, the presence of the heavy guns and howitzers enabled this one not only to neutralise the enemy's gun positions but also to damage and destroy the equipments.

An interesting example of the way in which opportunities could be seized within this fire plan is mentioned by Fortescue. There were two troops of Bengal Horse Artillery not allotted in support of any particular infantry or cavalry formation but held in reserve. They took part in the fire plan with the rest; but while it was in progress, the artillery commander saw that to move them to a position well forward in the left-centre of the battlefield would enable them to enfilade a Sikh battery that was proving difficult to subdue. The two troops were 2/3 and 3/2 Bengal Horse Artillery, and their forward position is shown on map S.

At midday the great line of battle moved smoothly forward, and as it approached its supporting gun positions the guns also moved forward and eventually reached a line of positions about 400 yards from the objective. It was during the final advance of the infantry that the only check occurred. There were two small villages – Bara Kalra and Chota Kalra, six hundred to eight hundred yards in advance of the Sikhs' position – that had not been included as targets during the preliminary bombardment. These were found to be held by determined infantry whose small-arms fire enfiladed the advancing infantry and the Horse Artillery troops as they pushed forward in support. This unexpected resistance caused the only serious losses to the attackers; but the combined action of gunners and infantry cleared the outposts and the whole line swept into the Sikh position, many infantry units not having to fire a shot. As Fortescue wrote: 'The general advance of the infantry turned the retreat of the Sikhs into a flight. They were throughly routed as they had not been since Aliwal, and, throwing away their arms, they dispersed in every direction.'

There is no doubt that this final defeat of the Sikh Army, with the loss of all its guns at the expense of so few casualties in the Bengal Army, was mainly due to the effective use that was made of a really powerful and well handled force of artillery. This was specifi-

cally stated by Lord Hardinge – Governor General during the first Sikh war – in his report in the House of Lords on 24th April 1849 in which he said '. . . so effectually had this arm of the service' (that is, the artillery) 'been employed, that the Sikh artillery, though managed as usual with great bravery, was, notwithstanding all their efforts, perfectly silenced; so that it was not necessary for the British infantry to fire in line, with the exception of two regiments of Europeans and four regiments of Native Infantry. With the exception of those regiments, not a regiment of infantry fired a musket shot, so considerable was the service rendered by the Indian artillery.'

It is interesting to compare this successful use of artillery with the ways in which it was used, similarly but not always so successfully, 66 years later during the war of 1914–18. In both cases, the aim was that of neutralising the weapons of the defender so that the infantry could occupy the objective. This tactic failed in the later war when the defender occupied a position in great depth and was well protected by field works and obstacles. At Gujerat, the Sikhs' position had little or no depth; and having received the full force of the artillery bombardment, all arms became incapable of resistance. It will be noted, however, that the unexpected resistance offered by the two village outposts that had not been neutralised was similar to that which the unsubdued machine-gun so often presented in 1914–18, to the discomfiture of the attacker.

Two further points concerning the battle of Gujerat are of interest in an assessment of the artillery firepower of that time. The first is that the complete subjugation of a powerful force of courageously and efficiently manned artillery – to say nothing of the infantry's defences behind it – was effected for the expenditure of 4,917 rounds from 72 guns. According to the Madras Records, the actual expenditure of each nature of equipment was:

30 6pr guns	2,019 shot	265 shrapnel	63 case
24 9pr guns	997 shot	220 shrapnel	31 case
6 12pr howitzers	87 common	167 shrapnel	0 case
6 24pr howitzers	69 common	106 shrapnel	8 case
10 18pr guns	539 shot	265 shrapnel	0 case
10 8-in howitzers	160 common	100 shrapnel	0 case

This gave the following remarkably small figures of expenditure of ammunition considered in the light of the destruction achieved:

6pr gun	77 rounds per gun
9pr gun	52 rounds per gun
12pr howitzers	42 rounds per gun
24pr howitzers	60 rounds per gun
18pr gun	58 rounds per gun
8-in howitzers	26 rounds per gun

It seems quite clear that this fire must have been most efficiently directed and applied.

The second interesting point is that this fire was spread over a period of $2\frac{1}{2}$ hours (Stubbs) or 3 hours (Fortescue). The main impedence to fire would presumably have been caused by smoke; and whether it was from that cause or because the fire was being applied very deliberately – or both – the overall rate of fire was about a quarter of the normal intense rate.

Conclusion

Firepower is a subject on which there is a dearth of the fully-established data that leads scientific study to uncontroversial conclusions. There has to be, of necessity, a great deal of speculation and a certain amount of guesswork – although in this book care has been taken to differentiate between assumption and established fact.

It is felt, however, that what emerges here is a pattern that can be seen to have run through the whole of the smooth-bore period – small pieces of evidence from a number of battles combining to give a consistent picture of the performance of smooth-bore weapons. And it is contended that the battle performances described are reasonably related to the theoretical capabilities of the weapons on which evidence is extensive and reliable. As always when the stories of battles are told, many unexpected and unpredictable factors are found to have arisen; but the determination of what must really have happened is often helped by the invocation of what the late Colonel Alfred Burne called 'the inherent military probability' in a particular situation.

If there is a weak point in many of the calculations made, it lies in the estimate of the number of volleys, salvoes or rounds fired in the engagement under consideration. In most cases it is possible to be certain of the maximum amount of fire that could have been applied, and so the minimum standard of effectiveness can be deduced. But it is often impossible to determine the lesser amount that may well have been fired, which would naturally have raised the standard of performance.

Thus it is usually possible to decide the average number of casualties caused by each weapon overall – and such figures can be taken as reliable; but the figures indicating the percentage of rounds ordered to be fired that were effective cannot be so well authenticated when the total number of rounds fired is in doubt.

It is quite clear that the effectiveness of any smooth-bore weapon firing an unstabilised projectile deteriorated with increasing rapidity as the range became longer. With the musket, that failing became noticeable beyond 100 yards; and with the guns it was apparent beyond about 800 yards – at which range there also began to be difficulties in laying on the small targets presented by men observed over coarse open sights. Yet the temptation to order fire at the longer ranges – and, even more, for soldiers to fire without orders – must often have been irresistible, particularly near the maximum effective range.

In an attempt to provide a constant datum, account was taken of only those muskets that were within 200 yards of their target. There is strong support for the assumption that this was the range beyond which the musket was making no real contribution to the firepower of a force. And it will no doubt have been noted that a considerably higher figure of effectiveness was attained on the occasions when a known amount of fire was applied at much shorter ranges only. It can therefore be concluded that there was a belt of a depth of between 30 yards and perhaps as much as 100 yards within which the musket could develop its maximum effect, and that from a range of 100 yards to 200 yards it was capable only of rapidly diminishing results. The same pattern can be seen in the case of artillery, but with correspondingly longer ranges.

All of this brings out the fact that, in the days of short-ranged weapons with a low rate of fire, the exact placing of the weapons and the timing of their use was of supreme importance. And it was in those respects that inspired command and leadership could convert what would otherwise have been an inconclusive slogging-match into victory. The skilful siting and movement of the outnumbered Allied guns and Wellington's quick perception and readjustment of the broken firing line at Talavera; the placing of Hawker's guns at Albuera; Wellington's anticipation of the lines of the French attacks at Bussaco and his movement of the defensive armament to counter them; the iron discipline that controlled, and the skill that directed, the musket fire of the eighteenth century; the careful and deliberate direction of the fire of the guns at Gujerat: all of these show that the outcome of a battle depended to a very considerable extent on the skill with which commanders placed and moved their firearms rather than allowing them to blunder into battle.

As far as smooth-bore small-arms are concerned, it does appear that the flintlock musket was a most inefficient weapon throughout the whole of its life from the middle of the seventeenth century to the middle of the nineteenth century. Some of that inefficiency was no doubt due to the faults of the firer; but by far the greater blame must be laid on the weapon itself, which was clumsy, unreliable and inaccurate even within its very limited range. In the middle of the eighteenth century, under the most favourable circumstances, in the hands of small numbers of highly skilled and well disciplined infantry and at very short range, it seems that perhaps 20% of the shots ordered to be fired caused casualties. Between 15% and 25% of the shots apparently misfired, and at least half of those that left the muzzle failed to reach their mark through a combination of inefficient distribution of fire, inaccurate aiming and, to the greatest extent of all, the eccentricity of the bullet.

How, then, can such low figures of effectiveness be reconciled with battle stories that so often describe one side firing its tremendous first volley and the whole of the opposing front rank falling before the storm? On the face of it, it seems difficult. But further thought reveals that there is no real inconsistency. Most of the casualties were probably caused in the front rank, which shielded those behind; and even allowing for some exaggeration in the reference to the 'whole' front rank, it was by no means unusual for a unit to suffer 30% casualties in the close combat of the eighteenth century. What does seem certain is that it was the opening volleys, fired with a clear view and under perfect control, that caused many more casualties than were inflicted in the following confused and smoke-impeded exchanges.

When considering the period of the Napoleonic wars, it must be remembered that the number of men armed with muskets in the great pitched battles was generally greater than that deployed in the wars of the previous century. Furthermore, the presence of large numbers of poorly trained conscripts in the French armies must inevitably have led to a deterioration in the standard of musketry. The overall effect of the muskets of the Napoleonic wars can therefore be expected to have been diluted by the greater numbers and, in some cases, degraded by less proficiency on the part of the firers. In calculating that effect here, an effort was always made to take into account only the muskets that could have been involved in an action and assume that they were not firing outside their extreme range of effective fire. The conclusions reached were therefore as favourable to the musket

and its firer as it was possible to make them. Nevertheless, it seems impossible to accept that more than about 5% of the bullets that could have been fired were effective, and the rate seems often to have been appreciably lower. The muskets could not have been less efficient than those in service in the previous century, and the conclusion must be that they were handled less well – the most likely fault having been engagement at too long a range, sometimes coupled with wild and undisciplined firing. There is no doubt that the inclusion in the calculations of muskets that were firing – as they certainly were – at ranges of over about 100 yards reduced the percentage of effectiveness as compared to that attained in the eighteenth century.

It has been asserted by some authorities, whose judgment is questioned with great reluctance, that the standard of musketry of British soldiers was generally higher than that of French conscripts. This is much to be expected: the British soldiers had carried out regular live firing practice, but the French conscripts had often never fired their muskets before being plunged into battle. And there are, indeed, some indications of such superiority in the figures that have been presented here, notably in the battle on the Ridge at Albuera; but the overall evidence put forward here is not strong enough to support a claim for universal superiority.

The low performance of the musket places the old controversy over the comparative merits of line and column formation for infantry combat in a somewhat different light from that which has often illuminated it. When the execution achieved by all the muskets was as low as it appears to have been, the difference between the number of casualties inflicted by a large number of muskets and those inflicted by a smaller number would have been a great deal less than the disparity in the numbers of muskets would suggest. Indeed, that difference may not have been obvious to those taking part in the battle. This may explain why the side with the weaker firing line was often able to prolong the fighting – particularly when it was possible to replace casualties continually from the rear, as could be done in a column. There is a good example of this in the action between Werlé's brigade and the Fusilier brigade at Albuera, where a force whose muskets were outnumbered by four to one was able to press home its attack over a period of twenty minutes by virtue of sheer weight of numbers.

An inherent weakness in all of these calculations arises from the incidence of a completely unknown number of casualties inflicted by the bayonet. If these impinged on the parts of the battles that have been discussed, it must follow that the effectiveness of the muskets was even lower than has been deduced. Efforts were made, however, to exclude actions that were known to have culminated in hand-to-hand combat on a large scale, and it is therefore thought that no great inaccuracy should have arisen from that cause. The plain fact is that the musket was a very poor performer – and one can sympathise with the Guards at Talavera when, after volley upon volley at the solid mass of Frenchmen in front that never seemed to grow smaller, they surged forward with the bayonet to show who was going to win that battle.

In attempting to assess the effectiveness of smooth-bore artillery, there was a danger in quoting average performance – for the circumstances under which the guns were operating varied much more widely than they did in the case of the musket and, in particular, the ranges at which the guns were fired varied to a far greater extent. Nevertheless, an average of performance makes a useful starting point; and that must have been what commanders and other planners had in mind when calculating the extent to which they could justify the inclusion of artillery in a particular force.

In the first place, there is ample evidence to show that the various impedences that could always be expected in battle led to a reduction of at least 50% in the number of rounds which could have been fired under ideal conditions. This reduction includes an allowance for technical failures and for the obscuration of the target or the proximity of friendly troops. This means that, when there is accurate information on the length of time during which the guns were fully engaged at maximum pressure, the probable expenditure of artillery ammunition in the nineteenth century can be calculated on a basis of one round per gun per minute for field artillery. Heavy artillery can be assumed to have fired at about half that rate. It must be emphasised, however, that the period of time referred to here is not that of the duration of the whole battle: it refers only to those times when the

artillery was presented with profitable or menacing targets. The artillery of the early eigteenth century could fire at between a quarter and a half of that rate.

The effectiveness of artillery fire varied somewhat according to the projectiles used, and it is best to consider each of these separately. There is no doubt at all that, from long experience, round shot was found to be the most effective projectile of the smooth-bore ordnance. This is confirmed by the consistent holding of a large allotment of round shot in ammunition echelons and also by the fact that in the field artillery the guns, which alone could fire round shot, always outnumbered the howitzers by at least two to one and normally by five to one. The effectiveness of round shot was due to the long zone, many hundred yards in length, within which it travelled at a destructive velocity below man-height. It was clearly more effective when the target could be taken in enfilade than when the fire was applied frontally, although the deep masses favoured by the French armies provided good targets for fire from almost any direction. An average of three or four casualties could be expected whenever a close formation of men or horses was within the zone of a single shot.

The ballistic performance of round shot must naturally have improved between the seventeenth and nineteenth century, notably due to gunpowder that burned more regularly, the better boring of gun barrels, and the production of more truly spherical shot. It seems likely, however, that such improvements had no very great effect on the lethality of round shot fire since at short or medium ranges this did not depend on extreme accuracy in the estimation of range and the application of correct elevation. The introduction of the tangent sight must certainly have improved the application of fire at long ranges.

Common shell and shrapnel required fuzes to burst them, and they depended for their effect on the precision with which the correct fuze setting was estimated and applied at the gun position and the accuracy of burning of the fuze. Greater errors were permissible with common shell than with shrapnel, but in both cases the fuzes introduced a complication that was absent from round shot. The amount of common shell that was fired was comparatively small, however, and would not have had a great effect on the overall effectiveness of artillery.

Convincing evidence on the effect of shrapnel shell is difficult to obtain. But it seems that when firing at targets in broken ground, as at Bussaco, shrapnel was probably more effective than riccocheting round shot; and its use was encouraged in preference to round shot at long ranges, where round shot tended to plunge and lose some of its long lethal zone. It must be assumed that when it was used in preference to round shot there was good reason for it and that its effect, in terms of the casualties inflicted by the spread of its bullets, was much the same.

There are few writers of military history who have not commented on the destructive effect of case shot at short range; and indeed, though its effect was certainly erratic, it must have been a most damaging projectile at short or very short range. It is probable that some 50% of the bullets fired could be expected to have reached their target at 200 yards; but when allowance has been made for the difference between a human mass and a practice target, it would be reasonable to assume that about half of those bullets would have taken effect. A single salvo of case from a British six-gun 6pr battery might thus have caused from 100 to 150 casualties and would have been the equivalent in effect of from four to six battalion volleys. The relative values accorded to case and round shot are indicated by the amount of each carried in the field. British light guns held 16 to 28 rounds of case per gun, whereas the French – who obviously relied upon it to a greater extent – held 50 to 60 rounds per gun.

When smooth-bore ordnance was at the peak of its performance in the first half of the nineteenth century, it seems that at ordinary fighting ranges – as opposed to long-range bombardment – the guns could expect to hit their targets with between one-third and two-thirds of the round or spherical case shot fired. This assumes that the target was a close formation of infantry or cavalry in the open and that the gun was well sited to do its job; but the figures seem to be well supported by the results of the actions that have been described. If it is assumed that each shot caused an average of three casualties, it follows that the guns could claim between one and two casualties for each round fired.

This estimate of between one and two casualties for every round fired can be translated into a claim

that each well-sited gun could have been expected to inflict between 60 and 120 casualties for each hour during which it was fully engaged at close or medium range – excluding, that is, long-range preliminary bombardment. The figures are purely averages from which many wide variations must have occurred. There were undoubtedly occasions when well-sited artillery was more effective – as in the case of Hawker's 9pr guns at Albuera; but when the figures are related to the periods of about an hour during which the artillery could have been purposefully engaged in the course of most of the battles of the time, the resulting estimate of 60 to 120 casualties per gun appears to be a credible reflection of the performance of efficient field artillery during the Napoleonic wars.

It is interesting to compare these figures with some quoted by Müller as having been recorded by Templehof and de Gros. Those authorities estimated that during the second half of the eighteenth century between 60 and 80 men were killed or wounded for every piece of ordnance deployed and, presumably, actively engaged. Their calculation provides some support for the figures suggested here.

Of interest in this connection is the table overleaf, which sets the total number of casualties inflicted in some of the battles of the Peninsular war against the number of guns in action. The casualty figures are the totals from all causes and were not all inflicted by artillery.

These figures indicate that, in nearly all cases, the Allied artillery was more effective than the French. And it is noteworthy that a larger number of guns seems usually to have recorded a lower performance. There were probably some diminishing returns here due to the fact that in these congested and smoke-clouded battles there was a limit to the number of guns that could be sited in positions from which they could contribute effectively. When Napoleon deployed 246 guns at Waterloo, for example, they could not all have caused 100 casualties per piece. On the smaller scale, however, this estimate seems to be well substantiated.

The ordnance improvement that had the biggest effect on performance was the elevating screw, introduced in the middle of the eighteenth century. This must have increased the rate of fire by a factor of at least two and probably more. Of less significance

Table showing total casualties relative to the number of guns in action in certain battles.

Battle	Phase	Allied guns	French casualties	French guns	Allied casualties	Remarks
ALBUERA	Overall	26	8,000	36 plus	7,000	
	Ridge battle	4–7	3,000[a]	24 plus 10 battalion guns	1,500	[a] 1,000 inflicted by guns at 140 per gun. Marked difference in effect of Allied and French artillery.
	Werle's attack	8–16	1,800	30	1,045	Difference as above.
TALAVERA	Overall	30	7,300[b]	66	6,200[c]	[b] probably about 80 casualties per gun.
	Ruffin's attack	5	1,500			[c] probably about 55 casualties per gun.
BUSSACO	Overall	36	4,400	38	1,252	
	Reynier's attack	12	1,970			French artillery ineffective.
	Ney's attack	24	2,428	24	500	Marked disparity in effect of artillery.

but valuable at long range and against small target was the tangent sight, which appeared at about the same time. It certainly seems that it was their increased rate of fire that led to the guns of the early nineteenth century being more effective than their predecessors. The improvement was due not to their being more accurate or longer ranged but to their ability to put more rounds on the target in a given time and also take better advantage of some of the fleeting opportunities for fire that presented themselves through gaps in the smoke of battle.

Throughout the period there was a steady improvement in the ways in which artillery was used. There tended always to be a division of the artillery into two echelons – one to provide close support to the infantry and cavalry, and one to be used under central direction. This division was perhaps more clearly marked in the early days because the heavier equipments were so clumsy that movement was difficult and the centralisation of control was unavoidable. As artillery became more mobile, however, there was less distinction between the two echelons; but whenever enough guns were available, commanders always liked to retain some under their own hands while decentralising a proportion of their resources for close support. In the British Army, in which there was often a shortage of artillery, commanders always retained the ability to redeploy or redirect the activities of guns that had been initially placed in support of units of other arms.

Thus far, the discussion of the performance of artillery has been confined to its work at what were called 'ordinary fighting ranges' – by which is meant at about 800 yards or less. It remains to consider the use of artillery at longer ranges since it was undoubtedly often called upon to fire outside the 800-yard limit.

The long-range preliminary bombardments carried out in the seventeenth century seem to have been somewhat aimless and very largely ineffective. Those of the eighteenth century were more purposeful, but it is a little difficult to find evidence of much greater effect. It seems that in the middle of the nineteenth century, however, counter-battery fire at long ranges rather suddenly became an efficient operation of war – as at Gujerat and, though it is outside the scope of this book, at Inkerman. On both of those occasions effective fire was developed at 1300 yards against gun positions – although it must be remembered that it was the fire of heavy guns and howitzers, which could be expected to have 30% more range than field equipments. Nevertheless, there is evidence here of the better sighting equipment already noted.

It is doubtful whether much was achieved by preliminary bombardments by light guns, up to and including 12prs, in the Napoleonic wars. But it would have been surprising if the guns had not fired in an attempt to cause harm as soon as their shots could reach the target; and Kipling's 'tricky trundlin' round shot' was an unpleasant companion even when near the end of its run. Indeed, there are instances of the effect of long-range fire against inexperienced or exposed troops – a well-known example covering both conditions being the ordeal of Bijlandt's Dutch-Belgian brigade at Waterloo. It is true that the accounts of nearly all battles seldom fail to include the damage done by the preliminary bombardment. Fortescue, in particular, gives many picturesque descriptions – such as when he writes of the French preliminary bombardment at Talavera 'tearing great gaps in' the British infantry on the left flank. Nevertheless, it does seem that there may have been some exaggeration of the physical results of this long-range fire even though its moral effect must have been daunting indeed. For although the actual number of casualties inflicted may not have been high – perhaps no more than two or three per cent – the sight of whole files being sliced apart or horribly mangled by single shots must have been a most discouraging start to a battle, particularly when no retaliation was possible.

The relative effectiveness of guns and muskets must have determined the numbers of each that formed part of all armies, acknowledging that a number of other factors such as the availability of ordnance and the ability to provide and feed horses to pull the guns and wagons had also to be taken into account. The ideal ratio between infantrymen and guns was declared by Napoleon to be 1,000 to 3. But that ratio cannot be regarded as exactly indicating their relative importance since, in the warfare of the period, it was essential to bring an adequate number of foot-soldiers into the field to hold their own in hand-to-hand combat and perform duties off the battlefield. However, representing a manpower ratio of about 100 gunners to 1,000 infantrymen, it does indicate the proportions in which it was considered that each arm could best contribute to the common aim.

Two more points should be made. The first is that the evidence presented and the conclusions drawn here are not intended to be interpreted as attempts to prove that either the gun or the musket was more effective than the other. Battles are not won by competition between the arms; and competent soldiers have always realised that success is achieved by the correct combination of all the resources available. Guns and muskets were always complementary weapons, operating to the best advantage in separate spheres – very clearly separated by the ranges within which each could work efficiently, so that in a particular stage of a battle it was often only one arm that could shoot at all. There was therefore little overlapping and no question of choosing which should play the major part.

The second point, touched on earlier, is that – certainly in the time of the smooth-bores – few battles were ever won solely by superior weapon power. Instances have been quoted in which greatly superior weapon power was opposed by determined and skilful troops and, although the side with greater firepower may eventually have won, the victory was long delayed and bought at high cost. It was ultimately not weapon power but will-power that won battles; and even though superior weapon power was a powerful lever, it was always a means to an end rather than the end itself.

This book does not pretend to have examined all aspects of the battles of the smooth-bore period. It is purely an analysis of the effect of the weapons used. But it is hoped that the results of the analysis may be seen to have a bearing on the course of the battles of that time.

Bibliography

Adye, Captain R. W., R. A., *The Bombardier and Pocket Gunner,* Eight editions between 1800 and 1827.

Baker, Ezekiel, *Remarks on rifled guns and fowling pieces,* 1823.

Balagny, Commandant, *Campagne de l'Empereur Napoleon en Espagne: 1808–1809.*

Becke, Captain A. F., R. A., *An introduction to the history of tactics 1740–1905,* 1909.

Belloc, Hilaire, *Six British Battles,* 1931.

Bond, Lieutenant Colonel H., *Treatise of military small arms,* 1884.

Cole, Lieutenant Colonel H. N., *Minden 1759,* 1972.

Colquhoun, Lieutenant J. N., R. A., *Practice results and military experiments.* Unpublished Manuscript dated 1814.

Duncan, Captain F., R. A., *History of the Royal Regiment of Artillery,* 1872.

Fave, *Histoire de l'artillerie,* 1871.

Fortescue, the Hon. J. W., *A History of the British Army,* 1889.

Girod de l'Ain, *Vie militaire de General Foy,* 1900.

Gleig, G. R., *The Campaign of the British Army at Washington and New Orleans,* 1847.

Gough, General Sir Charles, with A. D. Innes, *The Sikhs and the Sikh Wars,* 1897.

Graham, Brigadier General C. A. L., *The Story of the Royal Regiment of Artillery:* Sixth edition 1962.

Greener, W. W., *The gun and its development,* 1881. (10th edition 1910, reprinted 1972).

Griffiths, Major F. A., R. A., *The Artillerist's Manual and British Soldier's Companion:* Eight editions from 1839 to 1859.

Hamilton, Captain Thomas, *Annals of the Peninsular Campaign,* 1829.

Hogg, Brigadier O. F. G., *English Artillery 1326 1716,* 1963.

Horwood, Donald D., *The Battle of Bussaco,* 1965.

Howarth, David, *A Near Run Thing,* 1968.

Hughes, Major General B. P., *British Smooth-bore artillery,* 1969.

Jomini, General Baradi, *The Political and Military History of the Campaign of Waterloo,* 1853.

Kausler, Fr. de, *Atlas des plus memorables battailes, combats, et sieges,* 1831.

Lauerma, Matti, *L'artillerie de campagne francais pendant les guerres de la revolution,* 1956.

MacMunn, Lieutenant General Sir George, *Gustavus Adolphus, the Northern Hurricane,* 1930.

Mercer, General A. C., *Journal of the Waterloo campaign,* 1870.

Moltke, General von, *The influence of firearms on tactics,* 1871.

Muller, John, *A Treatise of artillery,* 1768.

Müller, William, *Elements of the science of war,* 1811.

Müffling, General Baron C. von, *History of the campaign of 1815.*

Napier, Major General Sir W. F. P., *History of the war in the Peninsula,* 1828–1840.

Oakes, Captain A. F., *The Artillery Officer's Assistant,* 1848.

Oman, Sir Charles, *History of the Peninsular War 1808–1814,* 1902–1930.

Wellington's Army, 1912.

Studies in the Napoleonic Wars, 1929.

Orr, Michael, *Dettingen 1743,* 1972.

Owen, Lieutenant Colonel C. H., R. A., *Elementary Lectures on Artillery.*

The Principles and practice of modern artillery, 1871.

Peterson, Harold, *Round shot and rammers,* 1969.

Rogers, Colonel H. C. B., *Artillery through the ages,* 1971.

Weapons of the British soldier, 1960.

Smith, Lieutenant Colonel C. Hamilton, R. E., *Aide Memoire: A sketch of the Science and Art of war,* 1850.

Straith, Major H., *Lectures on Artillery,* 1852.

Treatise on Fortification and Artillery, 1852.

Stubbs, Major General F. W., *History of the Bengal Artillery,* 1895.

Weller, Jac, *Wellington in the Pensinsula,* 1962.

Wellington at Waterloo, 1967.

Wellington in India, 1972.

Index